OUR MISSIONS IN INDIA

OUR MISSIONS IN INDIA

1834-1924

REV. E.M. WHERRY

GYAN

Published by

Gyan Publishing House
5, Ansari Road
Daryaganj, New Delhi-110002
Phone: 011-47034999, 9811692060
E-mail: books@gyanbooks.com

Distribution Network
gyanbooks.com
India, USA, Canada, UK, Australia

ISBN: 978-93-7097-000-7 (PB)

First Published, 1926

2nd Impression 2025

Printed at: Gyan Press, Delhi.

OUR MISSIONS IN INDIA 1834-1924
Author: REV. E.M. WHERRY

Our Missions in India

1834 — 1924

By

Rev. E. M. Wherry, M.A., D.D.

Author of the Comprehensive Commentary on the Qurán; Islam in India and the Far East; Islam the Religion of the Turk; The Sinless Prophet of Islam

For Forty-Six Years a Missionary of the Presbyterian Church, U. S. A., in India

1926

TO MY WIFE

CLARA MARIA WHERRY

COMPANION AND CO-LABORER

IN MISSIONARY SERVICE

FOR FIFTY-EIGHT YEARS

A Fore Note

THE Presbyterian Church in the United States of America was from the very beginning a Missionary Church. The first general assembly, comprising four Synods, met in Philadelphia in May, 1789. The matter of missions occupied the attention of this Assembly. The Synods were enjoined to secure two missionaries each, and present them at the next meeting of Assembly. The Presbyteries were urged to arrange for the taking of regular collections for missionary purposes. All around them were vast regions, occupied by European settlements and Indian tribes. There was need of a great missionary work among these. For three quarters of a century, a "Board of Correspondents" had been established in New York forming a kind of auxiliary to the "Scottish Society for the Propagation of Christian Knowledge." This Board of Correspondents appointed the Rev. Azariah Horton a missionary among the Indians in Long Island. Later on the devoted David Brainerd was ordained by the Presbytery of New York and became a missionary to the Indians of New Jersey and Pennsylvania. This occurred in 1744, but this zealous and indefatigable worker wore himself out in scarcely more than three years, dying at the age of thirty years. He was succeeded by his brother, the Rev. John Brainerd, who had visited his dying brother and who had comforted him by the assurance that his beloved Indian Christians would not be left as sheep without a shepherd. The salaries of these missionaries were provided by the Scottish Society, but their expenses were supplied by the Colonial Society from funds chiefly contributed by the American Presbyteries.

Such was the beginning of the Foreign Missionary Enterprise which now occupies so large a place in the hearts of American Christians. It was in the year 1831 that the Synod of Pittsburgh, which, from the day it was organized, had been distinguished for its interest in the missionary work, founded a society called the Western Foreign Missionary Society, and chose as its secretary the Rev. Elisha P. Swift. Mr. Swift was the pastor of a large congregation, but so great was his interest in the movement that he resigned his pastorate and devoted all his energy to the work of furthering the cause of Foreign Missions. The salary of this Secretary was provided by the liberal gift of the Hon. Walter Lowrie at that time the Secretary of the Senate of the United States.

In the year 1810, the American Board of Commissioners for Foreign Missions was established. The Presbyterian churches were interested in the work of this society. The feeling of denominational responsibility, however, soon led Presbyterians to believe that as a Church they had always regarded themselves as a Missionary Church, and had carried on missionary work among heathen tribes in America, they should have a Foreign Missionary work for which they should be solely responsible, they believed that they should thus cultivate a larger interest in the work of carrying the Gospel into all lands. It was, therefore, with no purpose of rivalry that this new Society was formed. Many churches and individual Christians continued to contribute to the American Board.

A few years after the organization of the "Western Foreign Missionary Society," the General Assembly established the "Foreign Missionary Society of the Presbyterian Church in the United States of America," and then the Western Foreign Missionary Society united with it.

This volume aims at giving a plain narrative of the missionary service rendered by the Presbyterian Church in the United States of America through its missions in India.

E. M. W.

Contents

Contents

CHAPTER I.

The Founding of the Lodiana Mission

THE Western Foreign Missionary Society, having decided to undertake a missionary work in India, sent a circular letter to the Theological Seminary in Allegheny, Pennsylvania, calling for volunteers. In reply to this call, letters were received from two students: Mr. John C. Lowrie and Mr. William Reed, offering themselves as missionaries. They were appointed to India in January, 1832. Mr. Reed was ordained by the Presbytery of Huntingdon, Pennsylvania, whose support they undertook. The Presbytery of New Castle, Delaware, undertook the support of Mr. Lowrie, and called a special meeting in the City of Philadelphia to ordain him to the ministry. This occurred in the First Presbyterian Church, during the sessions of the General Assembly, on the 23rd of March, 1833. Thus it appears that more than a year had elapsed since the appointment of these pioneer missionaries. Their time was spent in making addresses to the churches and in preparation for their work.

On the evening preceding their departure, a missionary meeting was held in the Second Presbyterian Church, Philadelphia, which was addressed by the missionaries and the Hon. Walter Lowrie, the father of Mr. John C. Lowrie. At this meeting were present also the wives of the missionaries: Mrs. Louisa A. Lowrie, a daughter of Thomas Wilson, Esq., of Morgantown, Virginia, and Mrs. Reed. A few days later (May 30, 1833), these missionaries with their friends went to New Castle on the Delaware River, and after a solemn service of prayer, they went aboard the good ship, the Star, and set sail for Calcutta.

Travel in those days by sail to India ordinarily covered a

period of four or five months. The course depended upon the winds. This obliged a long journey south to catch the trade winds. The passing through calms in the tropics often meant days of vexatious delay, the sails listlessly flapping in a wind too weak to fill them. The heat was oppressive; the waves, if any, glassy; or, worse still, no waves, only a smooth surface of glassy water. The only compensation was the unique opportunity to see some of the marine life; the nautilus with sail spread quietly moving on the surface of the waters; the jelly fish or the dolphins with their rainbow colors; and in the distance huge turtles floating and basking in the sun. The trade winds reached, the journey eastward was comparatively straight, bating the tacking north and south to overcome head winds or to counter the currents. Then came the days of the journey north into the Bay of Bengal. Here the current south seems to defy the wind in its struggle northward. The ship would spin along at the rate of ten or twelve knots on a course north-east, when the proximity of the Island of Sumatra would compel a change of tack to the north-west; two days have passed, when lo! they have made barely thirty miles on their journey! This illustrates the trials of the pilgrims of the sea, alleviated by fresh air and a sense of rapid motion. This has taken no account of the occasional storms, with skylights battened down, and the awful seasickness, often lasting three or four days; or it may be a sudden squall, lashing the sea into a white foam and after a few minutes leaving the storm tossed vessel in a calm, rocking up and down, right and left, fore and aft, an egg shell at the mercy of the waves!

At last the land head and a light ship appear and the weary travelers, after more than four months, are told they are near their destination. The journey up the Hugli River is like a holiday trip on the St. Lawrence. A day and a night and the anchor drops off Garden Reach. Four months and a half have passed, and now the journey by sea is ended. With thankful hearts they disembark and soon are welcomed by Mr. and Mrs. Pierce of the English Baptist Mission.

Through the generous kindness of these devoted missionaries, provision was made for our pioneer friends, during many months in Calcutta. Mrs. Lowrie had suffered throughout the voyage, seeming to rapidly decline in health. It was hoped that when she should land and secure adequate medical aid, she would recover, but though attended by the Calcutta friends with every care that love could suggest, she became weaker and weaker day by day, until within a few weeks the messenger came to call her to her Heavenly Home. She entered into rest November 21st, 1833, in the twenty-fourth year of her age. Her last hours were full of peace.

It seems strange that such a consecrated life should have been taken away before she could enter upon her chosen field of labor. This was, however, not the only disappointment that befell these pioneers.

Several months had to be spent in Calcutta in order to arrange for the long journey inland, and in deciding upon the field to be occupied. No little time was needed for the necessary correspondence in regard to this latter point. There were many wise counsellors near at hand: the venerable Dr. Marshman of the English Baptist Mission, a man of learning and of long experience in missionary work; Dr. Alexander Duff of the Free Church of Scotland's College now pushing his scheme for extending English education in India; the Rev. Dr. Corrie, a chaplain, who had spent some years in upper India; and several Christian gentlemen in connection with the English Government, who were acquainted with the people of India and their religious condition.

After careful inquiry and prayerful consideration, it was finally decided to begin the missionary work of the Presbyterian Church at Lodiana, an important city situated on the south bank of the Sutlej River, which was at that time occupied as a great military station of the East India Company's forces on the Punjab frontier. The chief reasons for this choice were the fact that hitherto missions had been opened in the towns near the seacoast and thence extended along the banks of the chief rivers. The territories as yet unclaimed by missionary societies were in the regions north and west. A call had been sent from Lodiana by Captain Wade, the political agent, urging upon the missionaries the importance of Lodiana as a centre for missionary work, being as it were a gate for entry into the Punjab and the regions beyond. The Cis-Sutlej States were mostly Sikh principalities, now under British protection. Hitherto no missionary work had been undertaken for this dominant people. It was virgin soil and therefore specially attractive as the sphere of a new mission.

The ordinary mode of travel north was by boat on the Ganges River. Accordingly boats were hired to carry the missionaries and their luggage, household goods and utensils. It was thought best to send Mr. and Mrs. Reed ahead, leaving Mr. Lowrie to follow on at a later date, but owing to the low water in the Ganges and the rapid approach of the hot season in Upper India, they concluded to remain in Calcutta until the next rainy season, spending the interim in the study of the language. A house was rented in Howrah and language study was begun. Seven months must now be spent in waiting.

Soon after entering upon this preparatory work, Mr. Reed began to suffer from fever and a cough, which the physician soon recognized as incipient consumption. Everything was done that could be done to stay the progress of that dread disease, when finally it was advised that he should return to America. Accordingly on the 23rd of July, Mr. and Mrs. Reed embarked for America, leaving their now doubly bereaved companion to go alone upon the long journey to Lodiana.

The strange fatality which thus beset this little band of devoted missionaries belongs to the mysteries of Divine Providence. Mr. and Mrs. Reed seemed to be very specially fitted for the pioneer work of a new mission. Mr. Reed was a graduate of Jefferson College, Canonsburg, Pennsylvania, After taking a course of study in the Theological Seminary in Allegheny, he spent some months preaching among the churches to arouse an interest in Foreign Missions. When he left his home with his devoted wife, they were followed by many earnest prayers. After a long journey, safely accomplished, he entered upon the work of language study, but in the midst of this work he was obliged to turn his face toward the homeland. The hope that a journey by sea might avail to stay the disease, proved vain. He rapidly grew worse and on the 12th of August he entered into rest. His body was committed to the deep near one of the Andeman Islands. Mrs. Reed and her little son reached their home in December.

Although thus early called to leave the work to which their lives had been consecrated, Mr. and Mrs. Reed had been permitted to take part in the pioneer work of choosing the mission field. His colleague makes mention of "his excellent judgment and good sense as being of great service in deciding on the question first to be considered. And his life of sincere, humble, earnest piety made his example one to be followed by his successors. It is his honor and reward that he was one of the founders of the Lodiana Mission."[1]

Mr. Lowrie now alone and in poor health was sorely discouraged. Alone, with no other companion than natives, and a journey of twelve hundred miles before him, amongst a strange people; could one wonder if he were discouraged? He did not falter. While preparation was being made for the home journey of his colleagues, he was busy arranging for the long journey north. He wrote in his journal: "I was made to feel that the trials of missionary life are often chiefly those of the mind. It is not the privation of comforts of home nor the outward hardships of his lot in his new sphere of life, but it is mainly the separation from friends, the loss of social and Christian privileges, the thoughts and longings of the mind for

[1] *History of A. P. Mission*, p. 165.

what must be foregone; the thousand visions of the imagination, by day and by night of what is far distant and never again to be seen; it is chiefly these things that are trying to bear. But trials can be supported with cheerfulness, if we are in the path of duty. I could not look in any direction without seeing multitudes of people without God and without hope in the world. . . . I could not hesitate to go forward."[3]

Mr. Lowrie's journey up the Ganges River to Cawnpore by river boat, and thence overland to Lodiana, was so characteristic as to justify a detailed description. He was not able to afford the more luxurious appurtenances of travel, which are mentioned in the accounts of the journeys of the governor-general to visit the up country provinces and native states: his was the journey of the average man, and that of his successors in the mission fields for many years to come. He tells the story in his book "Two Years in Upper India."

"Having engaged a twelve-oared budgerow, and another boat for the servants to cook on, and for part of the luggage, I had expected to start early this morning (July 25, 1834) on the journey to Lodiana. Bishop Heber speaks of 'two hours squabbling' with the boat people, when he was setting out on his tour of visitation. I found some trouble, both with the budgerow people and the freight or cook boatman. The former refused to prepare their meals on the boats, insisting on being permitted to cook on the budgerow, which, from the nature of the ingredients used by them and from the smoke, would have been very disagreeable. After they found that this point could not be gained, which, however, they did not yield until the matter was carried before the agents from whom I had hired the boats, then the people of the other boat set up a great jabbering about the place in their boat which should be assigned to the budgerow people for cooking. Each caste must cook by itself. We have now three places for cooking on the freight boat: one for me, at which also the servants cook; and one each for the crews of the two boats.

"We started with the tide, but made no progress, as the wind

[3] *Two Years in Upper India*, pp. 69, 70, 128.

was strongly against us, and we were obliged to 'come to' after two or three hours of hard work.

"*July 26*—We started again with the tide, about 3 P. M., but did not make much progress, mooring a few miles above Chitpur—five or six miles distant.

"*July 27*—We started early, hoping to reach Serampore by sunrise.

"*July 28*—We started again in the clear moonlight, about three o'clock A. M., and in the early part of the afternoon reached Chinsurah, twenty-two miles by water. The boatmen 'tracked' a good part of the way; that is, six or seven men went ashore, and pulling with a long rope, drew the boat along at the rate of two miles an hour. It is hard work; as the poor fellows have to cross nullahs, or arms of the river, frequently so deep as to require them to swim, and to walk often knee-deep in mud, all the time exposed to a hot sun. They relieve each other every hour by twos: that is, two of the men on board the boat take the place of two, who have been longest on shore. To keep their rope from becoming entangled by the bushes, and from dragging heavily through the water, they make it fast, almost fifteen feet above the deck, to the mast. As a considerable part of the vessel in the water is before the mast to which the rope is attached, and as the rudder is too small to be of much use, when the current happens to be very strong, there is great danger that the prow will be forced to one side or the other; and then there is still greater danger that the boat will be pulled by the men at the rope on its 'beam ends,' as the sailors say, on its side, and go down to the bottom. I describe the process minutely, for my most frequent dangers, and some of the greatest, were from this source. In many places the current dashes along with immense force at the rate of seven or eight miles an hour. The 'trackers,' bent almost to the ground, strain every muscle to pull the boat. The prow suddenly veers from the right direction; the boat is already half on its side; all on board sing out as loudly as possible to the men on shore to slacken the rope; and, if they hear it in time, all may be well enough; but, if not, the danger is very imminent that everything will be lost, except the lives of the reckless boat people, who seem to be an almost amphibious race. It would be no easy matter to drown one of them!

"When the wind is not favorable, 'tracking' is the common

mode of getting along; as they hardly ever make use of their long, awkward oars. Of course it is a very tedious mode of traveling. When the wind is favorable, they spread sail, contriving to fasten two or three sails, one above another, to the single mast in the centre of the boat. A strong wind will carry the boat against the current from twenty to thirty miles a day.

"*July 31*—Our boats were moored this evening just below the junction of the Bhagirathi and Jallinghi Rivers—branches of the Ganges, which here unite and form the Hoogley (Hugli). I found here another budgerow, and numerous native boats, all waiting for a change of wind.

"*August 5*—For two or three days, including the last date, the wind was quite unfavorable; so that we were obliged to 'lie to' without attempting to make any progress. On Sunday the wind increased to a violent gale, causing large waves on the river, which is here deep and broad. We were unfortunately moored to the lee-shore, so that the wind both dashed the boats against the shore and waves against the boats. It soon became evident that we should have difficulty to save the boats from being wrecked. In the other budgerow were a gentleman and his wife and their children. The lady becoming alarmed, insisted on leaving the boat, and it was well they did so, for it sank under the fury of the waves, in a few minutes after they had left it. A number of native vessels, and my freight boat, in which were some large boxes of things, shared the same fate. I had most of the valuable articles taken out of the budgerow, and with great difficulty it was just saved; but as the rain was pouring down in torrents, and the wind was very high, the books were much injured, the other articles damaged more or less, and, after three hours hard work in the rain, I got completely tired and wet. An English family happened to reside in the neighborhood, who received us kindly, and provided dry clothing."

These extracts from Mr. Lowrie's journal are sufficient to illustrate the trials and possible dangers of the river voyage. The compensating incidents were the varied and often most interesting scenery, the many towns and cities visited by the way, the intercourse with Europeans, and especially missionary families, located in the larger cities on the Ganges, and the many opportunities for Christian fellowship during these visits by the way.

On the 9th of October, 1834, Mr. Lowrie landed at Cawnpore, and immediately prepared for his journey overland. From this point, the luggage had to be sent up country on bullock carts for a distance of five hundred miles. Mr. Lowrie travelled by *dak,* i. e., by palanquin, carried on the shoulders of men, travelling, by relays day and night, at the rate of three or four miles an hour. Such a long journey would ordinarily oblige travellers to break journey from time to time. Mr. Lowrie's description of this kind of travel will interest the reader:

"At night the *Dak* traveller presents a singular appearance. Foremost are the 'bundle carriers,' of whom I have three, each man walking along with a peculiar fast gait, and carrying two bundles of twenty-five pounds each, swung at the ends of a stick over his shoulder. Then comes the traveller in his palanquin, borne by four men, who at each step make a peculiar unpleasant sound, a kind of grunt, by way of music; while four others run by their side; each set relieving the other about once in five minutes. But the most singular appendage is the mussalchi, or torch bearer, who runs along beside carrying a large torch, on which he pours oil every few minutes, making a fine light. Every ten or twelve miles a fresh set of men are stationed."

Mr. Lowrie travelled by way of Agra and Delhi, once capitals of the Moghul Empire. The distance from Cawnpore to Agra, one hundred and ninety miles, was covered in fifty hours. Here he stopped to visit the Taj, that marvellous mausoleum, built for the favorite wife of the Emperor Shäh Jahän, perhaps the most beautiful structure in the world. Underneath this structure lie the mortal remains of the Emperor and Mumtaz Mahal, the delight of the palace.

After visiting Akbar's fort, with the palace and mosque and other relics of the Emperor Akbar the Great, Mr. Lowrie proceeded to the City of Delhi, a journey of one hundred miles, which was accomplished in thirty-seven hours. He spent some days visiting the palace, mosques and tombs, travelling for miles through the ruins of former cities, which had been ruthlessly destroyed by the hordes of Tartars, Mongols, Afghans and Persians, who had followed one another like waves of the sea; each one building a new city for another to destroy. Climbing to the top of the famous Kutb-Minär, an immense tower two hundred and forty feet high, Mr. Lowrie was sadly depressed. He wrote in his journal:

"For miles and miles around, you see scarcely anything but the ruins of former greatness. One dilapidated palace, or mosque, or tomb after another rises in view, till you are almost depressed at seeing such manifold evidences of the feebleness of man."

Leaving Delhi, Mr. Lowrie travelled north to the City of Karnäl, one hundred and twenty miles journey, where he entered the territory of the protected Sikh States. His journeying was now almost at an end. On November 5th, 1834, he reached Lodiana.

The journey thus ended, after nearly eighteen months travel, would now be accomplished by steamship and railway in five or six weeks.

Of the four pioneer missionaries, only one was permitted to reach the mission field, a field unknown to those who had sent him, and yet a field soon to become a sphere of missionary endeavor of absorbing interest to the churches in many lands.

The possible fields open to the pioneers of the American Presbyterian Mission were many and diverse. The following sections of the country presented strong claims upon them: Assam, a vast region to the north-east, bordering upon Bhutän; Oudh and Rohilkand, a rich country stretching from the Ganges northward to Nepaul, then under a Muhammadan King with his capital at Lucknow; a third section was the Doab, the highly cultivated region between the Ganges and the Jumna

Rivers; and then the regions in central India, controlled by great warrior chiefs: Rajputana, the land of the Rajputs; and finally the boundless regions to the northwest; the Punjab, Afghanistan and Central Asia. This last was the field finally chosen.

The vast region lying between the Sutlej River and the Indus, the Punjab proper at that time, was under the rule of the famous Máhárájah Runjeet Singh. As yet no missionary was permitted to preach the Gospel in this Land of the Five Rivers. The East India Company had established a cantonment at Lodiana, near the south bank of the Sutlej River, marking the northwestern boundary line of the Dominion of British India.

Here was a field as yet unoccupied by any church. To the south and east were immense regions now under the British flag. To the north and west lay the land of the Sikhs, a sturdy people, independent in character, professing a religion largely monotheistic. Under the sway of the Sikhs were millions of Hindus and Muslims. Such a people afford to the missionary an opportunity quite unique for the planting of the Christian church.

This field was one of great historic interest. Here was the home of the first Aryan invaders of India. Here Hinduism had its birth. From the Punjab it slowly spread over the whole peninsula. It was here that the great battles were fought, which are described in the great Epic, the Mahabharata. It was through the Punjab that every successful invasion of India had ever taken place, except that of the British. It was here that the tide of Alexander's victories terminated.[3]

The first city to be occupied as a centre of missionary work was Lodiana. This was in great measure due to the advice of Sir Charles Trevellian, and also of Sir Claude Wade, then political agent stationed at Lodiana. Before leaving Calcutta, Mr. Lowrie had received formal permission to establish a mis-

[3] *History of A. P. Mission*, p. 41.

sion at Lodiana, and in anticipation of his coming, a small school had been started by the political agent and taught by a native teacher. The object of this school was the teaching of the English language. The expectation was that the missionary, on arrival, would take charge.

When Mr. Lowrie arrived in Lodiana he received a hearty welcome. Everything was done to make him comfortable and to make him realize that he had come among friends. His first duty was to make a survey of the field and to formulate plans for his work. He wrote in his journal:

"The present population of Lodiana is estimated at from twenty to twenty-five thousand, and is on the increase. When the navigation of the Indus is freed from the present restraints, which will most probably be within another year, the town may be expected to increase considerably, as it will then become one of the marts of trade with countries down the Indus. It is now a place of considerable business intercourse with the countries westward. Few towns have so varied a population in race and language. There are two regiments of infantry, and one troop of horse artillery here, commanded, of course, by English officers; so that nearly a hundred persons use the English language. There are probably two thousand five hundred people from Kashmir, who have found refuge here from famine and oppression, which have almost desolated their beautiful native valley. There are about one thousand Afghäns, who speak Persian chiefly.

"In regard to Lodiana, as a place for missionary operations, I still think it quite desirable to have a mission established here, of two families for the present; that is of two married missionaries. One of these, in addition to the Hindi, should possess a knowledge of Punjabi. The other, to Hindustani, or Urdu, should add Persian. After some time, perhaps one, two, or three years at the farthest, a press will most probably be nearly indispensable. At first, the missionaries will need to labor in a quiet way, avoiding professions of intention to convert the natives, but watching and improving the opportunities which I have no doubt will be constantly occurring for conversation, distribution of portions of the scriptures, tracts, etc."[4]

[4] *Two Years in Upper India*, pp. 113, 129.

It is easy to see that actual contact with the people, and counsel with Christian officers on the spot, had considerably changed the missionary's views as to the kind of work to be done. Indeed it seems certain that he had been sorely disappointed, and for awhile had questioned the wisdom of the choice of this field. He wrote:

"One thing has been much impressed on my mind, the importance of sending some person to make observation before a mission, of any size at least, is resolved on. I find that actual observation has corrected and modified my views of this field of missionary labor in no small degree; as I shall now describe:

"1. The way does not seem to be yet open for direct efforts, as it is, for instance, in the lower provinces.

"2. The manner in which the population is distributed is quite different from what I expected to find, judging from other parts of India.

"3. The proportion of those, who embrace the religion of Muhammad, is much larger than I had supposed, and they constitute the better classes of the people. . . . There is less prospect of their conversion than of any other class."[5]

Notwithstanding these doubts and anxieties, Mr. Lowrie had committed himself. He now set himself to do what his hand might find to do. He undertook to minister to the spiritual needs of the troops by conducting services in the church in the cantonment. He arranged to superintend the English school, he was expected to take charge of. He also undertook to conduct a school for the children of drummers, sergeants and native soldiers. This school especially seemed to afford an opportunity for evangelistic work.

After a sharp attack of malarial fever, with congestion of the liver, Mr. Lowrie was told by the army surgeon, that he would never be able to endure the Indian climate! Nevertheless he began the active work of teaching. Soon the attendance advanced from sixteen or eighteen to fifty. Of these "some were the sons of native chiefs and other respectable native

[5] *Two Years in Upper India*, p. 131.

gentlemen. Some of them were Hindus, others Afghans, others Kashmiris and a few Sikhs, speaking among them the Hindi, Hindustani, Punjabi, Pashtu, Persian and Kashmiri languages."[a]

The experience which this missionary had now acquired was sufficient to remove any lingering doubt from his mind as to this form of missionary endeavor. The daily influence upon the minds of the youth, the influence on their families, and the daily opportunity of correcting false views such as prevailed among them, added to the more important work of giving clear instruction concerning the Christian religion, made clear to him that Christian education was a key to the heart of India.

News now reached India that reinforcements were on their way to Lodiana. On the fourth of November, 1834, the Rev. John Newton and the Rev. James Wilson and their wives had sailed from Boston. With them also sailed the first single lady missionary sent out by the Presbyterian church in America, Miss Julia A. Davis.

Encouraged by the prospect of reinforcements to meet the plans he had made for two missionaries for Lodiana, Mr. Lowrie proceeded with the school work. His growing experience and success in this school and his vision of future endeavor may best be given in his own words:

"Several of these youths evinced no ordinary degree of capacity. All were uniformly respectful in their behaviour, and after a little training, became studious and some of them earnest in their attention to their books. It was delightful to look at their animated faces, and see their eyes kindle as they received knowledge daily, to which before they had been strangers. And when their confidence had been gained, they appeared to regard me with mingled respect and affection, and to receive my instructions with apparently perfect faith.

"I advert to this to show how invaluable are the opportunities afforded to a missionary by such a school for promoting the great object of his mission. He has a most hopeful charge, a

[a] *Two Years in Upper India*, p. 134.

company of youths, whose minds are as yet but partially under the influence of heathen opinions and associations. The influence of their families, out of school, is doubtless strongly unfavorable, but this weighty hindrance is, perhaps, more decidedly felt by adults than by children in India. And opportunities will occur every day of correcting the false views which prevail around them, and of imparting clear and connected instruction concerning the Christian religion, while all the teaching of the missionary is enforced by his example, and rendered almost sacred in the eyes of scholars by their views of his character."[7]

This hopeful outlook had, however, been scarcely realized, when a serious question arose, as to the possibility of continuing this work. Writing of this matter, he explained how that just in the beginning of his work in the school, there seemed to be a doubt as to whether this school could ever become a mission school. He wrote as follows:

"Now I found that among the Europeans in the upper Provinces, there was much apprehension about connecting religious instruction with the education of the natives; and some men, of liberal views too, were decidedly opposed to such a union, at least at this time. The general policy of the government colleges, in which the Christian religion is no more recognized than the Muhammadan or any other, should be followed with special care, it was argued, amongst a people, so partially under subjection to the British as the inhabitants of the Protected Sikhs States, and a people moreover of so much independence, not to say recklessness of character. The popularity of these colleges among the natives was everywhere acknowledged, but the successful religious institutions of learning in Calcutta, attended largely by native youths of the highest castes, were not so well known in the upper Provinces, or not considered as examples to be imitated where the circumstances were so different. As it was easy, starting from premises like these, to form quite an array of objections, which I doubt not were sincerely felt, against attempting to combine religion and education in schools for natives, religious prejudices would be aroused, disaffection might be created against the government, and the

[7] *Two Years in Upper India*, pp. 133, 134.

improvement of the natives be retarded by premature zeal; these were opinions which it is not strange that men should form in the peculiar circumstances of these Provinces.

"I esteemed myself fortunate in having to consult with a gentleman of such enlarged and correct views and of such general zeal for the good of the natives, as were evinced by the Political Agent at Lodiana. With many other men it might have been impracticable for me to have had any connection with the English School at that place, as I could not consent to take the responsible charge of an institution from which our holy religion was to be utterly excluded. After mature reflection, the school was fully placed under my control, and its studies were directed by a settled plan. No professions of our object were ostentatiously made, but on the other hand, no concealment of our views was attempted, nor was there any withholding of religious instruction. No alarm was awakened among either Hindus, Mussalmans or Sikhs: and the School, after a fair trial was considered a successful effort."[8]

Thus, the question, as to the opening of the Mission School at Lodiana, received a satisfactory reply. Education, including Christian teaching, became a primary agency for enlightening the minds of the people of that great Province. Henceforth education was to be an important factor in the Evangelistic enterprise of the Presbyterian Church in India.

The popularity of this school was so great that Mr. Lowrie was invited by the Maharajah Runjeet Singh to visit him in Lahore, the capital of his dominions. Having provided a suitable escort he brought the missionary in great state to become his guest. The object of this great Ruler of the Punjab was to induce the missionary to undertake an educational work at Lahore in order that the princes and young nobles might receive an English education. The proposal was that he should spend six months of the year at his capital. Mr. Lowrie was favorably impressed by the offer. He wrote:

"I should have been delighted to have accepted this proposal, if the state of my health would at all have justified my living

[8] *Two Years in Upper India*, pp. 138, 140.

on the plains; it presented a fine prospect of obtaining a standing and influence, which would have been invaluable to a missionary. And in reflecting on the past, I have been disposed to regret that I had not consented at whatever risk; but the physician's advice was imperative."[9]

Although unable to consent to the Rajah's project, the visit was not without important results. The missionary had made a good impression. The prejudices of the Sikhs against the Christian missionary were considerably modified, for during the long visit the missionary had many opportunities to tell the story of Jesus Christ and His salvation. The Rajah accepted the present of an English Bible and the translation of the Old Testament in the Punjabi language, and in the Gurmukhi character as published by the Serampore missionaries. Mr. Lowrie had frequent conversations with Muhammadans, the most prominent being Faqir Nur-ud-Din and Faqir Aziz-ud-Din, high officers in the employ of the Sikh Government.

After several weeks visit at Lahore, the missionary was sent in great honor to Lodiana. It is of interest to mention that the value of the costly presents,[10] given to Mr. Lowrie, form a first credit in the cash book of the Lodiana mission.

The new missionaries on their way from America had by this time arrived in Calcutta. The young lady, Miss Julia A. Davis, who had come out to undertake an educational work for the women of India, was met in Calcutta with the discouraging news that such work was as yet impracticable. Thus discouraged she severed her connection with the missionary party and became the wife of the Rev. Mr. John Goadby of the English Baptist Mission at Cuttack.

The missionaries were unable to leave Calcutta until the 24th of June, 1835. The slow method of travel by the river, already described, brought them to Fattehgarh about the end of October. Here they found tents awaiting their arrival, which

[9] *Two Years in Upper India*, p. 144.

[10] They were valued at R. 2183-10-5 ($1091.53).

had been sent from Lodiana by Captain Wade. The journey thence was in palanquin by stages of twelve miles a day, the missionaries distributing vernacular books and tracts by the way as they had opportunity.

On his return from Lahore, Mr. Lowrie continued his work of teaching and ministering to the spiritual needs of the English community. The example of the pioneer missionary at Lodiana has been followed, as far as possible, by his successors.

Owing to repeated attacks of malarial fever, Mr. Lowrie was obliged to spend the summer in Simla, a mountain resort some 7,000 feet above the sea. The physician had also insisted upon his seeking an entire change of climate by a visit to America. While in Simla he made a study of the country and its people, particularly the hill people of the Province.

Hearing of the near approach of the new recruits, he left Simla about the middle of November and went to meet them at a point about thirty miles northwest of Delhi. He then journeyed with them to Lodiana.

After some six weeks spent in canvassing the history of the mission to that date and advising with them as to the work and plans inaugurated by him, Mr. Lowrie bade farewell to many kind English friends, to the scholars in the school, and to his missionary brethren, commending each the other to the grace of God.

Leaving Lodiana January 21st, 1836, Mr. Lowrie, travelling by *dak* to Calcutta, had the pleasure of meeting with a third party of missionaries, consisting of the Reverends J. R. Campbell, J. McEwen, Messrs. J. M. Jamieson, W. S. Rodgers and Joseph Porter and their wives. It was a great pleasure to be able to help these brethren in their preparation for the journey up country, before leaving India. Embarking at Calcutta, he returned to America, landing in New York on the 28th of December.

Mr. Lowrie went home from India in the hope that he might be able to return again. This hope was not realized. Soon after his arrival he entered the office of the Presbyterian Board in New York as a secretary, in which office he was destined to spend a long lifetime. By voice and pen he labored for more than half a century for the cause to which he had consecrated his life. When he left India, he expressed the hope "that the mission established at Lodiana would be the morning star preceding the full day of Gospel light and influence among the interesting people of India." He lived to see his vision of a Mission at Lahore made real and he saw the Gospel carried to the borders of Afghanistan.

NOTE. The Rev. John C. Lowrie, D. D. was the son of the Hon. Walter Lowrie, sometime judge of the Supreme Court of Pennsylvania, a man who devoted his life to the cause of Foreign Missions as Secretary of the Board of Foreign Missions of the Presbyterian Church. Three of his sons became Foreign Missionaries. John went to India; Walter and Reuben to China. John C. Lowrie's whole life was spent in Foreign Mission service. Walter went to China in 1842, but in 1847 he was cruelly murdered by Chinese pirates. Reuben prepared himself to take his place, and went to China in 1854. He served for six years when he entered into rest.

The Lowrie family holds a place of highest honor in the annals of Foreign Missions.

E. M. W.

CHAPTER II.

The Missions Organized

THE pioneer missionary, having completed his work in India, committed the further development of his plans into the hands of the new missionaries, the Rev. James Wilson and the Rev. John Newton whose arrival in Lodiana has already been mentioned. Land had already been obtained,[1] whereon they now began to build two dwelling houses, a schoolhouse and a printing office for the accommodation of a printing press which had been purchased in Calcutta. The two dwelling houses were very plain structures, made of sun-dried brick with a thin covering on the outside walls and cornices of small burned brick, covered with lime plaster and whitewash. They consisted of four rooms, each 16 feet square, to which were added later on verandas and dressing rooms and bathrooms. The roofs were flat consisting of boards spread on wooden beams and covered with clay and plaster.

The schoolroom and printing office were placed on the west side of the compound and built in like fashion as the dwelling houses.

These buildings were most unsatisfactory, being squat on the ground, low in the ceiling and without proper ventilation. They partook of the general character of the European buildings of the day, suitable for the use of men who rented temporary quarters, never knowing when they

[1] Mr. Newton in a letter written December, 1862 to Dr. Lowrie wrote as follows: "You helped us to select a site for the Mission premises, where remains of some old brick kilns were still visible, on a small piece of land, which had been promised in 1834 by a native chief, for the use of the Mission. On his death, soon afterwards, without heirs, this land became subject to the disposal of the British authorities, and it was granted to the Mission by Captain Wade, Political Agent, early in the Spring of 1835." *The Foreign Missionary*, April, 1863, p. 309.

might be transferred to another place. Experience soon led the missionaries to build houses better suited to such a climate, which meant better health and longer life.

The threefold work now provided for was that of education, publication and the preaching of the Gospel whenever and wherever possible. This last form of work was in reality the first in importance, but, as we have already seen, was for several reasons as yet quite impracticable. Education had been begun when Mr. Lowrie took over the English school established by Captain Wade. Provision for publication was made, on the arrival of the second installment of the mission force, when the press was set up in the building now erected. Both English and vernacular type and matrices were brought from Calcutta. But before preaching and publishing in the vernacular languages was possible, the missionaries must acquire the requisite knowledge of the language. It came about, in the providence of God, that the only way as yet open to bring the gospel message to the people was to undertake the education of the people in the English language. The school was already in existence and some of the people were anxious to receive the instruction given. To be sure their main anxiety was to secure such knowledge of English as would enable them to secure service under the new government as writers and accountants. The monthly wage was only some forty or fifty rupees, but that was regarded as a large sum at that time, the mass of the people being glad to get regular service on wages of from five to ten rupees a month.

Accepting the advice of Christian friends, the missionaries carried on the school, realizing the need of much tact in their effort to maintain the religious ideals of a mission school. Quietly and with great wisdom, effort was made to win the confidence of the pupils and their parents. It was not until the second year of the school's life that the morning service, consisting of the reading of a portion of scripture and a prayer, was begun. Several people became alarmed and withdrew from the school, thinking they were now to be compelled to become Christians. The panic, however, soon passed away and the school went on its way as the pioneer for Western education in the Punjab. Although the school was always open to all classes, the majority of the pupils in the beginning came from Muhammadan families. This may have been due in some measure to an arrangement which enabled the school to offer small stipends to those who wished to prepare for Government service. A fund was started privately by the European ladies in the station to provide the money for these stipends. No guarantee as to repayment was required, except a promise made by the beneficiary himself, that when he should secure employment, he would refund the amount of the stipends received by monthly installments. It is much to the credit of the students that, with few exceptions, they refunded these stipends to the school. The Kashmiris being very poor were induced to permit their boys to accept these stipends and prepare themselves for Government service. Later on the Hindus and Sikhs, probably being influenced in the same way, and also stirred up by the action of their Muslim neighbors, began to send the larger number of pupils. Many boys came from long distances. A few were the sons of noblemen, who came riding on horses, carrying umbrellas! It will be of interest to the reader to learn something more of the scope of study and the subjects presented in this pioneer school. The following is quoted from the Report of the Lodiana Mission School:

"The school consists of two departments, called the Primary and the High School. The studies of the former are Roman Urdu; the First Books in a course of English reading, writing and the elements of Grammar and Arithmetic.

"The studies in the High School are English Reading,

Geography, English Grammar, Arithmetic, Evidences of Christianity, Algebra, Geometry, History of England, Chemistry, Political Economy, Surveying, History of India, Physical Geography, Mental Philosophy, Logic, and the Bible, together with written translations and compositions."

Concerning the curriculum the chronicler remarks: "This is the prescribed course; but no class has yet been induced to remain long enough to complete it."

Learning was not sought for its own sake, but as a means to secure emolument and an honorable position. To Christian men, who had sought an education at great personal expense and possibly some self-denial, loving knowledge for its own sake, this universal spirit of commercialism loomed up in their way, not only as a great disappointment, but as an obstacle in the way of their missionary career. Could it be possible that their lives were to be spent merely to provide *babus* (office clerks) to supply the needs of the Government? Was a service of this sort compatible with their calling as missionaries of the Gospel of Jesus Christ? What possible good could proceed from a merely secular education of Hindus, Sikhs, and Muhammadans, thereby fitting them to become powerful antagonists of the Christian faith? Such questionings led to much thought and consideration. Much valuable aid was received from the experience of their missionary friends in Calcutta, especially that of the great apostle and advocate of English education in India, the already venerable Dr. Alexander Duff. The result of this study was that education was continued with new zeal and carried on as a principal means of converting India's people to the thought, ideals and principles of the Christian religion.

The rapidly growing desire of the Indians for an English education was due to the definite purpose of the Government to educate young men to provide for the public offices native officials, who could understand and use the language of their English rulers. This would not only be most useful to those, who would otherwise be obliged to acquire a knowledge of the vernacular languages, of which there are more than forty, to say nothing of some five hundred dialects, but would result by and by in making the English language the language of learning and the medium of intercourse in the higher circles of all Indian society. Such schools would bring to the educated people of India a key to the treasuries of all the knowledge and science of Western nations, and particurlarly of the English speaking nations of the world.

From the missionary standpoint, therefore, it was not difficult to see the immense vantage ground that education of this kind would afford. As pioneers they would have the opportunity of bringing to many young men that culture of mind and heart, which would fit them for the highest places in the gift of the Government. Nothing else would so popularize the mission and dignify the missionary. Looking at this question from the standpoint of the missionary himself, what could be more interesting and attractive than the opportunity of speaking to boys and young men day by day for a period of years concerning the true religion and its way of life and peace for both time and eternity? The simple knowledge of Geography and History, of Science and Literature would surely create a revolution in the minds of those young men, leading them to abandon the false faith of their fathers. The result of merely secular education would be to create a generation of infidels. Mr. Lowrie, looking at this problem from the Christian standpoint, wrote as follows:

"The English language contains much that is evil, all that is good, studying it, thousands of influential native youth will abandon the religion of their fathers, perceiving that it is absolutely irreconcilable with the simplest rudiments of correct knowledge. But will they become Christians? Not necessarily. A large part of the influence that reaches the Hindu mind through the medium of our language has never received a Christian baptism. Many of those English ideas are engaged in demolishing the Hindu temples, but they do not build up the Christian Church. Left to the guidance of their own depraved hearts, without any light from heaven to direct their minds, these Hindu-English readers will become infidels, believers of no religion at all. Many of the Indians, especially in the Cities, where Europeans reside, and Indians, whose English education gives them great influence with their countrymen, are now of this character. . . . There is too much reason to fear the eventual prevalence of a pagan infidelity in India."[2]

Two generations have passed since these words were written. The experience and observation of all these years have abundantly justified this forecast, and have continually strengthened the hands of those who have maintained the cause of a Christian education alongside of the Government and the non-Christian schools and colleges, which have been established in every part of the Indian empire.

Returning to Lodiana: the English School there rapidly increased in numbers. It soon became necessary to add several Indian teachers. These were all non-Christians. Many of them were faithful and loyal to the school. Their presence gave confidence to the parents of their students and character to the school. The Christian teaching no doubt deterred some of the people from patronizing the school, but on the other hand the people generally were pleased to observe that the moral influence exerted upon their children greatly enhanced their prospects in connection with Government service. The routine of the missionaries, during the first year, was limited to the acquisition of the vernacular languages, the superintendence of the school, the building of their houses and other buildings needed for

[2] *Two Years in Upper India*, pp. 269, 276.

the school and the press, and the conducting of religious services for the English speaking community.

The third party of missionaries, already mentioned, after bidding adieu to Mr. Lowrie at Calcutta, proceeded on their way up country. The coming of so large a party, five men and their wives, opened the way to an extension of the borders of the Mission. In the Summer of 1836, the missionaries at Lodiana received a letter from Mr. Conelly, the Collector and Magistrate at Saharanpur, in which he recommended that city as a suitable station for some of the new missionaries who were then on their way up the Ganges. He at the same time made mention of a large house, lately occupied by one of the Civil officers, which could be bought for the paltry sum of four hundred rupees. This combination of circumstances seemed like a leading of Providence, especially as there were comparatively few places open in this field, and none so inviting as Saharanpur. Accordingly the house was purchased and made ready for occupation.

Saharanpur was a city of about 50,000 inhabitants and was the centre of a large agricultural district, with a population of 800,000, of whom about one-third were Muhammadans. The remainder were Hindus and out-caste peoples.

Another station occupied at this time was Subathu. The circumstances which specially led to the occupation of Subathu were also providential. During the Summer of 1835, while Mr. Lowrie was in Simla, he made a study of the hill tribes. Believing them to be simple minded and teachable, he thought Subathu would be a good centre for missionary work among them. This opinion he had mentioned in conversation with the missionaries at Lodiana. In the course of the Summer of 1836 they received a letter from Dr. Laughton, surgeon of the Gurkha regiment then stationed at Subathu, telling them that if a missionary could be sent there a good dwelling house could be purchased for the small sum of six hundred rupees. Already the need of a refuge in the mountains from the excessive heat of the summer was being felt. This invitation to make Subathu a mission station seemed a call of Providence. The invitation was accepted and the house was bought.

Subathu was a Cantonment station, where European regiments could be quartered during the hot season. It is surrounded by beautiful valleys and populous villages. The presence of a European physician made it attractive as a summer resort. It was possible for a missionary to live here, when life and health were impossible on the plains, and at the same time afforded a field for missionary work in the cantonment Bazar and the surrounding villages.

A third station was occupied during this year under circumstances illustrating the old saying: "Man proposes but God disposes."

The missionary party, already mentioned as being on their way from Calcutta, coming up country by river boats on the Ganges, arrived in Cawnpore. They had been overtaken by a storm just above the city of Bhagulpur, in which a boat containing the heavy luggage was blown over and sunk. A box containing some parts of a printing press was lost. At Cawnpore the missionaries learned that these missing portions could be obtained in Allahabad. It was decided to send one of the party, Rev. Mr. McEwen, to purchase the missing pieces. While in Allahabad Mr. McEwen was asked to conduct the Sabbath services held in the Baptist Mission Church for Europeans. The people were so pleased as at once to prepare an earnest request that Mr. McEwen and his wife be settled in Allahabad to render assistance in English preaching. The only other minister in Allahabad at that time was the Rev. Mr. McIntosh, sent by the Baptist mission at Serampore. Mr. McEwen was deeply impressed by this call and especially because of the wonderful opening for a new missionary work. Mr. McIntosh also urged upon the missionaries the great need of help in the work of preaching. After accomplishing the purchase of the parts of the press machinery, and also securing a practical printer for work at Lodiana, Mr. McEwen returned to Cawnpore and placed the call before his fellow missionaries, who decided that he and his wife should go to Allahabad to engage in English preaching, and await the action of the Mission meeting at Lodiana.

On the arrival of Mr. McEwen with Mrs. McEwen, at Allahabad, their reception by the people was most cordial. The field was seen to be so extensive, and the prospect for usefulness so encouraging, that the proposed arrangement was approved by the Mission; and Allahabad was now formally occupied as a Mission Station with Mr. McEwen in charge.

On arrival of new recruits at Lodiana, the new stations were recognized and the following definite assignments were made for the work at each:

Rev. John Newton and Mrs. Newton Rev. Joseph Porter[3] and Mrs. Porter	Lodiana
Rev. W. Rodgers[3] and Mrs. Rodgers Rev. James Wilson and Mrs. Wilson	Subathu
Rev. J. R. Campbell and Mrs. Campbell Rev. J. M. Jamieson[3] and Mrs. Jamieson	Saharanpur
Rev. James McEwen and Mrs. McEwen	Allahabad

At Allahabad, as in Lodiana, the first sphere of work open among the native population was that of education. a boarding school for girls was established, chiefly for orphans; and a day school for Eurasian children was opened. Mr. McEwen engaged regularly in English

[3] These three men had volunteered while in college and, on receiving their degrees of B.A., came to India. They were all afterwards ordained to the ministry by Presbytery.

preaching. In January, 1837, a church was organized with twelve members, and was called "The Mission Church."

The experience of this pioneer missionary at Allahabad was very similar to that of Mr. Lowrie at Lodiana. From his first arrival in India, Mr. McEwen suffered from ill health, and at length his strength declined so rapidly that it was considered advisable for him to return to America. He left India early in 1838, and spent the remainder of his life as a pastor in New York State. He died in 1845.

A printing press was now set up at Lodiana. The first outfit was very simple. Mr. Newton and Mr. Wilson while in Calcutta had visited the Baptist Mission Press. They were there advised to buy a press as a necessary adjunct to their work. Accordingly they purchased an old fashioned wooden press, such as was still sometimes used in those days. They also bought a font of type with paper and printing ink. These they got from the Baptist Mission Press, then under the superintendence of Rev. William H. Pierce, who had greatly befriended them as well as their predecessors.

Neither of these missionaries had any knowledge of printing, but Mr. Pierce gave them one of his Indian compositors to assist them in beginning the work. The Press building having been erected, they were ready to set up the press. The building had three apartments; one for the press and type, another for paper and printed matter, and a third for a bookbindery.

Mr. Newton had charge of the press; he learned from his compositor how to work the press and then he and the compositor taught some native apprentices. In this humble manner the first printing establishment in upper India was begun.

In the same year, 1836, two orphanages were begun in Lodiana; one for boys and the other for girls. Here again the beginnings were very humble. A girl was sent to the

Mission by the Magistrate at Karnal and a boy by the Magistrate at Delhi. This was the beginning of the two orphanages. By the end of the year the number of orphan girls increased to six. These were sheltered in a house built contiguous to one of the new mission houses and placed under the care of Mrs. Newton. The boys brought to the mission were provided for in another part of the premises and placed in charge of Mr. Porter.

The new missionaries at Saharanpur, Messrs. Campbell and Jamieson, with their wives, were necessarily engaged during the first year, in getting settled in their homes and in planning for their work. They also gave attention to language study. Here it may be mentioned that the missionaries at Saharanpur belonged to a denomination of the Presbyterian family, now denominated as Reformed Presbyterian. The arrangement between that church and the Presbyterian Assembly's Board of Foreign Missions was that the stations, including houses and land, were all alike to be held under the control of the General Assembly's Board in New York, while each denomination's representatives should be under the ecclesiastical control of their own Presbyteries. The allied body was expected to contribute to the Board in New York money enough to cover the salaries of their missionaries.

The first work that presented itself to the missionaries at Saharanpur was that of education. A school was started and for a time was quite prosperous. However, a serious mistake had been made in the beginning. They had been silent on the subject of Christian teaching. When later on they began to open the school with prayer, most of the students fled. The missionaries persisted and quietly went on with their work, and gradually the pupils began to return.

From this time and onward, when new schools were begun, religious services also began with the opening of the school.[4]

At Subathu, the missionaries, Messrs. James Wilson and W. Rodgers and their wives, found a comfortable home in the house which Dr. Laughton had secured for them. It was located in the Cantonment, which was a serious drawback, inasmuch as it might be claimed at any time by Army officers. For the present, however, the missionaries occupied it and began their work; the study of the vernacular language and preaching to an English congregation. A school for boys was opened in the native quarters. Mrs. Wilson began a school for Indian girls. This was the first school for native girls in North India.

The next year, Mr. Wilson was transferred to Allahabad to take the place of Mr. McEwen, whose failing health obliged his return to America. Soon after this it became necessary to transfer Mr. Rodgers to Lodiana. Mrs. Jamieson being in poor health in Saharanpur, Mr. Jamieson was sent to take up the work at Subathu. Mrs. Jamieson carried on the girls' school, begun by Mrs. Wilson. The character and importance of this school is thus noticed in the Mission Report: "Thirty-seven girls are on the roll, with thirty in attendance. Many of them can now read in the Hindi New Testament in the Deva Nagari character beautifully. They are likewise learning to sew, spin, knit, to make braid, &c. Some of them have made considerable progress in needle work."

This kind of work illustrates the service rendered by the wives of missionaries long before the more modern special

[4] Fifty years later, the Rev. John Newton, in his history of the Mission wrote: "So deeply has the propriety of this religious exercise impressed itself on the minds of the pupils, and perhaps on the parents, as contributing to the prosperity of the school that when a rival institution was organized eighteen years ago, by a combination of Hindus and Mohammedans, the classes at first being made up of pupils withdrawn from the Mission School, and having for its head master a young man, who had been educated by us, it was said to have been made a part of the daily routine for the regular studies to be suspended for a short time: when Hindus and Muslims assembled in separate rooms to get religious instruction from a Hindu Pundit and a Maulvie. *History of A. P. Mission*, pp. 29, 30.

service rendered by unmarried ladies began. With the work at Lodiana, Subathu and Allahabad in Girls' schools and Orphanages under the management of Mrs. Newton, Mrs. Wilson and Mrs. Jamieson, women's work for women had already made a good beginning.

On the 14th of October, 1837, a fourth party of missionaries sailed from America and arrived in Calcutta in the following April. These were the Rev. Henry R. Wilson, Rev. John H. Morrison, Mr. James Craig and Mr. Reese Morris, and their wives. The joy of their landing after so long a journey was soon to be clouded by sorrow . Some three weeks after landing, Mrs. Morrison was suddenly seized by that dread disease, Asiatic cholera. Her illness was accompanied by acute suffering and from the first she gave no hope of recovery. This she realized as she said to her husband: "Tell them all at home, much as I love them and much as my heart clings to them, tell them all I am not sorry that I left them all for Christ, though it be but to die in His service; no, tell them I rejoice that I have been permitted to enjoy the privilege." She died with the word "Glorious" on her lips. She was laid by loving hands beside the grave of Mrs. Lowrie.[5]

As soon as practicable, this party of missionaries journeyed northward, each to his destination. Mr. Morrison joined Mr. James Wilson at Allahabad and soon after took charge of the English Church services there. Messrs. Craig and Morris proceeded to Lodiana. Mr. Craig took charge of the school at Saharanpur and Mr. Morris was assigned to the management of the Mission Press for which he had special training.

The arrival of the Rev. Henry R. Wilson enabled the Mission to undertake the establishment of a new mission station at Fattehgarh, about two hundred miles northwest

[5] A memoir of this devoted young woman was prepared by Rev. E. J. Richards, and published by M. W. Dodd, New York.

of Allahabad. The providential circumstances which led to the choice of this station were as follows:

Two English officers had undertaken the care of a number of orphan boys, during the dreadful famine of 1837. One of these was Dr. Charles Madden, a pious physician at Fattehpur, who had 100 orphan boys. Being obliged by the failing health of his wife to leave the station, he was anxious to transfer fifty of these children to the care of a missionary. He proposed to make over the school building and apparatus and money to the value of one thousand rupees.

Captain Wheeler, a Christian officer at Fattehgarh had supported twenty orphans, but now was under marching orders. He had heard of the arrival of the American missionaries in Calcutta and became anxious to transfer his charges to them. It was therefore decided to accept the offer of these gentlemen, and accordingly they assigned Mr. and Mrs. Henry R. Wilson to Fattehgarh. The fifty children at Fattehpur were sent up to Cawnpore to meet the missionary. On arrival at Cawnpore the Wilsons realized that their work had already been provided for. Taking charge of the orphan children they proceeded to Fattehgarh and there found Captain Wheeler's boys awaiting them. They reached Fattehgarh, November 3rd, 1838.[6]

The Fattehgarh station included the City of Farrukhabad and the adjacent cantonment and Fort called Fattehgarh. Farrukhabad was the centre of a large and populous district, while Fattehgarh, some five miles distant, was the military centre with its European residents. The Mission station when fully organized comprised two communities with mission houses in each; Rakha in Fattehgarh and Barhpur near the city. Mr. H. R. Wilson established the orphange at Fattehgarh.

On the 12th of October, 1838, another party of mission-

[6] *History of A. P. Mission*, p. 110.

aries sailed from America for India, arriving in Calcutta in the following May. This party consisted of the Rev. Joseph Warren, Rev. James L. Scott and Rev. John E. Freeman, and their wives. Messrs. Warren and Freeman were appointed to labor in Allahabad and Mr. Scott at Fattehgarh. A printing press had been sent from America with this party; and as Mr. Warren had some practical knowledge of printing, he was made superintendent of the work of the press.

Mr. and Mrs. Scott reached Fattehgarh in August, 1839. The Orphanage at Fattehgarh now contained one hundred and nine orphan boys, twenty of this number having been given to Mr. Wilson by a gentleman in Bareilly, on condition that they should be known as the Rohilkand Branch of the Orphanage.

In order to provide manual training for the larger boys in the orphanage, six workmen were brought from Mirzapur to give instruction and aid in the art of carpet weaving. With an outlay of three hundred rupees, this new industry was inaugurated.[7]

On the 5th of August, 1840, the Rev. Messrs. John C. Rankin, William H. McAuley and Joseph Owen, together with Mrs. Rankin, Mr. McAuley and Miss Jane Vanderveer, sailed from Boston for India. Mr. Owen was assigned to Allahabad,—the other members of the party to Fattehgarh.

The arrival of Mr. Owen at Allahabad made possible the establishment of a High School for Indian boys. He had tarried long enough in Calcutta to make a study of Indian education methods. He was especially impressed by the work being done in the Institution of the General Assembly of the Church of Scotland, then under the superintendence of Dr. Alexander Duff. This institution had only been in existence for about ten years, but was attended by about

[7] *History of A. P. Mission*, p. 111.

six hundred pupils. The sight of such an opportunity to reach the heart of India filled Mr. Owen with profound admiration. It was, as he said, the most interesting thing he had seen in the great city. On arrival in Allahabad, he entered upon the duties of the superintendence of the first High School of that city.

The Mission property on the banks of the Jamna river at Allahabad was purchased about this time. It comprised a large compound of several acres in extent and a large double house, which was formerly the residence of the English magistrate. This building provided ample accommodation for two families, while the compound afforded a splendid site for the new school buildings. Messrs. Wilson and Freeman occupied the dwelling house. The extensive out-offices were remodeled to provide accommodation for the Girls' Orphanage. A house for the Boy's Orphanage was also built on the grounds. On the opposite side of the public road was a piece of land attached to this estate, and on this land was a building that had been part of an old mint. This old building was repaired and made a place for Hindustani worship.[8]

The Allahabad Orphan Asylum was at first begun to provide for children whose parents perished in the great famine of 1837-1838. This famine prevailed over the region on both sides of the Jamna river, from above Allahabad to the region of Delhi, causing a fearful destruction of life. The Government and private individuals did all that was possible to alleviate its horrors. Among other benevolent efforts, much was done to collect and feed the starving children, whose parents had either died, or had deserted them. Many of these children were afterwards restored to their parents or relatives; but hundreds, whose relatives

[8] *History of A. P. Mission*, p. 112.

could not be found, were handed over to various orphan asylums, which had been established by the Missions.[9]

In March, 1842, the Allahabad mission was further strengthened by the arrival from America of the Rev. John Wray and his wife. These took the places made vacant by the departure of Mr. and Mrs. Morrison for America, made necessary by the failing health of Mrs. Morrison.

Mrs. Morrison was not permitted to accomplish this journey. She was taken seriously ill in Calcutta and, after a lingering period of suffering, entered into rest on the 14th of February, 1843.[10] Mr. Morrison, with his three motherless children, proceeded to America.

The Rev. Levi Janvier and Mrs. Janvier, who were fellow travellers with Mr. and Mrs. Wray, were appointed to Lodiana. They had travelled from Calcutta to Allahabad by *dak,* the carriage being drawn by camels. They continued their journey by the same mode of travel to Lodiana. This marks a new era in travel, the river boat no longer had a monopoly. The Grand Trunk road, a metaled highway from Calcutta to Peshawur, built for military purposes, had superseded the river route, except for heavy freight.

Early in 1844, two more missionaries arrived from America; the Rev. J. J. Walsh and Mrs. Walsh. On the recommendation of the Rev. Henry R. Wilson of Fattehgarh, a new station had been opened at Mainpuri, a city situated some forty miles west of Fattehgarh. This was in some measure due to the zeal of a medical officer, Dr. Guise, who had interested himself in the Indian people and tried to help them by opening a school for boys. Mr. and Mrs. Scott of Fattehgarh were sent to take charge of the new station. On their arrival, November, 1843, the Civil Surgeon, Dr. Guise, gave them a hearty welcome not only

[9] Warren in *Missionary Life in North India*, p. 68.

[10] This was Mrs. Isabella Hay Morrison who was married in February, 1839. Mr. Morrison's first wife died in Calcutta in May, 1837.

to the station but to his own house, where they remained until the end of December, when the house they had engaged was ready for them. Dr. Guise transferred to Mr. Scott the school he had started. The school now grew so rapidly in numbers, that a new building had to be built for its accommodation.

It is interesting to notice once more that here as elsewhere the first form of evangelistic work open to the missionary was education.

The failing health of Mrs. Wilson of Fattehgarh now obliged Mr. Wilson to return with his family to America. Accordingly, Mr. Scott had to be brought back from Mainpuri to Fattehgarh to take up the superintendence of the orphanage and its industries. Mr. and Mrs. Walsh were sent to Mainpuri.

A number of stations had now been occupied in the Northwest Provinces. The distance between the Punjab and the Northwest Provinces was too great for convenience or economy. It was therefore found to be expedient to constitute two separate missions. Those in the Punjab and the Cis-Sutlej, Protected States form the "Lodiana Mission." The missions in Allahabad, Fattehgarh and Mainpuri were invited to form the "Farrukhabad Mission."

The solution of ecclesiastical problems in the early days of the mission is not without interest. Rev. John Newton gives us the following account of it:

"Of the party of missionaries which joined the mission in 1836, three were unordained. They had been sent out under the designation of *teachers*. They had all, however, the ministry in view; and having gone through a regular course of Collegiate study and obtained the degrees of B. A., they were prepared to prosecute their theological studies under Presbyterial direction. But there was no Presbytery in the mission field; and, in connection with the General Assembly, there was not a sufficient number of ministers to form a constitutional Presbytery. There were only two ministers in Lodiana, while the constitution required three. To meet this emergency it was agreed that the two (viz: Mr. Wilson and myself) and Mr. Campbell, one of the party referred to, who was a minister of the Reformed Presbyterian Church, should organize a Presbytery, and so be able to give formal ordination to the others, whenever the way for such ordination might be opened. Accordingly the Presbytery was constituted, and after the usual trial, the three candidates were ordained.

"The whole thing was of course irregular; but the anomalous position the missionaries were placed in seemed to them to justify it: and the principle of it has since been recognized by the proposed alliance of different Presbyterian bodies occupying the same mission field, for certain ecclesiastical purposes.

"The matter was soon after brought to the notice of the General Assembly and while the Assembly disapproved the measure, it gave informal validity to it, by acknowledging the three brethren — Jamieson, Rodgers, and Porter — as truly ordained ministers, and directing them, with the original two in its connection to constitute the Presbytery of Lodiana. This Presbytery in its first form was constituted in 1837. Its present form was assumed two or three years later.

"In 1838 another minister of the Reformed Presbyterian Church—Rev. Joseph Caldwell—joined the mission; and as two ministers, according to the law of that church, can form a Presbytery, Messrs. Campbell and Caldwell in due time organized the Presbytery of Saharanpur. That was in 1841.

"Not far from the same time, two Presbyteries of our Church were organized within the bounds of the Farrukhabad mission:—one the Farrukhabad; the other, the Allahabad Presbytery.

"Hereupon the General Assembly, in 1841, adopted a resolution by which the three Presbyteries of Lodiana, Allahabad and Farrukhabad, were to constitute the Synod of Northern India."[11]

Thus far in the history of the India Mission, compara-

---

[11] *History of A. P. Mission*, pp. 67, 68.

tively little had been accomplished in the way of conversions. The actual results of these ten years' labor cannot be tabulated in statistical form. Important centres had been occupied. Schools had been opened for non-Christian children, orphanages for both boys and girls had been established, and in them boys and girls were being converted and trained for service. Many of these were already proving themselves to be valuable helpers, as teachers and preachers. Christian homes had been created. Churches were organized, and the Gospel had been preached before thousands of Hindus and Muhammadans in widely scattered towns and villages. Excellent work too had been done among the Europeans, both civil and military. The scriptures had been widely distributed, the languages learned, books and tracts were being printed and published in several vernacular languages.

The great importance of the printing press in connection with missionary work had been demonstrated by the Baptist missionaries at Serampore. Under the inspiration of William Carey, William Ward and Joshua Marshman, the work of Bible translation and publication in the vernacular language had made astonishing progress. Scriptures and portions had been widely scattered in the cities along the coast, while many had found their way far up the navigable rivers.

For the missionaries, newly arrived in Calcutta, scarcely anything aroused more interest than the Baptist Mission press. As we have already seen, it was by the advice and help of the Rev. W. H. Pierce that Messrs. Newton and Wilson brought with them to Lodiana, a small wooden press with printing ink and paper.

After the erection of suitable buildings, this was made ready for work, but little could be done until the arrival of Mr. Reese Morris from America, who undertook the management of the Press. A few native compositors had been trained to do ordinary work and were now ready to begin work under the trained hand of the new superintendent.

The first publication at Lodiana was a Persian tract, entitled "A sermon for the whole world." It consisted of the Sermon on the Mount, with the last three verses of Matthew IV prefixed as an introduction. Other select scripture verses were added to set forth briefly the work of Jesus Christ as the Saviour of sinful men, the whole closing with the Apostolic Benediction in Hebrews xiii. 20 and 21.

The press plant was enlarged by importing from America two iron presses of the best make then known. The effort was made to print by lithography; but with indifferent success. Types were obtained in the Persian, Deva Nagari and Gurmukhi characters: manufactured for the most part in Serampore. Later on a type foundry was set up. The main purpose of the press was to print and publish Christian books and scriptures for evangelistic purposes. For a few years, the *Lodiana Akhbar (News)* was printed, as a kind of local Gazette in the interest of the Government. The languages employed were Urdu, Persian, Hindi, Punjabi and Kashmiri.

The missionaries began to write books and tracts, as soon as they had acquired the language. They used native munshies and pundits to aid in securing a correct idiom. Many books and tracts published elsewhere, were reprinted by permission. Up to the year 1844, fifty-eight thousand scripture portions had been issued. Of tracts 385,000 copies of some fifty-five original tracts had been printed, besides 75,000 reprints.

The principal authors were, John Newton, W. Rodgers, J. R. Campbell, James Wilson and Joseph Porter, for the Lodiana mission.

At Allahabad, the work of printing begun by Mr. Warren,

on his press, set up in a bath room, was for a year or two, merely a pastime while studying the language and a means of training his compositor, John.[12] In that small room John began his career as a printer on a catechism by John Brown of Haddington.

The work of the press at Allahabad increased slowly, as at Lodiana. The larger need there was a literature in Hindi and Roman Urdu. Messrs. Wilson, Freeman and Warren were specially active with their pens.

These humble efforts to begin the work of preparing and publishing a Christian literature in the vernacular languages of North India and the Punjab eventuated in the establishment of the publishing business of the American Mission at Lodiana and Allahabad.

One aspect of the literary work of the Punjab missionaries deserves special mention. The proper study of the language, preliminary to the writing of books in the vernacular, required various literary helps: Grammars, Dictionaries, Manuals, &c. The Punjabi language was absolutely wanting in any such helps. Accordingly the Rev. John Newton undertook the duty of providing such books. He first began by preparing a Grammar of the Punjabi language in English and Gurmukhi. His book grew up with his study of the language, and the aid of a good pundit. This work was published in due course and so became available for any one desiring to acquire a knowledge of the Punjabi language.

Later on he and his colleagues Joseph Porter and Levi Janvier undertook to compile an English and Punjabi Dictionary. Such a work necessitated a large acquaintance with the sacred writings of the Sikhs and many secular works in manuscript. This work occupied several years of

[12] John Jordan, who spent a long lifetime in the mission press, eventually becoming a joint proprietor with Mr. Caleb, and after acquiring a fortune, retired in old age, dying in 1918, respected by all. His body was carried by Christian young men to the grave.

study by men, whose hands were full of other forms of missionary work. The book when completed was used by civil and military officers as well as by missionaries for the next two generations.

Another kind of literature also had to be prepared: text books, in Urdu, Hindi and Punjabi. A manual of Geography and a History of the Punjab with brief descriptions of the chief towns and cities. These were published at Lodiana.

The creation of a Christian community brought also the need and the preparation of suitable books for old and young. Thus Christian literature grew up as a new intellectual product. Every man learned by experience the need—first his own need—of a certain kind of literature; and he set to work to provide for that need. As a result almost every missionary heard a call to literary effort.

The number of readers was as yet very small, especially in the villages; but to place in a village a copy of the scriptures, or a good book, was like placing a candle in a dark room.

The British and American Bible Societies were asked to publish the scriptures—the missionaries doing the necessary work of translating or revising needed for the various languages.

This work of preparing books and tracts continued year after year. The English and American tract societies were asked to publish and their response was most generous. Ere long the evangelist could carry with him considerable quantities of scripture portions, books and tracts in Urdu, Hindi and Punjabi.

The birth of a Christian community with its schools, training classes, Sunday Schools, &c., called for a special literature: Biography, History, Commentaries, Concordances, Theological treatises, with books for young and old. The preparation of such publications absorbed a large portion of the time and labor of the authors, revisers and printers. Like the rain and sunshine, which falling upon the newly sown seed, cause it to germinate and grow into golden harvests, so the quiet and often unseen influence of these devoted men, laboring in the solitude of the study has placed in the hands of coming generations of Christian workers the means of a wide extension of the Kingdom of God by means of the printed word of God and a Christian literature.

The distribution of Christian literature was at first comparatively easy. The paucity of books of any kind led many people to read Christian books with avidity. Even the printed papers used as wrappers were treasured by many and read over and over again. It was, however, difficult to induce people to buy books. In order to secure a wide circulation of religious tracts and books in the vernacular languages, it was necessary to circulate them free of charge. It is on record that the Lodiana missionaries gave away as many as 25,000 copies at a single mela at Hardwar.[18]

It was very common in the earlier years of the mission, for Hindus and Muhammadans to come to the houses of the missionaries for the express purpose of securing Christian books. In this way a large number of books were distributed annually. Through such channels many books were sent beyond the Sutlej into the Punjab long before the way was opened up for regular mission work. So too scriptures and books were sent into the closed lands of Afghanistan and Thibet. Thus the printed page frequently served as a pioneer to the advance of the missionary into regions beyond.

[18] *Report of the Lodiana Mission*, 1834-44, p. 36.

CHAPTER III.

Preaching the Gospel to Hindus, Buddhists and Muslims

IN the initial stages of missionary work in any foreign land, the missionary must spend a considerable portion of his time in the acquisition of the language. Until this has been accomplished, preaching, in the ordinary sense, is out of the question. It is well that it is so, because the period of language study affords an excellent opportunity for the study of the people and their manners and customs. The religions of the country too may be studied and such a practical knowledge of their worship, their rites and ceremonies may be acquired as will aid one in determining the best method of presenting the claims of the Gospel later on.

In the meanwhile, as we have seen, there is much to do of a very practical nature; the erection of dwelling houses, the opening of schools, the building of schoolhouses, the care of the poor and the orphan. As the language is being learned, many opportunities arise when one can tell the good news of the Gospel. First of all his own pure life, and that of his wife, in his home is a powerful witness. His care for the orphans and the needy ones everywhere around him, and his ministry to the sick and suffering, so far as possible, are sure to commend his cause to the people. Then he may distribute the scriptures and Christian tracts and books in the languages of the people, and thus interest many whose language he cannot yet use. By and by he will be able to say at least a few words of good cheer to those about him. Thus he will gain the confidence of his neighbors and will grow in the use of the language until he can venture on a more definite course of public address.

Such is the story of the early services rendered by the pioneers of American Missions in Upper India.

The first public proclamation of the Gospel was usually made in the open street. The missionary, taking his stand in some open place near a temple or mosque, begins to read aloud from the Bible in the vernacular. The people gather about him and listen respectfully. After awhile he addresses them upon the teaching of the passage read. The people listen with a manifest curiosity—struck perhaps by the novelty of a foreigner speaking their language. Perhaps one or more may be attracted by the message spoken. The interest of even a few hearers begins to arouse antagonism among the more zealous Hindus and Muhammadans. Some of these now begin to interrupt the preacher, asking questions calculated to excite controversy. And now, ununless the preacher is wise, he will soon find himself carried away from his objective and launched in the quagmire of a profitless controversy.

Such experiences as this soon led missionaries to secure, either by rental or by sale, a room or hall where the people might come and sit and quietly listen to the preaching. At some of the stations, houses or chapels were built for preaching purposes. Benches were provided, so that the people might be comfortable. Doors opened here and there to permit easy entry or departure.

At Lodiana a commodious church building was erected on a main thoroughfare, where regular services were held every Sunday afternoon. Audiences of three hundred people could be comfortably seated. In front was a broad platform with cement floor, where preaching in the open air could be carried on every day in the week, excepting Sundays. This church was provided with a good bell, the very ringing of which was a reminder that the Christian's God was worshipped in this city. A few Christians, the families of Christian employees of the mission, with the orphan girls, occupied the front seats. Back of them were school boys, Hindus and Muslims from the city and soldiers from the cantonment nearby. These services were usually impressive and were not only edifying to the Christian worshippers, but were also blessed to the conversion of non-Christians.

A very striking case was that of a Brahmin soldier, who after a long struggle and considerable persecution by relatives in the same company, who had become acquainted with his interest in Christianity, made up his mind to declare himself a convert. The Rev. Mr. Porter was preaching. His text was, "Behold, now is the accepted time, behold now is the day of salvation." The Brahmin soldier sat near the pulpit. As the sermon proceeded, he became visibly excited. Presently he arose and with a few rapid strides he reached the pulpit platform. This he ascended, and tearing the Brahminical thread from his neck, he cast it down and, with a loud voice, said: "That is a lie"; and then pointing his finger at the preacher, said "He is true." He then embraced him as his teacher! Bedlam followed. The soldiers trooped out of the church crying out, "That Brahmin has gone mad!—that Brahmin is mad!" The preacher then went on with his sermon. The Brahmin was not mad. He underwent much persecution, but remained steadfast.[1] His colonel was a Christian man, who took compassion on him, and made him an orderly so as to keep him under his protection. He fought through the Burmese war and, after discharge, became a preacher and eventually a minister in charge of a sub-station.

A similar church building was erected in Saharanpur, which was used during the week as a school house for boys. On Sundays it was used as a church. The same arrangement was made at other places. Chapels were built at Subathu and Meerut. The mission opened at the latter

[1] He was baptized and was called by the Christian name Matthias.

city was subsequently made over to the Church Missionary Society. At Simla, the Rev. J. M. Jamieson hired a house in the bazar, where he preached to the Hill men, coolies, who carried the sedan chairs used by Europeans popularly known as *jampans*—the carrier being called a *jampanee*. The services for the jampanees were held during the hours of divine service in the church. The opportunity was a good one, the jampanees at such a time being assembled in large numbers and always at leisure. The house, which was large, was often well filled.

The chapel movement began at Allahabad in 1840, when a small chapel was built in the Chauk (an open square used as a market place). The site was donated by Government, and the cost of the building, about seven hundred rupees, was contributed by friends in India. In 1844, a chapel was built in Kydganj, one of the large suburban villages of Allahabad. The money for this purpose was provided by a legacy left by a Muhammadan lady, who had embraced Christianity. This lady at her death, having no relatives, bequeathed her property to the mission.

In these chapels, services were held several times during the week; and in each, a vernacular school was also taught.[2]

These chapels supplied the immediate needs of the small Christian communities, but soon an effort was made to provide larger church buildings, wherein the Christians and their children, along with the boys and girls in the orphanages and Christian boarding schools might enjoy the ordinances of the church without the disturbing influences of non-Christians.

At Lodiana, such a church was built on the mission compound. Nearby was a tract of land, specially acquired as a place, where such Christian families, as were driven from their homes in the city or village, might build houses for themselves. This soon became a small village, known as

[2] *History of A. P. Mission*, p. 112.

"the Christian Village." It was convenient to have the church near by. Here services were held regularly every Sunday morning and on Wednesday evening. Periodical services in English were also held, to which European Christian friends in the station were invited.

The Mission Compound at Saharanpur proved to be very unhealthy owing to swamp land near by, in which swarms of mosquitoes were bred. Malarial fever was very prevalent. It was, therefore, determined to abandon it. A large tract of land was purchased on the opposite side of the city. New buildings were erected for dwelling houses and a Boys' orphanage. A church building was erected, accommodating both the Indian Christians and European congregations.

On the 5th of July, 1840, an Indian Church was organized at Allahabad, the ordinance of baptism having been administered, at the beginning of that year, for the first time in Allahabad, to a native of the country on profession of faith. Several others were baptized during the year. It was during this year, too, that for the first time, in Allahabad, the Hindustani language was used in administering the Lord's Supper.[3]

In the year 1841, a church was organized at Fattehgarh, with a membership of ten communicants, of whom four were Indians.

Mention has already been made of the formation of the Presbyteries and Synod. One of the first acts of the Presbytery of Farrukhabad was to receive under its care as a candidate for the ministry, Mr. Gopinath Nandi, a student of Dr. Duff's institution in Calcutta. After three years in study, he was ordained to the ministry. This was the first instance, so far as known, when in the entire East a native of the country received Presbyterian ordination.

Gopinath Nandi, a native of Calcutta, a Brahmin by

[3] *History of A. P. Mission*, p. 112.

caste, while a student in Duff's College, became a convert to Christianity. Many difficulties stood in his way, but he determined, cost what it might, to openly confess his faith. He was baptized by Dr. Duff on the 14th of December, 1832. After completing his studies, he became a teacher in the orphan school at Fattehpur, when, on the departure of Dr. Madden, that school was disbanded, he was invited by Rev. Henry R. Wilson to accompany him to Fattehgarh. There he was appointed head master of the new orphan school established there. We shall have occasion to make mention of this remarkable man more than once in later chapters of this history.

From this point and onward, we shall have occasion to chronicle the growth of the Indian church from within, the Indian pastors and evangelists relieving more and more the foreign missionaries from pastoral duty.

The duty of preaching the gospel far and wide pressed heavily upon the members of the missions, who had now become sufficiently acquainted with the vernacular languages to enable them to present the truth intelligently to their hearers. From a report of the Lodiana Mission in those early days we learn that it was a regulation of the mission that every missionary, able to leave his station, should spend a portion of each cold season in touring through the villages and towns of his district. In this way all the most important towns and villages within the bounds of the stations were visited—many of them often. The whole country was intersected by roads leading in every direction on which tours were made from the stations.[4]

Once a year the missionaries assembled for an Annual Meeting at some one of the stations. In order to have with them at their destination, as well as for the journey to and fro, proper accommodation, they took with them tents and necessary furniture. The journey was made by

[4] *A Brief Account of the Lodiana Mission*, 1834-1843, pp. 34, 35.

marching from village to village, where they could preach to the villagers and place in the hands of those who could read, books and tracts. The return journey was usually so planned as to enable them to reach new towns and villages. In this way, the journey to and from the annual meeting was allied to an evangelistic campaign. During the cold season when living in tents was tolerable, some of the missionaries, with their Indian assistants, made extensive tours visiting famous shrines, or fairs, where they were able to reach great multitudes of the people. One of the most famous places was Hardwar, situated at the point of exit of the sacred river Ganges from the Himalaya mountains. Here a great mela is held every year, in the month of April. Pilgrims come from all parts of India. Hundreds of thousands attend with the one great desire of washing away their sins in the waters of the sacred river. Once in twelve years a very great mela (The Kumb), is held, at which more than a million people gather together. Here are hundreds of Sadhus or Holy Men, naked but for a breech cloth, with bodies smeared with ashes, yet with a proud and supercilious bearing. A few of them would be found to be earnest seekers after some way of life, after the manner of the Hindu devotee. This mela was visited by missionaries because it afforded a unique opportunity for meeting people from all parts of India, to whom they could give the good news both by word of mouth and by means of scriptures and books, which the people might carry away with them.

Other sacred places were annually visited for evangelistic purposes by these pioneers. One was Thenesar, some 20 miles east of Ambala. This was the famous battle ground of the Karus and the Pandas. It was also the scene of some of the fiercest and bloodiest battles between Hindus and their Muhammadan invaders. Here gather together multitudes annually, at a great mela to avail themselves of the privileges of the sacred tanks wherein to purify themselves. From this place were scattered far and wide the gospel messages and the sacred scriptures of the Christian Evangelists.

One other, of the most famous melas, in India is the Magmela, held annually at the junction of the Jumna and Ganges rivers at Allahabad. A third river, the famous Saraswati, which disappears in the sands of upper India near Ambala, is supposed to flow under ground and to unite with the Ganges at Allahabad. This mela draws thousands of people from all parts of India. In all the years, this mela is noted for its multitudes of sunyasis, so called holy men, naked fakirs, wild fanatics with long hair in filthy matted locks, and faces and bodies smeared with ashes, a motley crowd, who come from everywhere. Fanatics come here bent on suicide. These fasten water vessels on their necks and, wading into the water neck-deep, deliberately fill the vessels with water until they sink carrying their bodies under.

The Rev. Joseph Owen tells us of a personal experience as follows: "I saw a wretched old man, who had cut his throat with a razor, lying gasping for life; he died soon after. The poor deluded creature was no doubt induced to kill himself in the hope that he would pass thence into paradise." He further says: "I never saw the people listen with more interest to preaching than they did here."[5]

Such scenes and such multitudes naturally draw the missionaries to this mela. Blinded and superstitious, as such multitudes are, many are more open to the gospel call than the great multitudes, who felt a call to attend the Magmela.

These missionary journeys often covered hundreds of miles, occupying months for their completion. The Rev. Joseph Porter with his helpers travelled from Lodiana as far as Fattehgarh and Agra, returning via Aligarh, Meerut,

[5] *The Foreign Missionary*, July, 1845, p. 105.

Saharanpur and Ambala, a distance of not less than 1500 miles, probably more, as he zigzagged his way from town to town, preaching to the people at every halting place.

This wide sowing of the seed of the word accomplished a most important purpose. Aside from the fact that some seeds fell on good ground and brought forth fruit, the public interest in the new religion was aroused. The work was pioneer and illustrates the mind and spirit of the missionaries, who felt themselves called to preach the gospel to every creature.

The Rev. J. M. Jamieson was stationed at Subathu because of the delicate health of Mrs. Jamieson. His house, being located in the cantonment, was liable to be requisitioned at any time. A new regiment was sent to Subathu and, in consequence, the Jamiesons had to vacate their house and find quarters elsewhere. In order to secure a house suited to Mrs. Jamieson's condition, they removed to Simla some twenty-five miles beyond. Both at Subathu and Simla, Mr. Jamieson became interested in the Buddhist Lamas or priests of Kanawr and Thibet. Numerous bands of traders annually came down from the mountain interior, or countries bordering on Thibet, to trade with the towns on the lower hills and even the plains below. Mr. Jamieson conceived the idea that if books and tracts could be prepared in the language of these merchants they might be sent into these hermit regions, and so the good news of Christ and His salvation be made known in those regions. He therefore undertook to acquire their language and then, with the aid of a Lama teacher, he wrote a booklet in the Thibetan language, which was a compend of the gospel story and the way of salvation. When this booklet was printed, he made ready for a journey into the Kanauri valley, and if possible into Thibet. He was fortunate in finding two English gentlemen, who desired to investigate the conditions of life in those remote regions. The party started on the journey towards the Thibetan border. Mr. Jamieson called at the Buddhist temples, visiting the Lamas by the way. He was anxious to learn the literacy of the people and find out what possible demand there might be for Thibetan literature in upper Kanawr, where the Thibetan language is used. He also desired to learn something of the adjoining country of Thibet and to discover the need of translations of the scriptures, and the facilities there might be for distributing them.

The journey led the party through Kotgarh, Rampur, and after twenty days' travel, on to Lipe, a village in Kanawr, situated on the upper waters of the Sutlej river.

In Lipe, Mr. Jamieson met twelve Lama priests. After conversing with them for some time and examining their books, of which several were very large, he presented them with some Thibetan tracts—the first Christian books in their own tongue they had ever seen. One of their number read fluently and all seemed pleased with their tracts.

From Lipe the journey was along the sides of precipitous mountains on a by-path quite dangerous. Passing by several towns they reached the prosperous village of Kanawr. This was a populous place surrounded by fertile, well watered fields, and was the site of a Buddhist monastery and nunnery. In the monastery were some twenty monks. Their library was large, containing two celebrated Thibetan works "Kah-Gyur" and the "Stan-Gyur," the former being a collection of 108 large volumes, and the latter of 225. These comprehend the principal works of the literature and religion of Thibet. They are principally translations from the sanscrit.

Mr. Jamieson then had the Lamas collected together and after making inquiries concerning their literature, religion, numbers and their need of books, he distributed tracts among them. They received them with apparent delight.

It was interesting to see so many of these learned and

veteran Buddhists reading in their own tongue for the first time, the way of salvation through the Lord Jesus Christ.

Continuing their journey they reached Poo, near the border of Chinese Tartary. Here they crossed the Sutlej by a very high and narrow bridge and, after climbing over rocks and piles of rubbish, they reached Dabling. To them this proved to be a Pisgah, whence they could see the Celestial Empire, but were prevented from entering into the forbidden territory. Accordingly they returned disappointed to Poo, and thence to Simla.

The journey was profitable however in experience, but the time did not then seem to have come to undertake mission work in Thibet. That work has since been done by the Moravian brethren at Poo and Kyelang.

Mr. Jamieson seems to have been the first missionary to visit Kanawr and the border of Thibet. Some years later Rev. John Newton and wife with Rev. C. W. Forman and wife visited the Kanawr valley. Mr. Jamieson continued to show his interest in the Lamas so long as he lived in Simla and Subathu. Mr. Jamieson, while in Simla, did a great deal of itinerant work, preaching in the villages. He almost annually visited the great mela at Hardwar. He also travelled back to Simla via Dehra and Mussoorie, a long journey of about one hundred and twenty miles. His familiarity with the Hindi language enabled him to preach to the natives in this region.

At Simla he spent some time in literary pursuits. Here he translated from the Urdu into Hindu the following booklets: "Poor Joseph"; "Two Old Men"; "Bob, the Cabin Boy"; "What Is Your Religion?"; "Salvation Not by Works," and "Notes to Pilgrim's Progress."

During Mrs. Jamieson's illness, the mission house at Subathu was occupied by a military officer, but on the removal of the regiment the house was again available, and

Mr. Jamieson reoccupied it. He reopened the Boys' School. Two of his old inquirers applied for baptism, assuring him that his work had not been in vain.

It was while he was here, that he had sought permission to open a new station at Ambala, but not being able to secure a house there, he felt that the reopening of the work at Subathu was the will of God. He then planned a school with hostels where village boys might come and board themselves during the week bringing food from home. He also wished for a poor-house, believing that such institutions would attract the people from the nearby villages. However the sudden death of his wife, under an attack of cholera, obliged his return to America on furlough to provide for his children. He had succeeded in building a poor-house, in which there were 35 or 40 inmates. He also built a church of stone, thirty feet by twenty-four, for the use of Europeans. The money for both the structures, he raised among friends in India.[6]

[6] *Foreign Mission Church*, p. 154.

CHAPTER IV.

Barriers Removed—The Punjab Occupied

THE time had now come when the doors so long closed against the entry of the gospel into the Kingdom of the Punjab would be opened. Maharajah Runjeet Singh had a long struggle before he finally brought the many Sikh chiefs under his control. He was quick to see and to appreciate the value of European munitions and tactics in warfare; and, accordingly, he employed a number of French officers to drill his officers and troops on western lines and to teach his artizans how to manufacture small arms and ammunition and to make cannon for heavy artillery. His efforts were so far successful, that he easily restrained the efforts of the Afghan amirs to invade his territories. Within his own border, the power of the Moslems was completely broken. He was jealous of the British whose victorious advance had continued until they had reached the Sutlej River. To accomplish this they had set up a protectorate over the Sikh states east and south of the Sutlej. As the lion of the Punjab saw the red of English dominion spreading over the map of India, he instantly apprehended its further extension over his own borders. However, he entered into a treaty with the British Government and acknowledged their protectorate over the Cis-Sutlej Sikh principalities, which he faithfully observed. He strengthened his army until it numbered 90,000 infantry besides 30,000 horse and artillery numbering several hundred pieces. His borders were protected by forts built by competent engineers. His rule extended north and west to the borders of Afghanistan and Baluchistan and included Kashmir. He was lord of the Land of the Five Rivers. All Europeans were excluded on political grounds, excepting a few in his employ. The religion of the state was the Sikh religion, the faith of Nanak and the Ten Gurus. Islam in the Punjab was crushed under an iron heel. Christianity was excluded. The missionaries at Lodiana longed for the day when they might enter the Punjab. Books and tracts in the languages of the people were carried beyond the Sutlej but not by Christian hands. An effort was made to test the matter of the closed door by sending an Indian Christian over the river to Phillaur, eight miles distant. The messenger was Mr. Goloknath, a catechist. This first apostle to the Sikhs stopped near the fort and began to preach the gospel. He was at once arrested and thrown upon his back and a millstone[1] was placed on his chest. He was told to wait there until it was determined what should be done with him. After some hours, the Sikh officers decided to send him back to Lodiana in safety with a warning not to return. This mild decision was no doubt due to a desire not to give offence to the English at Lodiana.

The great Rajah died June 27th, 1839. His body was cremated. Nine of his wives and concubines were burned alive on the funeral pyre. The ashes were scarcely cold when conspiracy and counter conspiracy began. The heir apparent, Kharak Singh, a weak-minded man, reigned only four months, when he was deposed and soon after died under suspicious circumstances. He was succeeded by Nau-Nihal Singh, a worthy prince who had distinguished himself in military service. He was enthroned with great pomp, but on the same day he was killed while riding on an elephant, by a portion of an arched gateway falling on him as the animal crushed his way through. The next in succession was Rajah Sher Singh. He was foully assassinated in 1843. His son and heir to the throne, with his wives and every member of the royal family, was slain, that no rival to the youngest and favorite son of Runjeet Singh might remain alive to contest his right to rule. The palace was taken and Dhulip Singh, the only remaining son of Rajah

[1] The household mill made of two stones each weighing 30 pounds.

Runjeet Singh, a lad of ten years old, was proclaimed to the throne. Troops were sent off to guard all river crossings and all the opposite party (except General Ventura, who escaped) were made prisoners. Rajah Dhulip Singh was put on the throne and Sirdar Hira Singh was made Prime Minister. Six hundred persons were slaughtered on both sides.

Things went from bad to worse. The queen mother, Jindan Kaur, a woman of great energy, carried on the new government, but did not have the support she wanted from Hira Singh, the Prime Minister. This man feared the Sikh army (called the Khalsa), and sought relief by leading most of the army towards the Sutlej River.

This action of the Sikh army, which was known to be anxious to cross swords with the English army on the Punjab frontier, naturally led the English to be prepared for an attack. The English army numbered 30,000 with 70 guns. They were stationed at three points: at Firozpur under Sir John Littler, at Ambala under Sir Hugh Gough, the Commander-in-Chief, and Lodiana under the Governor General. On the 11th of December, the Sikhs began to cross the Sutlej, near Firozpur, led by Lal Singh, with cavalry under Tej Singh 30,000 strong. On the 18th of December they attacked Sir Hugh Gough at Mudki, a village twenty miles south-east of Firozpur, and, notwithstanding the Sikhs had surprised the English while at breakfast, they were defeated with great slaughter. During the night they retreated to Firozshahr, a village midway between Mudki and Firozpur, where they entrenched themselves and mounted over one hundred guns. Tej Singh, with his cavalry, stationed his army between Firozpur and the new battle line to prevent the English General Littler from reenforcing General Gough. However, the English succeeded in getting 5,000 soldiers from Firozpur.

The English attacked Lal Singh on the 21st of December at three in the afternoon, and after a bloody battle, the Sikhs retreated to Subraon. Tej Singh only discovered his error in watching General Littler, when later in the day he arrived at Firozshahr and learned that Lal Singh had retreated. After some hesitation he followed the retreating army to Subraon. Here the Sikhs entrenched again and awaited reinforcements.

The English had lost heavily. There was also a delay, which encouraged the Sikhs to send an army towards Lodiana to intercept reinforcements coming from Ambala. They camped at Baddowal near Lodiana. Sir Harry Smith was sent from Firozpur to protect the Ambala contingent and its heavy artillery, but wished to join the Lodiana garrison before attacking the Sikhs. His way led through Baddowal, and so, when he arrived there he found the Sikhs, who at once attacked him. He, however, managed to bring his army in safety to Lodiana without serious loss.

On the 22nd of January, the Sikhs left Baddowal and went to Aliwal some fifteen miles from Lodiana. Both armies had received reinforcements. Sir Harry Smith marched to the attack and defeated the Sikh army at Aliwal, driving it into the river where thousands were drowned.

The decisive battle was yet to be fought. On the 10th of February the battle of Sobraon was fought. The English with 15,000 troops attacked the Sikh army 30,000 strong with 70 guns behind their fortifications. The fight was furious, but the English captured position after position and by midday had secured a complete victory. The Sikhs retreated to a bridge of boats on the Sutlej River, when a panic resulted in thousands being drowned.

The English forthwith crossed the river and established themselves at Kasur. The Khalsa had been defeated and soon peace was proclaimed.

During the course of this brief, but bloody war, the missionaries and civilians and all European and Christian people were filled with anxiety and fear. One evening a marauding expedition of the Sikhs set fire to some buildings on the further side of the city. The ladies of the station, including Mrs.

Janvier, took refuge in the fort for that night. The next day the commanding officer sent off Mrs. Janvier and the orphan girls with the native Christians to Saharanpur.

The success of the British forces at Aliwal put an end to their fears and quiet was restored. That there was good reason for the anxiety is evident from the fact that the government reimbursed the losses of the missionaries due to their removal from Lodiana to Saharanpur.[2]

The English school had been broken up owing to the invasion of the Sikh army, but now the students began to return. By the end of the year the ordinary work of the mission was in full swing.

New responsibilities were now laid upon the missionaries. The war resulted in bringing in the day for which they had waited for more than a decade. The British had entered the Punjab and had annexed to their possessions all the region lying between the Sutlej and the Bias Rivers, both in the hills and the plains. This brought under the British flag many large towns and scores of villages where the gospel might be preached without hindrance.

Accordingly the board in New York was urged to send large reinforcements.

In the meanwhile the Rev. Joseph Porter was sent to Jalandhar to secure land for a school building. Mr. John Lewis was appointed to be the head master of the new school. Tents were pitched on the site and the school was begun without delay. European officers contributed most liberally toward the erection of a school building, in which also religious services might be held.

Thus the door so long shut against the gospel was now open, and, as we shall see, the way was soon to be made clear for the establishment of missions at Lahore, Gujrauwala and Rawal Pindi.

---

[2] See *The Foreign Missionary*, October, 1846, p. 18.

CHAPTER V.

Expansion in North India

PERHAPS the most encouraging work of the North India Mission in the early forties was that of the orphan schools at Fattehgarh. For the boys' orphanage, it was imperative that the education given should be practical, if any Christian community were to be established. Effort was made to secure a piece of land near by upon which married orphans might be settled. The government made liberal response, and gave a plot of land on very generous terms. This was divided into lots; and homes were provided for married couples.

This was preliminary to setting up a tent factory, which would provide for the practical training of the orphan boys; and which would also become a lucrative investment for the Indian Christians.

Rev. J. L. Scott and Mrs. Scott were now transferred from Mainpuri to take charge of the boys' orphanage and its industries. Mr. Scott took hold of this work with great energy. The industries were organized on a business basis. A joint stock company was formed and Christians were induced to invest their savings to form a working capital. Contracts were taken from the government for the manufacture of tents for the army. Along with the making of tents was the weaving of carpets. Every boy was obliged to spend a part of each day in the tent factory. Thus they were able to earn something each month toward the expense of their education.

In October, 1844, the seat of government for the Northwest Provinces was transferred from Allahabad to Agra, the former capital of Akbar the Great. This transfer seriously affected the mission at Allahabad. Many English friends, who had rendered very efficient aid by their sympathy and financial support, were now removed to Agra. But this loss to the work in Allahabad proved to be a gain, when during the next year it was decided to begin mission work in Agra. This decision was due partly to the fact that Agra afforded a large and important field for evangelistic effort, and partly because the friends who had so generously aided them in Allahabad, assured them that in Agra like help and sympathy would be extended to them.

Accordingly, the Rev. James Wilson, of Allahabad, and the Rev. John C. Rankin, of Fattehgarh, were transferred to Agra to begin the work at the new capital. The American missionaries were now brought in touch with the religion of Islam, and both of them became pioneers in the direct work of evangelizing the Muslims of India. Mr. Wilson had been engaged in producing a vernacular literature since he entered the mission at Lodiana. He wrote in Urdu the following booklets: "On the Future State"—"Nicodemus the Enquirer"—a translation of Gauladet's "Child Book on the Soul"—a translation of the "Confession of Faith" and the "Westminster Shorter Catechism." His most important work was the annotated edition of the Quran in Roman Urdu, prepared for special use among missionaries and Indian Evangelists. His preface to that edition attracted special interest because he therein advocated the view that the "Man of a fierce countenance" mentioned in the prophecy of Daniel (Chapter VIII: 23) is Muhammad, and that the vision of the chapter relates not to the Roman apostasy, but to the rise, progress and fall of the religion of Islam.

It was at about this time that Mr. Rankin wrote his book on Muhammadanism, which was one of the first books published on the Muhammadan controversy, in the Urdu language, in which the character of the Arabian prophet was compared with that of Jesus Christ.

Agra was at that time the centre of the conflict. The Rev. C. Gottleib Pfander, Rev. William Smith and Samuel Theodore

Leupholt of the Church Missionary Society, with James Wilson and John C. Rankin, were the champions on the Christian side. The outcome of this controversy was the conversion of several men of note, who became leaders in the days following. Christian literature became enriched in the writings of Dr. Prander's "Balance of Truth," "The Key to Mysteries," and the "Way of Life,"[1] which have been translated into the Persian and Arabic languages, and continue to be standard works on the Muhammadan controversy.

The North India Bible Society was organized about this time and Mr. Wilson was elected its secretary, with headquarters in Agra.

Mr. Wilson's arduous life as a missionary for seventeen years began to seriously impair his health. Early in 1857 he returned to America. Mr. Wilson was one of the pioneer missionaries of the Presbyterian church in the United States of America. He served in four stations, being a pioneer in each: Lodiana, Subathu, Allahabad and Agra. He was scholarly, a man of sound judgment, a good preacher and wise administrator. His inability to return was felt to be a serious loss to India.

The first Sikh war resulted in the annexation of the Jalandhar Doab to the British Dominions, thus pushing the boundary line on from the Sutlej River westward to the Bias. The youngest son of Maharajah Runjeet Singh, Prince Dhulip Singh, a boy of ten years of age, was recognized as heir to the throne. Major Henry Lawrence was appointed Resident at Lahore and a British force was detailed to garrison the Punjab for a period of eight years.[2]

The spirit of the Khalsa had been humbled, but not broken. Early in 1848, two British officers were treacherously murdered in Multan. This was the signal for a fanatical ris-

---

[1] These three books are known in Urdu as *Mizan ul Hagg—Miftah ul Asrar—* and *Tariqul Haiyat*. They have been published in several editions. The first two have been revised and emended by Rev. Dr. St. Clair Tisdale, some time missionary in India and Persia. E. M. W.

[2] *Encyclopedia Brittanica*, Article "India".

ing of the Sikhs against British rule. "The Khalsa army again came together and once more fought on even terms with the British. On the fatal field of Chilianwala, which patriotism prefers to call a drawn battle, the British lost 2,400 officers and men, besides four guns and the colors of three regiments. Before reinforcements could come out from England, with Sir Charles Napier as Commander-in-Chief, Lord Gough had restored his own reputation by the crowning victory of Gujrat, which absolutely destroyed the Sikh army. Multan had previously fallen; and the Afghan horse, under Dost Muhammad, who had forgotten their predatory antipathy to the Sikhs in their greater hatred of the British name, were chased back with ignominy to their native hills. The Punjab henceforth became a British Province.[8]

The Punjab was annexed April 2nd, 1849. The boy King, Rajah Dhulip Singh, was deposed and given an annual allowance of 50,000 pounds. He retired as a gentleman to Norfolk, England.

During these months of turmoil and anxiety, the missionary work continued as usual. Soon after the annexation of the Punjab, a letter was received by the missionaries at Lodiana, sent by Dr. Baddely, a Christian surgeon at Lahore, urging them to move on to the capital without delay, assuring them that every encouragement might be expected from the Lawrences and Mr. Montgomery and others. Accordingly the Rev. John Newton and the Rev. Charles W. Forman were appointed by the mission to take up the work of establishing the mission in Lahore. Accompanied by Mrs. Newton, they arrived in Lahore on the 21st of November, 1849.

As the Christian community had urged the establishment of the mission, an appeal was made for financial aid, with the approval of the Board of Administration and the Governor General. In response thereto, the sum of Rs. 4,238 were contributed. A suitable house was secured in the city as a tempo-

[8] *Encyclopedia Brittanica*, Article "India".

rary residence. In this house an English school was begun on the 19th of December. It began with three pupils, all being Hindu Kashmiris, two of them having been formerly students in the mission school at Lodiana. The number gradually increased until it became necessary to find more capacious quarters. Happily a soldiers' chapel built by an English gentleman at his own expense had been placed at the disposal of the mission, and being well adapted to the uses of a school the classes were transferred to it. The number of pupils rapidly increased until, at the end of the year, the attendance amounted to eighty. Of these fifty-five were Hindus and twenty-two Muslims, and three Sikhs. Racially the eighty ranked as Punjabis thirty-eight, Kashmiris three, Bengalis seven, Hindustanis twenty-eight, Afghans three and one Baluch.[4]

It was at first proposed to open a vernacular as well as an English school. This would have meant a school in which the Persian as well as the Urdu language would have been taught by non-Christian teachers, as had been arranged at Lodiana and Jalandhar. The Urdu language having been constituted the language of the courts, as now required by the government, it was certain that it would become more prominent as the years would go by. For this as well as other reasons, it was determined to employ an Urdu teacher and make the study of Persian and Urdu a part of the school course. Thus was begun a policy which has characterized all mission schools in the Punjab ever since. The same plan has been adopted in government schools also.

The Lahore School was from the first conducted in the strictest sense on Christian principles, agreeable to the prospectus put forth by the missionaries on their arrival at the station. Every effort was made to procure class books, which recognized the Divine authority of the Christian religion and

[4] *Lodiana Mission Report,* 1850, pp. 25, 26..

studiously inculcated its doctrines as truths which all men should understand.

Besides this, one of the daily studies of the higher classes was the New Testament. From the first the school was opened with prayer, and although the pupils were distinctly told that they were not required to be present at the prayer service, few, if any, deliberately absented themselves from it.[5]

Thus began the work of Anglo-vernacular education in the capital of the Punjab; a work consistent with the policy of the mission, inaugurated at Lodiana at the founding of the mission, a work which has eventuated in revolutionizing the moral and religious thought of multitudes throughout the provinces.

The plan of evangelization comprised not only education, but also preaching, or the expounding of the claims of the Christian faith by word and the printed page. It was, however, expedient for the present to limit public preaching to the regular church services, intended primarily for European and Indian Christians. For non-Christians, the evangelist depended upon personal work, by which is to be understood speaking to one or more individuals, in a shop or dwelling place or courtyard. Opportunity was afforded by the desire of the people to know why the missionaries had come, or to hear what they had to say. This usually afforded an opportunity for presenting copies of the Scriptures (usually portions), or of books to any who could read. The religious services connected with the schools, especially the Sunday service, usually held in the school hall, drew some people from the neighborhood. The next step was to hire a shop in the bazar, where the preacher could converse with the people and distribute tracts and books to those who could read. Later on, more public meetings became possible, and were held in chapels erected for the purpose.

Such meetings in the cities attracted many visitors, who

[5] *Lodiana Mission Report*, 1850, p. 26.

would invite the missionary to visit them at their homes in the country. By a natural evolution, the desire to carry the Gospel to the numerous towns and villages, led them to undertake extensive tours. Some similar tours have been described in a previous chapter, but up to this date none could be undertaken in the Punjab before the conquest of the Jalandhar Doab.

The first tour made in the Punjab of that day is described by Rev. Dr. C. W. Forman. The barriers set up at Lodiana by the scruples of English officials seem to have been completely broken down. Mr. Forman wrote April 19th, 1849, as follows:—

"Immediately after the close of the late war, Mr. Newton, Goloknath and myself went into the Punjab upon a missionary tour, our chief object being to attend a mela, which was to be held at Jawalamukhi, a town in the hills, about a hundred and twenty miles northeast of Lodiana. We crossed the Sutlej, the southern boundary of the Punjab, about eight miles from Lodiana. Our road then, for sixty miles, lay through a beautiful fertile plain, with wheat almost ready for the harvest. At the end of a four days' march, we arrived at Hoshyarpur, a town near the foot of the hills. Having procured mules at this place, to carry our tents, books, etc., we entered the hill-country. After crossing one range of hills, we came into the Dunor valley, three or four miles in breadth, which runs the whole length of the Himalaya Mountains. Leaving the valley, we arrived at Jawalamukhi in less than two days' march.

"Jawalamukhi is situated in the valley of the Bias, a mountain stream, at the foot of a hill, twelve or fifteen hundred feet high. The appearance of the town is very different from that of the towns on the plains. The streets are paved with stones; the houses are large; many of them detached from one another, and surrounded by little yards, or gardens. There are many temples in the place, built of hewn stone; and tombs of the same material, built in commemoration of widows, who were burned with their husbands' bodies. The town belongs entirely to the Faqirs (mendicants), and is regarded as one of the most sacred places in Northern India. On the side of the hill, at the foot of which the town stands, several small flames were discovered issuing from the crevices in the rock. The people, of course, regarded this as the manifestation of a Devi (goddess), and they gave her the name of Jawala, and the place the name of Jawalamukhi, or the Face of Jawala.

"Pilgrims began to frequent the place, and faqirs built huts above it, with the double purpose of being near so holy a place, and collecting alms from the pilgrims. As the number of the pilgrims increased, the number and wealth of the faqirs increased. At present there are several colleges of them, living in large, well built stone houses, upon the sides of the mountain, and in the town. They number probably three hundred and own property to the value of many thousand dollars.

"We were at Jawalamukhi more than five days. Each day, preaching was kept up for five or six hours. Great numbers came here every day. Generally as many as could hear the speaker with ease were present. Sometimes so many were assembled, that those furthest off could with difficulty hear anything that was said.

"The people listended quietly and attentively. It is not unworthy of being noticed, that Mr. Newton, upon one occasion, had a congregation of women, who listened attentively to him through a whole sermon.

"I have never witnessed so favorable an opportunity of making the gospel known. A few promised to come to Jalandhar, or Lodiana, to receive further instructions.

"The feeling manifested towards us was most friendly. No one seemed displeased by our presence, although the greater part of our work was done at the gate of the shrine."[6]

This very graphic account of a missionary tour to a sacred place is but one of many that might be quoted. It illustrates one phase of service common to every station and every mission in India. In this service the Indian preachers were especially efficient.

A further extension of the Lodiana Mission was determined upon at the annual meeting of 1847. The City of Ambala, an important military centre seventy miles southeast of Lodiana, had been mentioned as being well situated for a new mission station. It lay about midway between Lodiana and Saharanpur.

[6] *Foreign Mission Chronicle*, September, 1849.

It was located near to the great capital city of Patiala, and not more than thirty miles from the historic battlefield of Thenesar.

Accordingly arrangements were made to station Rev. J. M. Jamieson there on his return from America.

While in America Mr. Jamieson married Miss Eliza McLeary, with whom he sailed for India, arriving in Ambala on the 5th of April, 1848. A house was rented until land could be procured. A large house was also rented in the city for a school. The old difficulty of introducing religious services led to the withdrawal of more than half the patronage, but later on the requirement was accepted and the school continued with 60 in attendance.

A church was organized with a membership of six.

The following year Mr. Morrison was transferred from Subathu to Ambala, especially to aid in the district work, Mr. Jamieson's time being absorbed in the work of building a dwelling house. He also succeeded in getting a hospital and a poorhouse built, entirely by the local government and managed by a local committee, the missionary visiting occasionally to give religious instruction.

The building for the City Boys' School was finally completed in 1853. The main hall in the building became available as an assembly room for the Indian congregation.

A regular service was also conducted in the Sadar bazar in the cantonment. This was for European and Anglo-Indian Christians connected with the army.

On the transfer of Mr. Morrison to Lahore in 1850, Mr. J. H. Orbison[7] was placed in charge of the city mission school at Ambala city.

The work undertaken at Allahabad underwent no change because of the transfer of the provincial government to Agra. Each department of service, education, preaching, and pastoral work, and the school and orphan asylum continued as before.

[7] Rev. James Harris Orbison arrived in India in 1850. He labored at Lodiana, Ambala and Rawal Pindi.

In October, 1846, the government closed its school in Allahabad. The mission was then permitted to occupy the government school building and to make use of the school furniture and library. This school had about seventy pupils in attendance, but the report now went forth that the pupils were to be made Christians. In consequence of this false rumor, many pupils left the school. Nevertheless, the Bible was introduced into the school, in spite of the prejudices of the scholars. The government had excluded it from their schools, and naturally its introduction was looked upon with suspicion. After a few days, however, the first class, reading in English "Milton's Paradise Lost" and not understanding the allusions to man's first act of disobedience, asked permission to examine the Bible account of man's fall; and so the Bible was gradually introduced into all the classes. Two months later an examination was held and every class was found to have made a beginning in Bible study.[8]

The missionaries connected with the school at this time were the Rev. Joseph Owen and the Rev. James Wray. In writing about this school, Mr. Owen speaks of it as "The College." He says:

> "This institution was established, and for some years supported by the British India Government; its objest being the education of native youths in the English language and learning."

From this statement, it is plain that the original design of this school, like that of the Lodiana school, under the political agent, was to train men for government service. When, therefore, the missionaries undertook to give a more liberal course of instruction the patronage underwent a change. Mr. Owen wrote:

> "The Bible and Christian books have been introduced, the heathen holidays discountenanced, and a radical change accomplished in the religious character of the institution. What

[8] *History of A. P. Mission*, p. 117.

will be its future history, it is not easy to predict. Probably it will be chiefly attended by boys and young men of a different class of the community; but at any rate, it will no longer be a great hindrance to the spread of the gospel. With the Divine blessing it may become a powerful agency for good."[9]

How the hearts of these faithful workers would have rejoiced, could they have foreseen the splendid college now occupying the old campus of the Allahabad Mission School.

Mr. and Mrs. Wray, by reason of ill health, were soon obliged to return to America. They left in 1849. Mr. Owen, left alone, persevered in his work. He clearly foresaw the vast field for Indian employment in public offices, and the consequent new impetus towards the English education given in the mission schools. Railway projects were commencing and engineers had already been sent out to survey routes from Calcutta to the northwest. The telegraph would inevitably follow.

Near the close of the year 1846, a new addition to the mission was made by the arrival of Rev. David Irving, Rev. A. H. Seeley and Mr. Munnis and their wives.[10] These were all stationed at Fattehgarh, some to take the places of those who were to be removed by sickness and death.

Mrs. Scott's health began to break in 1847. She went to the mountains in hope of recovery, but, this failing, she left in November of the same year, with her two daughters and a daughter of Mr. and Mrs. Freeman, and sailed for America. Although very feeble, and yet realizing how much her husband was needed at his post, she urged him to remain behind. She died at sea, leaving the motherless children to complete the journey, cared for by strangers.

Mr. and Mrs. Irving spent several months in connection with the orphanage, still in charge of Mr. Scott, who labored alone for three years, caring for the financial and industrial

[9] *Foreign Missionary*, 1847, Letter of October 21, 1846.

[10] Rev. J. H. Morrison of the Lodiana Mission also came with this party.

work of the Christian village. Of this period of his life Mr. Scott wrote:

"It has been a time of trial, perplexity, suffering and sore bereavement, during which I have, in the midst of many discouragements, been endeavoring to do my part in the external service of the sanctuary."

In addition to the tent factory, a plant for the production of saltpeter had been started. This last adventure proved a failure and resulted in a loss of Rs. 2,500. Friends in the mission made good this loss, and the tent factory continued to be prospered.

The health of Mrs. Irving having failed, the McAuleys were placed in charge of the orphange and the school for non-Christian boys.

A year later Mr. and Mrs. Irving returned to America, but were destined to spend a long life in the service of foreign missions, Mr. Irving having been made a secretary of the Foreign Missionary Board in New York.

In 1848, the Rev. Alexander A. Hodge and Mrs. Hodge arrived in India. They were appointed to Allahabad, where Mr. Hodge was placed in charge of the mission high school. Two years later they were obliged to return to America, owing to the failure of the health of Mrs. Hodge. Mr. Hodge, afterwards Dr. A. A. Hodge, was elected professor of systematic theology in the Theological Seminary in Allegheny City, Pennsylvania. Later on in life, he succeeded his very distinguished father, Dr. Charles Hodge, as professor of systematic theology at Princeton, New Jersey. In this capacity he had an important part in the training of missionaries during his lifetime. What seemed to be a great loss to the cause of missions, proved to be a great gain.

The year 1850 was marked by a further serious loss to the mission force. Mrs. Freeman, who had so courageously sent her daughter home to America, soon after fell a victim to the Indian climate. Mrs. Freeman was distinguished for great gentleness of character. Mrs. Scott, her friend and co-worker, was remarkable for great firmness and decision of character, shrinking not from any sacrifice that duty seemed to demand. While in full health she made a journey to the hills alone, with her infant son in search of health, travelling a distance of five hundred miles by *dak* in ten nights. When her physicians advised her return to America, she determined to go alone, because she felt that her husband was needed at his post. When parting from her husband, she said:

"I trust we shall meet again here below, but if not, it will all be ordered aright by our covenant-keeping God."

Mr. and Mrs. Freeman accompanied Mrs. Scott to Calcutta, leaving in her care their daughter. As Mrs. Freeman was taking her little daughter in her arms for a last embrace, Mrs. Scott pressed her hand and said: "Trust ye in the Lord forever; this," she added "has ever been my motto, and I have never trusted in vain." Thus they parted; those two saints of the Lord, soon to be reunited.[11]

This tender eulogy emphasizes the great loss to the mission by the removal of two such saintly women.

Soon after the death of Mrs. Freeman, Mr. Freeman returned on furlough to America.

It was at this time that most important aid came to the mission in the person of two German laymen, Messrs. Adolph Rudolph and Julius F. Ullmann. These gentlemen had been trained by the famous Father Gossner, and came to India in a company of thirty lay missionaries, who were to carry on a mission at Chapra, in Bengal. This company represented various trades. There were carpenters, tailors, masons, farmers, etc., one an apothecary. They were to receive from home about eight dollars a month each, and were expected to live in native houses and to practically support themselves. Within

[11] Mrs. Holcomb in *History of A. P. Mission*, p. 119.

three years, about half their number had died. Most of those left alive deserted the place and found employment elsewhere. Some of them joined the Church Missionary Society. One, Mr. Adolph Rudolph, joined the Lodiana Mission, and the other, Mr. Ullmann, the Farrukhabad Mission. Mr. Rudolph was stationed first at Saharanpur and a little later at Lodiana, where he was ordained to the ministry and spent a long life of faithful service as pastor of the Indian church and superintendent of the high school, and manager of the press. He was a great itinerant preacher. Having some knowledge of medicine, he was for years the good doctor in city and village.

Mr. Ullmann, in the North India Mission, was ordained to the ministry at Farrukhabad. He labored as a preacher, teacher, author and translater of the Scriptures into Hindi. As a writer of hymns he was most successful. Much of the hymnody of the Indian church is from his pen.

In 1850, another Indian was licensed to preach as an evangelist. He was popularly known as Babu John Hari. His parents were Muhammadans and became Christians under the teaching of the famous Henry Martyn, while he was chaplain at Dinapore. The father took the name "Henry" from love of his spiritual guide, but was familiarly called Hari (Harry). The son was given the name John, and thus came the name John Hari. He was a most valuable worker. Under Dr. Warren, he was connected with the Allahabad Mission Press and became a skilled translator.

In this way, the gaps in the depleted ranks of the mission were filled.

In December, 1850, a large reinforcement from America arrived in Calcutta, consisting of the following persons: The Rev. Robert S. Fullerton and Mrs. Fullerton, the Rev. D. Elliott Campbell and Mrs. Campbell, the Rev. Lawrence Hay and Mrs. Hay, the Rev. H. W. Shaw and Mrs. Shaw. Messrs. Hay and Shaw were appointed to Allahabad; Mr. and Mrs.

Fullerton to Mainpuri; Mr. and Mrs. Campbell to Fattehgarh; and Mr. Orbison to the Lodiana Mission, for service at Ambala City.

The following year the mission force was further depleted by the return to America of Mr. and Mrs. McAuley, on account of ill health. In consequence of changes due to these retirements, Mr. Walsh was transferred from Mainpuri to Fattehgarh and Mr. Scott from Fattehgarh to Agra, where, in addition to his ordinary duties, he became secretary of the North India Bible Society.

In the end of this year (1851), Mr. Scott went on leave to America, and in consequence Mr. Warren was transferred from Allahabad to Agra. He was elected in Mr. Scott's place secretary of the Bible Society. Mr. Hay was made superintendent of the mission press at Allahabad. At the close of that year, Rev. J. E. Freeman returned from America bringing Mrs. Elizabeth Freeman with him. The Rev. J. F. Ullmann and Mrs. Ullmann returned from England. Messrs. Freeman and Ullmann were stationed at Fattehgarh.

This chapter illustrates some of the vicissitudes of missionary life in these early days. The sanitary condition of the cities was far from satisfactory. The absence of railways made it difficult to escape the intense heat of the plains, resulting in much sickness and death among both the wives and children. Then the great majority of the missionaries were new to the country and were necessarily obliged to give attention to the study of the languages. New fields of labor were constantly being opened up, and the feeling was strong that entry into these should not be delayed, lest the doors should close. The result was that the forces had to be scattered and much time had to be given to the building of houses and the organization of schools and other institutions. It was as yet a day when foundations were being laid. The day of rapid progress in evangelization was not even near at hand.

CHAPTER VI.

Anglo-Indian Education

A NEW era in the history of India was marked by the introduction of western science and economic appliances; canals, railways and the telegraph, improvements, which were destined to revolutionize in a considerable degree the thought and life of India. As we have already noted, some of the older missionaries had anticipated the advantages which would thus accrue to their endeavor to evangelize the people. The forecast of the great pioneer in English education for India, Dr. Duff, was now beginning to be realized. The educated Indians had demonstrated to their countrymen the vast importance of western science, in consequence of which the mission schools were being crowded with students anxious to secure the places now being opened to those who knew English.

Schools for girls had been established and some progress had been made in the education of the women. Protestants had as yet done but little for the education of European and Eurasian girls in India. Pure European children had been sent home in childhood, only to return when their education had been completed. Roman Catholics had provided for a limited education for this class in their schools for boys and in their convents for girls. But they scarcely aimed at more than a primary education for girls, including some knowledge of music and art. The boys were expected to occupy places as clerks and subordinate officers, in the public service. The girls were fitted to be wives, who would by their accomplishments make their homes attractive. All this would combine to strengthen the hold of the Catholic Church upon them.

On the removal of the government offices from Allahabad to Agra, there was therewith an influx of European and Eurasian people, employed in government offices at the new capital. The Presbyterian missionaries at once recognized the imperative need of a good English school for this class, as well as for the children of Protestant missionaries.

An earnest endeavor had been made to establish a Protestant academy at Agra, with both male and female departments, but after a year or two, the school suddenly collapsed.

The following statement, taken from Dr. Warren's "Missionary Life in Northern India," describes how the American mission was enabled to solve the problem of a school for Anglo-Indian children.

"Soon after the failure of the Protestant academy, its friends, especially the late Mr. Thomason, lieutenant governor, began to wish that our mission would undertake its revival. They represented to Mr. Wilson that it would succeed only as a mission school; and that there was no other mission then able to undertake it. Mr. Wilson had had some thought of this kind before, and now began to lay plans for the undertaking. He advocated the renewal, in some shape, of the Protestant academy, and spoke of his hope that a theological seminary might grow out of it eventually. The want of men, and the want of a principal for precisely such a school, led to postponement.

"Mr. Wilson was obliged to return to America before anything was settled; but he left the scheme as a kind of legacy to his successors. When Mr. Scott took his place at the station, he too began to advocate the plan. With the help of the secretary to the late academy, he wrote and printed a pamphlet on the subject, which was circulated amongst all missionaries in India, and secured their almost unanimous approval of the scheme. He was encouraged to send the plan to our executive committee in New York.

"When the matter was thus laid before the executive committee, they approved the scheme and requested Mr. Fullerton to leave Mainpuri and commence a boys' school at Agra. They also expressed an intention to send out another man to aid him. This order reached us at the close of 1851, shortly after my arrival in Agra. As the committee intimated a desire that a commencement should be made during that cold season, Mr. Fullerton removed his family in February, and the school was opened on the second day of March, 1852. We began it in a small hired bungalow, near the Presbyterian Church with six scholars.

"Although I was not expected to take any part in the instruction of the school, yet Mr. Fullerton insisted that I should take upon myself the greater part of the arrangements to be made for it. With the advice of several friends, I published a small pamphlet as an advertisement. In this we announced the principles, plans and arrangements for the school, and made an appeal to the public."

It was decided to so lower the fees as to admit a large number of children, whose parents were unable to pay the high fees charged in the former school.

The Presbyterian Church at Agra, organized largely of the members of the church in Allahabad, lately transferred to Agra, undertook to pay Mr. Warren for his pastoral services. The board in New York appropriated money for the rent of a house for Mr. Fullerton. The church agreed to advance one thousand rupees towards the purchase of a house large enough for Mr. Fullerton and the school. The lieutenant governor contributed one thousand rupees, which, with other generous gifts, enabled Mr. Warren to purchase a suitable building and to put it in repair before Mr. Fullerton arrived. The school filled up so rapidly that, by the beginning of 1853, the house was too small for both school and Mr. Fullerton and his family, so that provision had to be made for Mr. Fullerton in a house near by.

The Rev. R. E. Williams, a friend of Mr. Fullerton, came out from America to aid in the work of this school. Mr. Williams was made principal, and, with an East Indian head master and other assistants, the school grew till it had nearly one hundred pupils, some of them coming from the Punjab and others from Benares. The school was for boys only.

Mr. Scott's scheme contemplated a school for both boys and

girls. The mission board in America had only sanctioned a school for boys.

"But Divine Providence immediately began to press us onward in further measure for the education of that class of people. Two intelligent European girls were taken in hand by Mrs. Fullerton, and partly supported by some good ladies, in order to save them from being sent to the nunnery school. A poor East Indian widow begged of Mrs. Fullerton to allow her two daughters to attend also. Then some neighbors, who could pay for the privilege, begged to be allowed to send their children. This, Mrs. Fullerton was induced to concede, so that she might hire an assistant. She procured the attendance of a young woman and began a private school, not promising to continue it longer than it should suit her own convenience. She soon had fifteen pupils.

"A good lady at Agra, the wife of a civilian, interested herself in the girls, who were unable to pay for an education. She soon found several; whereupon she begged donations and subscriptions, and got two other ladies to join her to form a committee."

This work proved so much of a success, that she was able to aid not only the girls but also the boys.

With the aid of the lieutenant governor and other English residents, a large house, just opposite the boys' school, was purchased and paid for. The home board then recognized this school also. Both these schools soon became boarding schools.

Mr. Warren, who did so much to further these schools by securing the money for the buildings, pays the following tribute to the work of Mrs. Fullerton:

"It is but right to mention the zeal and devotedness of Mrs. Fullerton in connection with the girls' school. The labor involved in the care and instruction of the school, is very great, and the responsibility and the care of female boarders would not be easily borne, without any pecuniary recompense, by anyone less heartily engaged in the Master's service. She has displayed the greatest patience, under misconstructions and evil reports, even bearing to be asked if she considered her work to be mission work! But she already has an installment of her reward; spiritual fruit has been produced; and the marvellous transformation of character, which results from her influence over the girls, must be highly gratifying."[1]

These schools had a brief career under the founders, owing to the Sepoy rebellion, which obliged the missionaries and the students to take refuge in the fort. At the close of the mutiny, the mission was obliged to reconstruct its work, in the process of which Agra was abandoned as a mission station.

But, in the meanwhile, another institution had been founded. It was in the year 1854, that a number of Christian gentlemen combined in an effort to establish a Protestant school for European and Eurasian girls at Landour in the Mussoorie Hills. One of the prime movers in this enterprise was the Rev. John S. Woodside, Presbyterian missionary in Dehra. Money was collected and a grant of Rs. 13,000 obtained from the government, wherewith buildings were procured in Landour. The Society for Promoting Female Education in the East, with offices in London, was induced to undertake the conduct of the school. Qualified teachers were sent out to India and the school begun. For some twenty years the school was popularly known as the "Company School," but rightly called the Woodstock School. It was then purchased by the Woman's Foreign Missionary Society of Philadelphia, U. S. A., who undertook to support the institution, in the special interest of missionaries' children, but open, with some restrictions, to the public also. For two years it was superintended by Rev. David Herron, D. D., of the Dehra Station, with Miss Mary Pratt as head mistress. In 1877 Dr. J. L. Scott and Mrs. Scott were sent out from America to take charge as principals of the Woodstock School, with Miss Mary Fullerton as assistant.[2] From this time and onward, Woodstock rapidly developed so as to become a high school and finally a college for women, wherein the daughters of missionaries of all Protestant de-

[1] *Missionary Life in North India,* Warren, p. 212.

[2] Mr. Scott had been in Agra and Miss Fullerton's mother established the Agra Girls' School, as noted above.

nominations along with the girls from Anglo-Indian families receive an education under Christian auspices.

In the year 1875, a school for the poorer class of Europeans and Eurasians was begun at Ambala by Miss Julia Bacon. This school met a real need at the time. A year later, it was transferred to Kasauli in the mountains in order to secure a better climate. It became quite popular, and continued to grow in usefulness until the year 1883, when, owing to the failure of Miss Bacon's health, she was obliged to return to America, with no hope of being able to return. No one being found to take the school, it was closed.

From this time and onward, a certain number of indigent European girls have been admitted into the Christian Girls' School at Dehra. The statements thus briefly made cover more than a generation, a period sufficiently long to test the wisdom of the missionaries, who ventured to contravene the judgment of many—yea the great majority of good people in the homeland and in the missions in India. There were many who were obsessed with the idea that work for the evangelization of the heathen could not be consistent with the endeavor to bestow spiritual blessing upon nominal Christians. They could engage enthusiastically in educational work for Hindus, Muslims, Parsis and Jews; or for native converts, but would look askance at any proposal to undertake any special work for "Eurasians." The fact that the founders of our missions in India were led in the Providence of God to preach to Europeans and to open a school for Eurasian boys, did not seem to have impressed them as a guidance of the Spirit of God, leading them to an important principle, which was illustrated in the story of Paul and his companions when they went forth to evangelize Asia Minor and Europe: that principle was to go first to the Jews and their proselytes and then to the heathen. The example of the pioneers at Lodiana, Subathu, Lahore, Saharanpur, Allahabad, Agra and Fattehgarh, who conducted services and even organized churches for Europeans and

Anglo-Indians, proves their sense of obligation to their Christian brethren, dwelling in the midst of idolaters and Muhammadans. The logical inference was that they should also care for their children as for the children of their own families and of the native Christians.

The missionaries early realized the need of school privileges for their own children. Without such school, they were either obliged to separate from them, leaving them alone among relatives or friends at home, and go back to the mission field; or, to separate husband and wife, the wife remaining at home for the children's sake, while the husband returned to carry on his work as well as he could, without the sympathy and help of his wife. Hundreds of devoted men and women endured these separations and privations. Hundreds of children suffered the loss of the loving ministries of their own parents, or at least of the father, by reason of the necessity of such separations.

The only apparent alternative was for both parents to retire with their children, in the homeland, for the sake of their education. Here other difficulties confronted those who adopted this course. The long absence from America served to incapacitate some of them for the home work, so that employment seemed to be denied them.

The successful work accomplished in the Woodstock School and College brought relief to the missionaries, enabling them to keep their children with them until they could enter high schools or colleges in America. For some a college education also became quite possible in India. Thus in helping others, the missionaries helped themselves.

Another great benefit resulted from this educational work. Many, if not all, of these Anglo-Indians were destined to spend their lives in India. Education for their daughters meant elevation of the intellectual and social status of the community. Some of them have been introduced into the mission service as teachers and Bible women. Mrs. Adam Anthony, an Anglo-Indian, opened the first school for Indian girls in the city of Agra. She was educated in the Agra girls school for Eurasians already described. Woodstock has educated many of her own teachers. Many more have gone into some of the highest callings in life. All have contributed to the uplift of India's millions in civilization and national life.

CHAPTER VII.

Bible Revision and Publication: Survey of Progress

THE translation and publication of the Bible at Serampore and Calcutta by the Baptist missionaries accomplished a great work, especially in Bengal. The translations into the languages of Upper India, however, were very defective. This was due to the fact that natives, who were employed for translation work were not always competent for the work. They translated from the English Bible, instead of the original Greek and Hebrew text. The result may easily be imagined.

With a view to provide better translations in the Hindi and Urdu languages, the missionaries of the Church of England, and of the London Missionary Society, at Benares founded a society for the publication of tracts and scriptures in the vernacular.

An attempt to set up a press at Benares having been found to be impracticable, they fell in with the plan of the American missionaries at Allahabad to establish a press. This plan left the missionaries at Benares free to give themselves to the work of translation and revision.

The Presbyterians at Allahabad had in mind the same work. The first meeting of the Synod of North India was held at Fattehgarh in November, 1845. Three years later, it was convened in Agra; at which meeting a resolution was adopted urging the necessity of preparing Urdu and Hindi translations of the standards of the church, and also emphasizing the importance of revising the Urdu and Hindi scriptures. From this time forth strenuous effort was made in both the North India and Punjab missions to hasten this most important work.

This movement culminated in the establishment of the North

India Bible Society, auxiliary to the British and Foreign Bible Society, in Agra, in the year 1845, of which the Rev. James Wilson was the first secretary. The secretary of the Hindi sub-committee was the Rev. Joseph Owen. He undertook to revise the Hindi version of the Old Testament, made by the Rev. William Bowley of the Church Missionary Society. The whole was carefully compared with the original Hebrew. So many alterations were necessary as to make it almost a new version. The first volume, which comprises Genesis to the Second Book of Kings, was printed at the Mission Press, Allahabad, then under the superintendence of the Rev. L. G. Hay.[1]

The first edition of the Urdu Old Testament (called the Shurman and Hawkins Edition) had been printed at the Allahabad Mission Press, under the supervision of Rev. James Wilson. A new edition was now wanted, but for this some revision was necessary. For this work a committee was appointed consisting of the Rev. J. A. Shurman, of Benares, and Rev. Joseph Warren, of Allahabad. When the work was about half done, Mr. Shurman died. Mr. Warren carried on the revision, with such help as he could get. The New Testament was revised by a separate committee.

Rev. Joseph Owen, having been set free from the "College" which had prospered so well under his guidance, gave himself to literary work. He revised the New Testament in Hindi; he translated into Urdu the Confession of Faith and the Apostles' Creed; wrote a work on Theology and a Commentary on Isaiah and the Psalms, with a new version of the Psalms in Urdu. He also edited and published a volume of sermons for Indian Christians; eight of these sermons were written by Rev. Joseph Warren.

At Lodiana, the larger part of the New Testament with the Psalms, translated by Mr. Newton, was published in the Punjabi language. A book of psalms and hymns in the Urdu language was prepared by the Lodiana missionaries, with the

[1] See Moffatt's *Story of a Dedicated Life*, p. 128.

assistance of Rev. William Bowley. Mr. Janvier and Mr. Ullmann were also busy preparing a hymn and psalm book, suitable for use in the churches.

The writing and publishing of books and tracts also went on apace. The Rev. Joseph Warren was the author of the following books in Urdu:

"Eight Lectures on the Eighth Chapter of Proverbs,"

A tract on the New Birth,

A translation of Gauladet's "Ruth,"

Translations of Watts and Henry on Prayer,

"Dairyman's Daughter"—"The Young Cottager"—Flavel's "Fountain of Life"; and Hodge's "Way of Life."

These were published for the American Tract Society.

At Lodiana were printed large editions of scripture portions in Hindi, Urdu, and Punjabi—also a few in Persian and Kashmiri. These were published for the North Indian and American Bible Societies.

The preparation and publication of tracts in Urdu and Punjabi was a considerable part of the work of the older missionaries. The Punjabi books and tracts in the most part were written by the Rev. John Newton. The Urdu tracts were written or translated from the English by various members of the Mission. The number published up to 1856 was approximately 350,000.[2]

It was still the custom to distribute scriptures and religious books and tracts free of cost. The effect was learned from inquirers and from its influence in the increased number of people who gave up idolatry; and in the discovery of small bands of non-Christians who had formed new cults, each one borrowing something from Christianity.

As we are approaching a period in the history of our missions in India which, while threatening their very existence, would introduce a new era, it will be profitable to note the progress already made. More than two decades had passed

[2] For further particulars, see Appendix I.

since the founding of the pioneer mission at Lodiana. Two wars had swept over the Punjab. The Khalsa Raj had become subject to British rule and all parts of the Punjab were now open to missionary work. Subathu, Ambala, Saharanpur, Dehra, Jalandhar, Lahore, Gujranwala and Rawul Pindi were already occupied as stations of the Lodiana Mission. The ban against the preaching of the gospel had been removed, and now the messengers of the gospel were permitted to proclaim the message of mercy everywhere. Extensive journeys were made from Lahore to Peshawur and from Jalandhar to Hardwar. The printed word in Urdu, Hindi and Punjabi was scattered by thousands of volumes in all the larger towns and in all the sacred places.

The schools especially had made wonderful progress. In Lodiana, the school was attended by 279 pupils, and only ten of these received a stipend. The school at Jalandhar had 233 names on the roll, with an average attendance of 201, under the supervision of an Indian evangelist. At Ambala, notwithstanding strong opposition by the Brahmins and great apathy among the people, the school had 115 pupils. The schools in Lahore, only six years old, had 575 pupils in attendance. Schools had been established at Gujranwala, Gujrat and Rawul Pindi and were superintended from Lahore. At Saharanpur, 70 boys were under instruction. At Dehra 150 boys were enrolled.

In addition to these schools for some fifteen hundred boys, there were several orphan schools for boys and girls, day schools for Christian girls, besides a few schools for non-Christian girls.

The course of study in these schools comprised the following subjects: Reading, Writing, English Grammar, Geography, Arithmetic, Algebra, Geometry, Prose Composition and Poetry. In the vernacular, the course included Persian Urdu, Arithmetic, Geography, English History, Geometry, Mechanics and Natural Philosophy.

In almost every station, the missionaries undertook the superintendence of the poor-houses, leper asylums and, in times of famine, they distributed the relief funds. At Lodiana, the poor-house accommodated from twelve to twenty persons; the lepers were housed in huts by themselves. At Ambala, lepers, the lame, the blind, the maimed and the infirm of every description were cared for. The number averaged 200. At Lahore the poor-house ordinarily accommodated 175, with about 30 outdoor paupers. Maharajah Dhulip Singh constituted a fund for "the care of poor travellers, sick persons, etc." In Dehra, at the earnest request of a local committee, the missionaries undertook to superintend an asylum for lepers with 40 inmates. Such benevolent institutions have had the hearty interest of missionaries in all the years since, and from among the poor and especially the lepers, many souls have been saved.

Even after the lapse of nearly a quarter of a century, the number of converts was small. Nevertheless, organized churches were set up at all the stations.

In most of these churches, the missionaries were the pastors. Weekly prayer meetings were held, and usually a monthly concert of missions, in which effort was made to conserve and inspire a missionary spirit.

A few Indians had been taught privately and after examination by the Presbytery were duly licensed to preach; and still later they were ordained to the ministry as evangelists.

In due course, the Presbyteries were invited to form a Synod. Meetings of these ecclesiastical bodies were regularly held, but as yet all business was conducted in the English language. Nevertheless, the foundation of an Indian Church had been laid. All matters of discipline were transacted by the sessions of the individual congregations. That discipline was strict, both as to the reception of members and in dealing with offences against morals and religion.

Such a summary of results, however, does not adequately

depict the hard work of the missionaries. The acquisition of the languages, used in the field, was a serious undertaking, lasting from one to three years' labor for each. For one of the languages (the Punjabi), it became necessary to prepare a grammar and a dictionary, neither of which had ever before been written, even in the vernacular. As yet there was not a usable version of the scriptures in that language. This work was undertaken by the Rev. John Newton, with the assistance of the Rev. Levi Janvier and Rev. Joseph Porter. These men enabled the British and American Bible Societies to publish the four Gospels and the Acts of the Apostles, Genesis and twenty chapters of Exodus, and the Psalms in the Punjabi language. Besides this, a considerable literature in books and tracts, was published in the same language.

Thus far this survey has had relation to the Punjab Mission. The mission in the northwestern provinces was an extension of the work begun at Lodiana. First Allahabad was occupied. A little later on, Fattehgarh was made a station. Then Mainpuri was occupied and Fattehpur with the Rev. Gopinath Nandi in charge. Last of all Agra, the new seat of government for these provinces.

Flourishing schools were established at Allahabad, Fattehgarh, Farrukhabad and Mainpuri. Orphan schools for boys and girls at Allahabad and Fattehgarh. A girls and boys boarding school for European children at Agra. A leper asylum at Allahabad and an industrial school in Fattehgarh.

The mission press at Allahabad was now busily engaged in publishing scriptures and religious books and tracts.

In the early months of the year 1856, a great many changes occurred in the various stations. In the Punjab Mission, two of the older missionaries, Messrs. Rudolph and Jamieson, were obliged to go home on furlough. This necessitated the transfer of Mr. Newton to Subathu and of Mr. Herron to Lodiana. Similar changes took place in North India: Mr. Walsh went to America on sick leave. This made necessary the transfer of

Mr. Freeman from Mainpuri to Fattehgarh to take charge of the orphanage. Mr. Ullmann was sent from Fattehgarh to Mainpuri, Rev. A. O. Johnson was placed in charge of the high school at Farrukhabad.

Notwithstanding these changes, the outlook at all the stations was good. The schools were flourishing and daily becoming more popular. The literary work under Messrs. Newton and Janvier in the Lodiana Mission, and Messrs. Owen and Hay at Allahabad was proceeding apace. The preaching in town and village was carried on with great zeal. In the Punjab the number of tours was larger than usual. Some of these were made by Mr. Newton in the Jalandhar doab before and after the annual meeting. Qadir Bakhsh and Mr. Daniel visited the towns and villages to the northwest and southwest beginning at the Sutlej River. Mr. Newton went out again in the direction of Jagraon, at which place and in the vicinity he preached several weeks. Mr. Janvier and Qadir Bakhsh travelled in the direction of Saharanpur via Kamaun, Sangol and Sarhand Bassi: Isa Dàs and Basant went to Anandpur and Qadir Bakhsh to Rupur. Mr. Newton again visited Lahore and Firozpore, while Qadir Bakhsh went to Kashmir.[3]

In addition to these tours, the usual visits to the melas were made closing with a visit to Jawalamukhi, to which the scripture reader Isa Das went with Mr. Newton, who had come down from Subathu for the purpose. Particulars as to these visits cannot now be given. The most interesting visit would be that to Kashmir. Some details of this may be given in another chapter.

The missionaries at Saharanpur travelled three hundred miles on a tour to Jalandhar and back again. Their tour to Hardwar, where they spent a week at the mela, was accom-

[3] Qadir Bakhsh was a convert from Islam, a native of Kashmir. He made an annual visit to his native state to preach the gospel. The account given here is taken from the *Annual Report of the Mission* and is intended to illustrate the evangelistic zeal of missionaries.

panied by unusual interest. Many professed to be inquirers and took with them copies of the scriptures.

The Rev. Goloknath, accompanied by Mr. J. B. Lewis and Abdullah, visited Dasuah in the Hoshyarpur District, Kartarpur, Nur Mahal, Kapurthala and Jawalamukhi.

In the North India Mission, the missionaries, touring from place to place, found unusual interest among the people. They were much encouraged in their work.

Thus a cordon of mission stations, or centres of work, had been stretched along the foot of the Himalaya Mountains for a thousand miles. Schools, churches and chapels, asylums, orphanages, presses, Bible and Tract societies were actively at work. Christian converts were as yet comparatively few, but wherever the European stood up to preach, there were with him Indian Christian workers to testify to the power of the gospel to save.

The interest of the churches in America and Britain had been aroused; and prayer and praise ascended to God for his blessing on the missions in India. Other societies had joined hands to aid in the good work begun in the northwest and Punjab. The pioneers of the American United Presbyterian Church had arrived in the Punjab. The Church of Scotland had also begun its work at Sialkot. Dr. Butler of the American Methodist Episcopal Church had fixed upon the new Province of Oudh and Rohilkand as the sphere of a new mission. Friends in India, in the civil and military service, showed a lively interest by their liberal contributions for the support of the work.

But even then clouds began to obscure this brightness of their prospect, and the rumblings of the disturbed elements portended a storm.

CHAPTER VIII.

Sepoy Mutiny in North India

NOTWITHSTANDING the peaceful conditions which characterized the vigorous and masterful rule of Lord Dalhousie, and the quiet in which the great mass of the people dwelt, there were many circumstances which caused anxiety in the minds of the more thoughtful. Many men in high places could not be oblivious to the many signs of unrest in the army. The blind confidence of European officers in the native regiments, who were ready to resent any suggestion of disloyalty, only added to the fears of the more discerning among the civilian population. Stories too were afloat of conspirators, who were poisoning the minds of the people, as well as of the Sepoys. Faithful servants among the natives warned their masters that trouble was at hand. They told of the mysterious distribution of *chapaties* (unleavened wheaten cakes) among the people. This was a sign that something serious was to be expected. Many Europeans were alarmed, but what to do they knew not. The missionaries and the Indian Christians were anxious for their families as well as for their work.

A new governor general had recently arrived in India, affording discontent an opportunity to propagate itself. The Rev. Joseph Owen, of Allahabad, who had been in India seventeen years, was more able than many to understand the inner life of the Indians. On the tenth of March, 1857, he wrote in his journal as follows:

"Our new governor general lacks the pre-eminent ability of Lord Dalhousie, and we are approaching a crisis,—a crisis in which a man of pre-eminent ability will be required."

A little later he wrote again:

"There are signs of trouble abroad in the native community.

The Sepoys are becoming troublesome and mutinous. Hitherto the matter has been dealt with leniently, but the probability is that it must be put down with a strong hand."[1]

The allusion here was probably to the feeling of dissatisfaction among the Sepoys in the newly annexed province of Oudh; and to the ominous discontent of the Delhi Muhammadans, when they saw their King threatened with deposition; and especially to the mutinous conduct of some of the Bengal army regiments at Barrackpur and Berhampur, obliging their disarmament. At Ambala, too, there were signs of insubordination. Numerous fires of incendiary origin began to alarm the people. Similar occurrences were reported from other centres. Alarmed by these reports, some of the missionaries prepared for a sudden flight to some place of refuge. Their chief anxiety was for their Indian Christians, who would become the first objects of attack, by the enemies of the Europeans. The Muhammadans of Allahabad were talking of their desire to massacre all the infidel English. Every Indian Christian instinctively felt that a rising of the Muhammadans would mean a purpose to exterminate the Christians.

Whilst taking all precautions against a surprise and even providing for a possible flight, the missionary communities including the Indian Christians were instant in prayer to God for his grace and help in time of need.

It was on the ninth of May, 1857, that some Sepoys (native soldiers) belonging to the 3rd Cavalry, stationed in the cantonment at Meerut, refused to use cartridges in any way whatsoever. A report had been circulated that the cartridges were polluted by an application of a mixture of cows' blood and hogs' fat, in order to destroy the caste of both the Hindu and the Muhammadan Sepoys. This absurd story seems to have been believed by the Sepoys, who would not use the cartridges, even when told they need not use their teeth to open them. They were tried by court martial and sent to prison. The next

[1] *Story of a Dedicated Life*, pp. 138, 139.

day, Sunday, May 10th, "when the British soldiers were getting ready for church, the comrades of the prisoners broke into the jail and set them free. In the ensuing darkness and confusion, the mutineers got away to Delhi, and the criminal classes of the town and vicinity sacked and burned the officers' bungalows."[2]

During the night the mutineers rode to Delhi, where they were joined by the troops. After killing their European officers, they seized the fort and the arsenal, and soon had the entire city under their control. They then proclaimed the old King[3] as their Emperor. This was the signal for revolt all over North India.

It is not necessary to enter into any detailed description of the mutiny, which is so well narrated in every history of India. It will suffice to follow the fortunes of our missionaries and the Christian communities created by them.

The mutiny broke out at Lodiana early in June. The only missionaries in the station were Mr. and Mrs. Reese Thackwell. Mr. Janvier had been obliged to go to Landour, on account of illness in his family, where he was kept during the fearful scenes of the summer.

All had been quiet during the month of May, but it proved to be the calm before the storm. "There were evident tokens of a deeply-seated fellow-feeling on the part of many of the people in the city, particularly the Muhammadans, in the advancing rebellion; and when early in June, a large body of mutineers from Jalandhar, reached Lodiana, they found a crowd ready to join them in their work of plunder and devastation. Through a gracious providence a body of loyal Sikhs, being part of a regiment formerly raised in Lodiana, had just arrived and partial defense was thus realized. The treasury in cantonments was fortified, and there Mr. and Mrs. Thackwell, with other Europeans, obtained shelter; but those who

[2] Keene's *History of India,* Vol. II., p. 226.

[3] Bahadar Shah, the last of the Moghuls.

had come for rapine and blood soon found opportunity on the mission premises for the former, while the Lord in his mercy interfered to prevent their attaining their speecial object in the latter. The church, in the city, where for years the gospel had been preached, often to seriously attentive listeners, was set on fire. The schoolhouse shared a similar fate; and with its library, extensive, and valuable philosophical apparatus, and depot of books for sale, became a desolate pile. The Depository on the mission premises, with its contents of many thousand volumes of books for distribution, was reduced to ashes. Its broken and blackened walls alone remained. The bindery, with its large stock of printed sheets, binders' tools, and materials to the value of several thousand rupees, shared a similar fate. The paper room, with a large supply of printing paper newly stocked, and the church on the mission premises, were set on fire; the former destroyed, the latter much injured. The dwelling houses were rifled, windows broken, and an attempt made to fire one of them, where an additional stock of books for distribution had been stored, after filling the Depository: but most providentially it failed."[4]

"On the arrival of the mutineers, the native Christians and orphan girls fled, and found shelter on the premises of one of the Cabul princes, living in the neighborhood. Thus the Lord was pleased to preserve the lives of all our company. Their houses were rifled and some of them set on fire; but not one of themselves was permitted to be injured."[5]

---

[4] *Twenty-third Report of the Lodiana Mission*, p. 5.

[5] Mushi Nazamuddin, afterwards foreman of the Lodiana Mission Press, and an employe at the time of the mutiny, gave the author of this history a circumstantial account of the way in which the orphan girls escaped from the mutineers. He said that he and his brother Ghulam Qadir, on realizing the danger which threatened the girls in the orphanage, hurried to the orphanage and led the girls through the Mission garden and out to a number of tumble-down offices belonging to the Cabul prince above mentioned. They told the girls to sit perfectly quiet until the soldiers had left, and they would not be noticed. Still further to protect them they threw brush up against the doors of the house where they were hidden. They then fled to the city to protect their own homes, but they were afraid to tell what they had done and so were never known as the saviours of the orphan girls.

As soon as the Cabul prince heard of the fact that the orphan girls had found a refuge on his premises, he loudly proclaimed himself as the protector of the Christians. That he was wise in his generation became evident when he received fifty rupees monthly as an addition to his pension. I had this story also from Ghulam Qadir. E. M. W.

The magistrate receiving additional troops was enabled to execute summary justice upon the incendiary population, which had joined hands with the mutineers and had burned and robbed not only the property of the missionaries but also of the merchants in the city. A few hours after the rebel soldiers had departed on their way to Delhi, twenty or more of the marauders were hanging by their necks on gallows erected along the main street of the city.

Much of the stolen property was recovered and agreeably to an old law of the country a tax was levied on the inhabitants, to make good the losses that the mission and other parties had sustained.

Martial law was now proclaimed and the removal of ladies and children from the disturbed districts was ordered. Accordingly Mr. and Mrs. Thackwell, with the orphan girls, left for Ambala, and soon after went to Kasauli in the Himalaya Mountains.

By the first of October, the missionaries were able to return to Lodiana. The school was reopened in the Murray Ganj Chapel, which had been spared, and there also the Sunday services were held. Soon the work of repairing buildings was begun under the supervision of Mr. Thackwell. As far as possible, the ordinary work of the mission was entered upon with thankful hearts.

A sad bereavement, however, befell Mr. Thackwell, who lost his young wife and infant child.

The missionaries at Saharanpur were urged by the civil authorities to send the women and children to the mountains. Some of them went to Dehra and others to Landour, where they remained until the following October.

At Jalandhar City, the experiences of the missionary, Rev. Goloknath, and his Christian staff was strangely in contrast with what has been recorded concerning the stations east of the Sutlej River. In his annual report Mr. Goloknath wrote as follows:

"The work of educating the youth of the place has been carried on during the year as usual. The number of scholars on the roll on the first of August was 317. The outbreak of the Sepoys in May did not affect the attendance of the pupils in the smallest degree; the same number that had come to school before the three native regiments at Jalandhar cantonment mutinied, still continued to attend after that event.[6] This same quiet and immunity from danger characterized the mission community at Lahore, Subathu and Rawul Pindi. The missionary work was carried on with some regularity, notwithstanding the turmoil due to the mutiny."

It has been noted, in all histories of this period, how wonderfully loyal the Sikhs in the Punjab were, who only ten years before had fought so valiantly against the government they now supported so bravely.

These circumstances of peace and safety were no doubt due in great measure to the prompt and wise action of Sir John Lawrence, the lieutenant governor of the Punjab, and his coadjutors. The disarming of mutinous regiments at Lahore, Peshawur and Campbellpur and the prompt suppression of the outbreak at Sialkot, together with wise administration, combined to give confidence and a sense of security to the people, and so lead them to trust the government, which knew how to be generous as well as just.

We must now turn to occurrences in the North India stations, where was enacted a series of tragedies, which filled the Christian world with horror.

The success of the mutiny at Meerut, on the 10th of May, and the capture of the Delhi fort and magazine the next day, was immediately followed by uprisings all over North India. The missionaries and their friends at Allahabad, Agra, Fattehgarh, Fattehpur and Mainpuri were filled with dismay and direst forebodings of evil. The records preserved, showing the experiences of the missionaries and the native Christians are somewhat fragmentary, but the journal of Mr. Owen affords

[6] This remark applies to the missions under review. Far different was it with the American and Church of Scotland mission of Sialkot.

the reader a reliable and often graphic account of what occurred at Allahabad. We are indebted to the late Rev. James C. Moffatt, D. D., professor of church history in the Princeton Theological Seminary, for the preservation of Mr. Owen's journal, as found in his biography entitled "The Story of a Dedicated Life." Mr. Owen's family being absent in America, he was permitted to remain in Allahabad for some weeks after the outbreak, and to take an active part in the care and defence of the women and children, and in shepherding the scattered members of his flock.

There were no European troops in Allahabad. The defence of the fort and its magazine had been committed to a few companies of Sikhs, who remained loyal throughout. Reports were coming in continually that the people in the city were willing to join the sixth regiment in their plan to break open the jail and to plunder the city and to kill all European residents. The native Christians reported that there was a panic and religious frenzy in the city, and that the missionaries would be the first objects of attack.

On the 31st of May, Mr. Owen received a letter from Mr. Freeman, of Fattehgarh, bringing intelligence that all the missionaries in Delhi had been murdered, and that among the victims there were not less than two hundred Europeans and East Indians. Railway officials in Allahabad had been warned of their great danger, and many had gathered together in the station expecting an attack. A message came in the next day from Sir Henry Lawrence at Lucknow announcing the rising of the Sepoys there on the 30th of May.

On the 5th of June, news came that the Sepoys had risen at Benares, and it was feared that they would make a dash at Allahabad. All Europeans were now ordered into the fort and arrangements were made to meet the mutineers. Mr. Owen wrote:

"We are all gathering up a few articles of clothing to take

with us into the fort: *No bed, no baggage; light kits the order of the day.*

"On Friday night, June 5th, I assisted in watching the fort, with a company of volunteers, for we had no European troops and were quite at the mercy of the Sepoys and the Sikhs. Of course I got no sleep that night, and went home to our bungalow on Saturday and got a good rest under the *punkah* (fan). All there was so quiet that I felt strongly inclined to remain next night. Gopinath and his family had spent two or three nights in the fort, but thought themselves more insecure there than at home. They had fled from Fattehpur to Allahabad for safety. They were extremely afraid, not only of the Sepoys, but also of the Sikhs. I tried to get them to come in on Saturday night, but they chose to remain. I left Kallan (his servant) there, with an order to make them as comfortable as possible.

"All seemed to be expecting something that night, and were on the alert. The volunteers, amounting to some eighty, were divided into three squads: one to protect the flagstaff, where it was supposed an enemy might attempt to scale the walls, another to protect a weak point on the Jumna River, and the third to be with the main guard at the gate. At nine o'clock the volunteers met and were told off to their respective duties for the night. The moon was full and shining beautifully. It was impossible to realize, when coming through the bazar, that danger was near. The shops were open, and the people were quietly at their occupations.

"On Saturday evening, about nine o'clock, Court walked up to me, as I was standing near the old pillar, remarking: 'You must not be surprised if we have something tonight, for the telegraph wires from Benares have been cut in the midst of a message.' He requested me at the same time to stay with the ladies, if anything should occur.

"I came up and joined in worship with the Hays and Munnises, and was on my way back to the tent, when we began to hear a rattling of musketry in the cantonments. The alarm was immediately sounded, and all the volunteers rushed to their posts. I ran up and gave notice to our friends. They were soon out on the balcony, where, in a few minutes all the women, leaving the tents, were collected. Hay, Munnis and I, then closed all doors leading from the stairways and stood with loaded pistols, ready to shoot down the first native, who might attempt an assault upon the ladies and children. We saw a native, sitting quietly among the ladies, with a sword in his hand. We disarmed him and turned him out in double quick time. The rattling of musketry continued about half an hour, the sound reaching us from various points between cantonments and the bridge. We thought the mutineers had probably got in and made a combined attack at those various points. We hoped they were getting a good cutting up.

"The officers' wives were, of course, deeply anxious about their husbands, who were in the midst of all that firing. One after another came to me asking, 'Do you think the Sepoys will be loyal?' I could only say, ' I hope so.' Others were highly indignant that any such questions should be asked, or that the least doubt should be entertained of their loyalty.

"Some time after the firing ceased, we saw a gentleman coming from the main gate of the barracks. Hitherto we knew nothing of what had occurred. I went and opened a door and called him. His first words were: 'Alexander is lying dead outside, but tell Mrs. Harvard and Mrs. Simpson that their husbands are safe here in the fort, although Colonel Simpson's horse has been riddled through with bullets. The sixth regiment Sepoys are in open mutiny.'

"There was a general rush to me to know what had happened. The ladies, who a few minutes before were so strongly standing up for the Sepoys, were utterly confounded. I went to Mrs. Simpson and delivered the message I had received. She seized my hand and fell on my arm with a loud cry. In a few minutes Colonel Simpson came up, with his clothes covered with blood, and gave an account of his almost miraculous escape.

"I must, however, mention what occurred at the gate, before the colonel came up to his quarters, which was the turning point with us in the fort.

"One hundred Sepoys at the main gate, who were mounted on the main guard, were commanded by Lieutenant Brasyer to give up their guns. Two nine pounders were brought close to them and the torches were ready to touch them off in case of disobedience. The volunteers were also before them with loaded muskets cocked and fingers on the triggers. At the command to pile their arms, there seemed a slight hesitation, but they soon gave them up, then partly rushed back to them, but, finding themselves overpowered eventually yielded. This was the critical moment for the four hundred Sikhs to join them, had they been so disposed. Had they done so, not one of us would have escaped. The massacre would have been universal, and then the fort with its vast magazine and armory would have been in the hands of the mutineers and the whole of the northwestern provinces must have gone from under British rule. You may imagine our relief and joy when word was quietly passed on to us, 'THE SIKHS ARE STAUNCH,' . . . The Sepoys were all ready to start an outbreak in the fort, for their muskets were loaded, and, contrary to orders, were capped, and in this condition were taken from them. It may be said that, under God, we owe our safety to Lieutenant Brasyer especially and to the volunteers. Most of these are railway people, and for securing them we owe all thanks to Mr. Hodgson, who sent out train after train and brought them in from a distance of more than twenty miles. Their presence did much to turn the scale in our favor."

The next day, the outbreak in the cantonment began. An alarm was sounded by the mutineers, and thereupon their officers, who were at dinner, rushed out to see what had occurred to cause the alarm. They were shot down before they reached their posts, only three escaping alive. Then bedlam broke loose. The bungalows were rifled and burned. The treasury was broken open and the money taken. The next morning the mission houses were destroyed. Mr. Owen wrote in his journal as follows:

"The morning passed on, and until eleven o'clock our bungalow appeared from the top of the barracks all safe. In reality, however, it was not so. From an early hour the Pathan of Durgabad, from whom we rent the land, and to whom we have shown nothing but kindness, was there with some hundreds of low caste Muhammadans, plundering all our property and burning our books. Of this I knew nothing at the time.

"Mr. Spry (the Church of England chaplain) appointed a short service at twelve o'clock in the veranda of the barracks. Just before it began, I ran up to the top of the barracks, and saw the smoke rising from the roof of our bungalow. It caused a bitter pang, but I was enabled with calmness to look up to

God and say: 'All is right, thy will be done.' As we sat at worship in the veranda, I could see the column of smoke rising from the roof. . . . The service was short and attended by few. Most of the gentlemen were engaged in guarding the fort. Several ladies were overwhelmed with grief at the recent loss of their husbands.

"The burning went on during the whole of Sunday, and no effort was made from the fort to arrest it. Some sixty or seventy of the first families (Europeans) arrived from Benares, and were brought across the river by a steamer that happened to be here. In the afternoon, the rebels came close under the fort and burned a bungalow at Arail. The incendiaries continued the whole night unchecked."

Another chapter from Mr. Owen's journal reveals to us in a graphic manner the experiences of hundreds of people, when they had learned the vast extent of their losses. We quote as follows:

"Here I am in the fort, living in a small tent, with all the property I have left in the world, comprised in a few changes of clothes, my Hebrew Bible, Greek Testament, Turretin's Theology, Witseus' Economy of the Covenants, and a few other odd volumes. All my furniture, my library and most of my private manuscripts and papers, have been consumed. Our dear Jumna house has been burned. The church has been robbed, also the mission 'College,' and the whole place completely sacked. The native Christians have been scattered I know not where. I can only see the place from the ramparts of the fort, but cannot go through to inquire; nor yet have I been able to ascertain the particulars of their condition. We feared that they were all murdered, but hear that their lives have been spared. The stations and cantonment of Allahabad are in ashes. Mr. Hay's house[7] has been burned, and we hear that the press has also gone. Scarcely a bungalow seems to have been left. The work of conflagration is still in progress. Day and night new fires are added to the vast scene of desolation and smoking embers. Here we are shut up in the fort and not an effort has been made to arrest the work of destruction."

A Muhammadan priest set up the standard of Islam and

[7] This was situated on the cantonment side of the City some four miles distant.

proclaimed himself lieutenant governor under the King of Delhi. Many atrocities were committed on the helpless women and children. The trials of those who took refuge in the fort were terrible. Mr. Owen explained:

"We are almost starving here, living on half rations. We can get nothing from the outside. The people of the town seem determined to starve us out; at least the Muhammadan portion. They have forbidden supplies of any kind to be sent in. The commissariat was very badly supplied, and we are all suffering. The heat, too, is excessive, and the filth allowed to accumulate is abominable. I have no quarters, but sleep in a tent at night. I have no furniture, but my dear books are a sad loss, for I do not know how to get on without them, but God will provide."

Refugees came in every day with reports of rapine and murder. The rebels were having a glorious revel at the station. Brandy was sold at a half cent a bottle and champagne was still cheaper. Colonel Neill came in from Benares that evening.

The next day the gallant colonel with his fusileers cleared the way to the Ganges. Mr. Owen was then informed that more troops were soon expected to arrive, but that all ladies and noncombatants were to be sent by boat to Calcutta.

Mr. Owen received permission to remain behind. He describes the departure of his colleagues and others as follows:

"I accompanied the Hays on board this evening, truly sorry to part from them. They have been very kind to me. I love and esteem them, the more I know them, and shall feel very lonely without them, but I believe they are in the way of duty in going. The flatboat, on which they are going, is crowded with people; the steamer also is crowded. A number of armed volunteers protect both steamer and flat boat. Major Cory, an officer of the late 'Illustrious Sixth,' goes as military commander of the whole.

"There are not cabins for one third of the passengers. Screens and curtains are fitted up all over the decks, and the poor people are jumbled in as thick as they can stand."

All of the members of the American Mission who now remained in Allahabad, besides Mr. Owen, were Rev. Mr. Munnis, Mrs. Munnis and their children.

Among the passengers on the flatboat were Rev. Gopinath Nandi and his wife and children, who had been left in Mr. Owen's house the night of the outbreak.

He had wandered about the place, after the sacking of the mission compound, in great distress. He had been robbed of all his money.

"At last he fell into the hands of the Maulvie, who had set up his government at the gardens. He was kept in the Serai (Inn), with his feet in the stocks four days and four nights. His poor wife was dragged by the hair of her head on the stones and greatly bruised. Their persecutors threatened several times to kill him, and having found out that he was a Christian padri, they were very bitter against him, but he stood firm and witnessed a good confession. Young Ensign Cheek, who was wounded on the night of the outbreak and who had been wandering about, hiding sometimes in the jungle, sometimes on trees, sometimes standing in the water, was suffering most excruciating pain, while with Gopinath in the Serai. Not the least of his sufferings was from thirst, and almost night and day he was calling for water. In the midst of his sufferings, he exhorted Gopinath to stand firm, saying: 'Padri Sahib, hold on to your faith. Don't give it up.' When the Muhammadans saw Gopinath trying to show kindness to Cheek, they put him at a distance and tried to prevent all further intercourse between them. Poor Cheek died this evening from exposure and long neglect of his wounds."

Hearing that Ensign Cheek had a relative at Bansurah, Mr. Owen went to the hospital to see him and to ask if he had any message to his friends, but found him past speaking. Thus died the young man, who stayed the faith of the Indian Evangelist.

The missionaries and ladies with the children, who embarked at Allahabad, in due course arrived safely in Calcutta. Mr. Hays and his family proceeded to America, where Mr. Hay spent a long and useful life in the home mission field.

The missionaries at Mainpuri, Mr. and Mrs. Ullmann, had

fled for refuge to Agra. The missionaries there, with the children in the boarding school, took refuge in the fort, Mr. and Mrs. Ullmann with them. The mission houses at Mainpuri were plundered and burned. The chapel was also destroyed. The new schoolhouse escaped destruction, because the Rajah wanted it for a court house.

At Agra, the torch was applied to all European buildings. The building for the normal school, for the education of native teachers was first set on fire, and in a short time five miles of the station were lit up by the flames of burning buildings. People continued to flock into the fort for protection, until the resident population numbered six thousand. Many more were cared for during the day. The missionaries were all able to render substantial help in caring for the wounded, who were brought in from the battle fields in the neighborhood. Their suffering was real, for while safe within the old fort of Akbar the Great, their discomfort was not only due to the crowded condition of the refuge, but to the want of food and constant anxiety for friends outside.

CHAPTER IX.

The Tragedies of Fattehgarh, Agra and Allahabad

THE fort at Fattegarh was at this time manned by a regiment of Sepoys, most of whom were full of the spirit of mutiny. The colonel in command, encouraged by the professions of loyalty on the part of the older soldiers, vainly hoped he might be able to quell the spirit of the younger men and prevent an open rupture. However, rumor of mutiny and slaughter of Europeans at Mainpuri, Fattehpur, Shahjahanpur and other stations, aroused the feeling of sedition to such a pitch as to make flight absolutely necessary. The missionaries were reluctant to leave the Indian Christians, but these urged them to flee for safety. They rightly judged that the Europeans would be helpless to defend either them or to save themselves, if they remained.

The missionaries in Fattehgarh were the Rev. Messrs. J. E. Freeman, D. E. Campbell, A. O. Johnson, R. McMullen and their wives, with the two children of Mr. and Mrs. Campbell. As soon as the news came of the flight of the missionaries from Mainpuri, and the report that the mutineers were marching on Fattehgarh, the missionaries assembled at the home of the Freeman's collecting such garments, etc., as they could carry with them. They all wrote farewell messages to their relatives in America, trusting that they might find their way in the mails. One of them wrote:

"You cannot imagine the anxiety of mind this insurrection has caused us. We are living every day in expectation that it may be our last, but we have the blessed consolation that if we are to die it will be as missionaries to the heathen. Who would desire a more glorious death? May God in his mercy prepare us for whatever awaits us! The friends of missions at home will be sorry to hear that all missionary labor is suspended at present. What the future will be, we cannot tell, but we trust that this insurrection will result in opening still wider the door for the spread of the gospel of Christ."

"June 2nd—Bad news: all is growing worse. The insurgents have arisen all around us, and we are trying to get a boat, in which to make our escape. . . . In a few hours we fly. The whole country is now in arms. Farewell! Farewell! Perhaps you may never hear from me again."[1]

In the evening the missionaries went to spend the night with their English friends, the Guises and Macleans, who lived near the boat landing, where their boat was anchored for the journey down the Ganges. The night was spent in prayer for the Christians they were leaving behind them. It was hard to leave them in their defenceless condition and exposed to the fury of wicked men. They could but commit them, as well as themselves, into the hands of their merciful heavenly Father.

The boat which they had secured, was an ordinary river flat-boat, fitted up with a deck cabin, which would provide some protection from the intense heat of the hot season. Such boats were provided with sails, but these were of little use on the down journey, the boat being allowed to float with the current.

On the morning of the fourth of June, the little band took their seats in the boat, their luggage being placed in three other boats. Others were waiting in their boats to accompany them. They now numbered one hundred and twenty-six souls. The river was low, and often the current carried the boats near the shore. The shore being high afforded opportunity for sniping by any one having firearms. Many of the men on the boats were armed, but were only formidable to villagers.

They were unmolested until they reached the village of Kamalganj, about eight miles below Fattehgarh. Here the villagers were seen preparing an attack. Armed with clubs they

[1] This last letter of Rev. A. O. Johnson is quoted from Walsh's *Martyred Missionaries*, p. 268.

stood on the bank, intent on plunder. But the sight of so large a party of Europeans led them to allow them to pass unmolested.

At the next village, they found a number of Sepoys and desperadoes, who opened fire upon them. Some of the party on the flotilla returned the fire and the boats passed on. This was at Singarampur, at which the missionaries had frequently preached, when in attendance upon an annual mela, where thousands of people came to bathe in the sacred river.

The next village where they were attacked was Kasimpur, a Muhammadan village. The channel of the river being near the village, the villagers fired a volley, wounding a man on one of the boats. Elated with this success, they fired musket after musket. To silence them, and enable the boats to pass, the Europeans returned the fire killing eight of the villagers. The villagers continued to follow the boats, firing whenever the boats came near enough. Thus they went amidst fear and hope until the evening of the sixth of June, when they fastened to the shore in order to cook some food. Here a Zamindar, or landlord, mustering his men, surrounded the party, telling them they were at his mercy and that resistance was vain. He did not meditate murder, but he wanted money. On the payment of one thousand rupees, he allowed them to pass on and even gave five men as a guard. Four of these soon deserted, but the party continued their journey towards Cawnpore. They travelled day and night for two days, without meeting with further obstacles. But, unfortunately, on the evening of the eighth of June the boat ran aground on an island midway between Bithur, the capital of the Nana Sahib, and Cawnpore. Here they were stranded at the very mouth of the lion's den, but they knew it not, as yet. They had not heard of the defection of the Mahratta Prince, the Nana Sahib. They had not heard of Sir Hugh Wheeler's being besieged in his own trenches. In these circumstances, they did the worst thing they could have done, by sending a letter addressed to General Wheeler, asking his assistance to get from the boat to his camp.

The letter was carried promptly to the Nana Sahib. Of course no help came. They remained on the island for four days, when a body of Sepoys came near by and fired several shots at the boats, killing a child and a lady and a native nurse. The whole party then left the boats and took refuge under some trees on the island.

Seeing no way of escape, one of the missionaries proposed prayer, saying that the day they had so long dreaded, was probably at hand. Mr. Freeman read a portion of scripture and then offered a prayer. After the prayer, Mr. Campbell addressed them all, urging them to lay hold upon the salvation offered to all in the gospel. Just then a boat load of Sepoys arrived and made them all prisoners.

The story of Debi Deen, one of the native Christians, who had gone with the missionaries from Fattehgarh, and who had been sent back by Mr. Campbell to warn any others, who might be following them, of the danger, adds some particulars to the narrative of Mr. Walsh. Debi Deen says that

"When the party reached Nawabganj (five miles above Cawnpore), they saw with spyglasses, guns placed on the banks, to oppose their progress down the river. They could hear the booming of the cannon in Cawnpore and knew that the Europeans were defending themselves. There they remained two days, being unable to get down the river or to obtain assistance. At last hundreds of desperadoes, Sepoys and cavalrymen and cultivators from the villagers, men, women and children, surrounded them. The Europeans fought as long as they could, the ladies loading and the gentlemen firing the muskets. A round shot from the shore broke a hole in the large boat, on which they had all been obliged to take refuge. The boat began to sink, and all were obliged to get out on the island, the ladies holding their children in their arms under the scorching sun of June, the hot winds blowing full blast. They directed the servants on the boat to destroy all the weapons and to throw them into the river. They were soon beset by multitudes, who took their watches, all they had in their pockets, their hats, shoes, stockings, coats, everything, except a slight covering from the waist downward. Then all were put into a large boat and brought to the Cawnpore side. Debi Deen saw the whole party brought to the shore; the ladies brought off first and made to sit on the ground. Then the gentlemen were brought off and tied with a long rope, arm to arm. The Sowars (mounted police or cavalry) rode near the ladies, while they were thus sitting on the ground. The ladies joined their hands together and in an attitude of entreaty begged for their lives. The Sowars replied to their prayer in abusive and obscene language, and shaking their swords over them, told them that not one of them should live. When the gentlemen had all been tied together in a ring, the ladies were placed within the ring, and all were marched off. Mr. Campbell gave a farewell salute to the native Christians, who gazed after the company, till the bazar, through which they were taken, covered them from view."[2]

This story explains why, when one boat had gone ashore, the other boats could not have been used to escape down the river. It also made clear why the Europeans could not defend themselves with their guns, their munitions having run out, and their weapons having been destroyed that they might not fall into the hands of the mutineers. They had made a heroic endeavor to defend the women and, when nothing was left, they surrendered, well knowing that no mercy awaited them.

They were placed in a house and guarded as prisoners for the night. The next morning they were marched to a parade ground near by and there ruthlessly put to death.

Mr. Owen visited Cawnpore soon after the English army had avenged the death of the many Englishmen slain there. While there, he met an Indian, who told him that,

> "He saw a number of European ladies and gentlemen with their children being killed by Sepoys and Sowars, on the plain in front of the Sevada Kothi, the house formerly occupied by Perkins. The Sepoys shot them with their muskets and the Sowars with their pistols, and then they cut them in pieces with their swords."

Thus perished a devoted band of martyrs, whose bodies, with those of their European companions, were tumbled into a well

[2] *Story of a Devoted Life*, pp. 204-206.

near by; over which has been erected a beautiful canopy, with an angel figure guarding the place, where lie the precious remains, to await the trumpet of the Resurrection Day. Mr. Owen's informant declared that the Nana Sahib was present on horseback and superintended the gruesome butchery.[3]

If the statements given above are correct, this tragedy occurred a fortnight before the slaughter of Sir Hugh Wheeler and his devoted company of soldier martyrs and their women and children, who perished on the 27th of June. It is possible that the Nana kept all his prisoners until after the capture of General Wheeler and his force and that the slaughter of his prisoners occurred when General Neill and his army was about to enter Cawnpore. Amid the many conflicting reports, it may not be possible to give the exact order of events, but the main facts, as to the faith and hope of these martyrs, which enabled them to be steadfast unto the end, remain as already given. Their witness was not in vain. "The blood of the martyrs is the seed of the church." Two generations have since drawn courage and strength from these devoted saints. In their lives and in their sufferings and death have been lessons of faith and devotion for Christian men, women and children in every church in the Christian world. Christians do not now gaze so much at the beautiful marble figure of the angel standing over the well at Cawnpore, where in thought the mortal remains lie buried, but see the glorified saints radiant in joy, wearing crowns of victory.

But the tragedies of Fattehgarh were not complete. When the missionaries left in their boats, it was hoped that the Indian Christians might escape, but it soon became evident that the fanaticism of the Muhammadans would not spare them unless they would apostatize.

The orphan boys and girls fled to the villages. Some were made captive and were never heard of again. Some of the

[3] *Story of a Dedicated Life*, p. 207.

Christians went as far as Cawnpore, wandering from place to place, and were at last only too glad to return again. The blind girls from the orphan asylum, and one boy, a leper and blind, were some days and nights together without shelter, and had the most scanty fare, and yet only one died. Their infirmity was their defence. Others in the Christian community had won a martyr's crown.

"Prominent among this number was Dhokal Parshad, the head master of the mission school in Farrukhabad. When he and his family fell into the hands of the mutineers, and life and liberty were offered, if they would renounce Christianity, he answered: 'What is my life that I should deny my Saviour? I have never done so since the day I first believed on Him, and by the grace of God, come what may, I never will.' When a Sepoy approached him, sword in hand, he meekly bowed, and his head was severed from his body by a single blow. His wife and children were also put to death."[4]

The sufferings of the missionaries and the Indian Christians were often those due to long continued anxiety and suspense. An extract from a letter written by the Rev. David Herron from Dehra Dun, will sufficiently illustrate many similar experiences:

"The news of the massacre at Meerut and Delhi and other places reached us in quick succession, and threw us into a state of the utmost alarm. The native troops in the regiment stationed at this place had not yet proved their loyalty. With the exception of one company, which was left to guard the station, they were marched off at once to Meerut. For six weeks after they left, we had not a word of reliable information from them. It was, however, rumored by evil persons, who wished to excite rebellion among those who were left, that the regiment had mutinied and gone to Delhi; and again that they were on their way to this place to murder the Europeans. The natives be-

[4] Another report had it that Dhokal Parshad, wife and family were blown from a cannon.

lieved, and, in some instances, said publicly that English rule was at an end. The Mussalmans, especially, became quite bold and impudent. The inhabitants of some districts in the plains, just below us, had formerly been robbers by profession. For more than half a century, they had been prevented from following the vocation of their ancestors, and had been confined to the cultivation of the soil by the strong arm of the English Government, but as soon as they thought that the pressure of the government was removed, their hereditary spirit of plunder revived, and in large bands they attacked and sacked towns and villages. The mails were all stopped, and we were thus cut off from communication with any quarter for some time. You may fancy our consternation under these circumstances. We did not know but that we might be attacked any hour of the day or night, by mutineers, or Mussalman fanatic or predatory hoards; and yet a few Europeans, who were in the station, felt it to be necessary to go about as usual and keep up the semblance of authority before the eyes of the natives, even when there was no power to uphold it, had it been called in question. Mrs. Herron and I moved into Brother Woodside's house, which is a two-storied building. Our plan was, if suddenly attacked, to escape to the roof, and there defend ourselves as long as we could. At night we had a guard on every side of the house to give us warning of the approach of danger. These guards were of course natives and sometimes we felt almost as much afarid of them, as of any others. There was only one servant about the house in whom we had confidence. We let him know all our plans.

"One night, one of the servants rushed into the rooms, where we were sleeping and cried out that the Sepoys were around the house. Mrs. Woodside seized one of her children and Mrs. Herron the other, and, according to our plan, fled to the roof, Brother Woodside and I bringing up the rear, each carrying a double-barrelled gun, the servants mentioned above accompanying us with the ammunition, which consisted of a flask of powder, a box of gun caps, some balls and fifteen or twenty cartridges. Our first impression was that all the bungalows of the station were on fire, there happening to be more fires on the mountains and in the Doon, burning up the old grass before the rains.

"After this the ladies and later on the native Christians were sent up to Landour, in the mountains, the missionaries remaining to aid in guarding the station. Hearing that the Jalandhar mutineers, after sacking the Mission premises at Lodiana, were coming to Dehra, it was determined to go out with such forces as could be gathered together and attack them. The mutineers, however, were hurrying on to Delhi; and Dehra had no further trouble."

At Allahabad, many of the Christians had found temporary refuge in the fort (as we have already seen), but those who remained in the city were great sufferers. Some of them had been so terrorized as to be driven to repeat the Muslim creed: " 'There is no God but Allah and Muhammed is the Apostle of Allah.' This they did to save their lives and the lives of their children. Even Yunas repeated the Kalima and so did Mrs. Gibbons and others. Not one of them except Gopinath Nandi showed the spirit of a martyr."[5] Gopinath Nandi"s account of the persecutions of Indian Christians, written from Calcutta and published in the *Foreign Missionary* of September, 1858, is as follows:

"We were without clothes, having only a piece of rag about a foot wide and a couple of feet in length, and the children were altogether naked. Everything we had was plundered, even the very clothes on our bodies, by the villagers where we took shelter before we were brought into the presence of the Maulvi. In place of clothes, if you were to have put dirt and mud, of which we had abundance on us, it would have been correct. Then we had three children two about six years old, twins, and a baby of one year."

This description of Rev. Gopinath Nandi and family, as they appeared when brought before the Maulvi governor in Allahabad, was given to correct a beautiful illustration in which the party was represented in full dress. Mr. Gopinath Nandi goes on to say:

"The saving of our lives was a miracle. Other dear Christians, both European and native, were exposed to similar dan-

[5] This is the statement of Mr. Owen. It completely belies the frequent declaration that "no Indian Christian had apostatized during the mutiny." I think very few did. Many died for their faith. E. M. W.

gers, but most of them were slaughtered. No less than ten or twelve times, we were brought to the very brink of the grave. Everything appeared against us. The sun beat upon us with all its powerful rays, the hot wind pierced like deadly arrows, the sword hung ready to fall upon us, to sever our heads from our bodies, starvation and nakedness brought our mortal frames into a state of wretchedness; yet none had power to hurt us, because such was the will of our Heavenly Father. Again the trials were so great and incessant that nothing but the grace of God alone kept us faithful. The Maulvi, when he failed by argument to bring us to renounce the Christian faith, brought forward all the threats, which a wicked heart could invent. He threatened to cut off all the limbs of our bodies, and thus to torture us to death; but when he saw that these even had no effect to change our creed, he then promised to give us riches, land free of rent, and other worldly grandeurs; but thanks be to God, he soon received a negative answer.

"The Maulvi then tried to lead Mrs. Nandi to abjure the Christian faith, but failed. She thought she was doomed to die, and began to teach her little boys in the hearing of all, with such pitiful eloquence as to apparently touch the hardened hearts of her persecutors. The Maulvi ordered us to be taken into the prison and kept for a future occasion. Thus came we out through our fiery trials, praising and glorifying Jesus for giving us grace and strength to confess Him before the world.

"A short account of the Fattehpur native Christians, I am sure will not be uninteresting. All of them, with their families, remained in the Mission premises to the last moment. When the mutineers attacked and burnt all the houses, they then fled in different directions. Some of them, after hiding in the jungles for more than a month, came to Allahabad for shelter: as to the others, no one knows whether they were killed by the mutineers, or fell victims to the climate. A man and his wife, who had been baptized and admitted into the Christian church, were caught by the mutineers. One of the man's hands was cut off, and the woman, after being savagely treated, was shorn of her hair. The English, arriving in time, saved their lives."[6]

Many more cases might be cited to illustrate the martyr spirit of Indian Christians during these terrible persecutions. It is only just to say, that among the Hindus, and especially the

---

[6] *The Church Mission Gleaner*, July, 1858.

lower classes, many were found ready to give refuge to the Christians. One old Muhammadan Maulvi, an employe of the Mission, living near, hid seventeen orphan children in his village; and, on the return of peace, he brought them all back to the Mission. Similar cases have been reported in the Fatteh-garh District. These succorers of the helpless followers of Christ have not gone unrewarded.

CHAPTER X.

The Reorganization of the Missions

THE Lodiana Mission suffered no loss of life at the hands of the Sepoy mutineers. Many buildings had been wrecked. The press building, book depot and paper godown were burned. The printing presses were broken and the type scattered. The school buildings were in ruins. The missionaries were unable to return until October.

At Lahore, the work of the Mission suffered some interruption, but at no time was it entirely discontinued. The same was true of Jalandhar and Rawul Pindi. Similar conditions obtained at Ambala, Saharanpur and Dehra. Little could be done until the missionaries should return to their several stations and assemble at the Annual Meeting. On their return, the work was continued on the same lines as before the outbreak.

At Lodiana Mr. Thackwell was authorized to repair the houses which had been damaged and to rebuild the schoolhouse. The means for this rather extensive work were amply provided in the indemnity given by the government.

The missionaries went out as usual, accompanied by their Indian helpers, to preach the gospel in the villages. Even in Lodiana, where recently so much violence had been manifested by the destruction of Mission property, bazar preaching was conducted as usual. The people came and listened with usual interest. Here then, it may be truly said, that no reorganization of the missionary work was necessary. At all the stations the work went on as usual.

Far otherwise was it in the Missions in the Northwestern Provinces. There everything was in confusion.

The Mission Chapel in Mainpuri was a ruin, the Mission bungalow had been plundered and burned, and the ground had been appropriated by the Rajah, who had rented it to Zamindars (farmers) for cultivation for sixty-two rupees a year. The new school building had escaped the general destruction as it suited the Rajah, during his reign of terror, to use it as his Court of Justice."[1]

The Christians at Fattehgarh, who had fled from their homes, hearing that the English had defeated their enemies in several places, began to return. Finding no one there, who had any special interest in them, they wrote to the missionaries at Agra, asking that some one might be sent to them. It was decided to send Mr. Fullerton. Mr. Ullmann had been sent to England to superintend the publication of the Bible in Hindi. Mr. Fullerton therefore visited Mainpuri on his way to Fattehgarh. This had been his first station and home in India. His heart was greatly saddened to see the desolation there.

"On reaching Fattehgarh, he found it the headquarters of the Commander-in-Chief. Ten thousand soldiers, and nearly as many camp-followers were encamped there; while oxen, buffaloes, horses, camels, elephants, artillery wagons, baggage wagons and private conveyances filled every available spot. The Mission bungalows, the old Church, the tent factory and the Christian village were all in ruins. The walls and spire of the new church were still standing, but the roof had been destroyed and everything movable taken away. The orphanage was filled with oxen, the drawing-room of one of the bungalows held an elephant, and other parts of the building were used as stables for oxen. Even the little cemetery had not escaped desecration. Mr. Fullerton found it filled with oxen, and the tombs marred and broken."[2]

At Agra, Allahabad and Fattehpur, a similar state of chaos marked the mission premises and the Christian villages. They had suffered the loss of all things. The entire work of the Mission had to be organized anew.

It was not, however, as if nothing had been accomplished. The missionaries were now men of experience. They knew the

---

[1] *History of A. P. Mission*, p. 126.
[2] *History of A. P. Mission*, Mrs. Holcomb, p. 127.

language and the people. They had by them a Christian community whose faith had been tried in the fire. A few had lapsed, but all such returned deeply penitent and newly consecrated for the work.

Early in 1858, a conference was held in Agra, which was attended by most of the surviving missionaries (connected with the Farrukhabad Mission). It was then decided that Messrs. Scott and Fullerton should remove from Agra, to Fattehgarh and Farrukhabad respectively, and that Mr. Williams should go to Allahabad.

This action of the Mission meeting forecast the abandonment of Agra as a station. The removal of the Government from Agra back to Allahabad no doubt influenced this action. The feeling that inasmuch as four of the missionaries and their wives had been slain, and two more had gone home with their families, Mr. Hays to America and Mr. Ullmann to England on special duty, retrenchment was necessary.

In regard to this action of the Mission, Rev. E. Williams wrote to the Board in New York, March 15, 1858, as follows:—

"The urgent wants of Fattehgarh, the number of native Christians there, their destitute condition both temporal and spiritual and the importance of the station in every view, seemed to render unavoidable our action in removing Messrs. Scott and Fullerton thither. To us and to the church at home, Fattehgarh must always henceforth possess an interest above any of our other stations, as having been the residence of our martyred friends. It was not, indeed, the scene of their death, but it was there that they had preached and prayed and taught: it was there they left the impression of their devoted lives; and in this way the ground had been more clearly and deeply consecrated in the memory of the Church than it would have been by their blood.

"Shall Agra be given up? Should it continue the seat of Government, which is not impossible, I suppose you will say decidedly No! The importance of having a missionary here to represent our Board in the Committee of the Bible and Tract

Societies, you will appreciate, and I need not attempt to illustrate it.

"Should Agra cease to be the seat of government, it will still be a large military station. But that fact apart, it is a great city; and however strongly occupied by the Episcopalians and Baptists, its crowded streets and suburban villages afford ample scope for the labours of our Board too. It would be a pity to see our graveyard, 'God's acre,' desecrated and our beautiful church turned over to a common use.

"I may add that it is situated near enough to the native city to be a favourable basis for missionary operations."[3]

After a strong appeal to the Board in New York, and to the church for reinforcements, Mr. Williams paid a tribute to the Indian martyrs as follows:

"Perhaps no instances of trials more terrible or of steadfastness more wonderful are recorded in the martyrologies of the early Church than some which the Christian annals of these troubles will furnish. Inspired patience—meek forgiveness, sublime faith, persistence in the confession of the Son of God even unto death; such as Neander would have loved to describe and to dwell upon as manifestations of the inner life, have been all exemplified in this land, within the last few months, by men and women who, not long ago, were bowing down to idols, without God and without hope in the world. Surely there is encouragement in such facts and surely the appeal which they present will not be disregarded."

These words reveal at once the sad prospect of sacrificing the Agra station and the strong reluctance to give up so promising a field of labor.

In January 1858, Mr. Owen went to meet his wife in Calcutta on her return from America. Owing to disturbed conditions in Allahabad he left his wife with friends in Calcutta. After an arduous and somewhat adventurous journey up country, he arrived safely in Allahabad. In his journal he wrote:

"We entered the Mission Press Compound shortly before one

[3] *Foreign Missionary for June,* 1858, pp. 21-22.

o'clock this morning . . . Babu John Hari and Mirza and other native Christians were soon up, and came to assist in taking my things off the van."

Here he met the Rev. James Kennedy of the London Mission at Mirzapur, who had gone to Allahabad to minister to the Christians there. Mr. Kennedy has left on record an interesting account of what he saw, and of what Mr. Owen saw at Allahabad. He had gone from Mirzapur to Allahabad in response to a letter written by a leading Christian.

"All the missionaries having left some months ago, I was particularly desirous to visit the native Christian community at that station. As I travelled, I saw traces of the dire rebellion, which had been raging for some months, in burnt-down houses and well-nigh desolate villages. On reaching Allahabad, I saw for the first time, on a large scale, the desolating effects of the mutiny. Most of the houses of combustible material, were easily burnt down, but there were several flat-roofed houses, with beams and stones laid over them, which were not so easily destroyed. In some cases, resolute and too successful efforts were made to destroy even these, but the toil was found too great, and a few houses escaped with the destruction of the furniture and fittings of every description. Among these were the station Church and the principal chapel of the American Mission. It is quite melancholy to walk over the place and see house after house in ruins, with nothing to be seen but pieces of charred wood and tottering walls and then to remember how many, who occupied these houses, had been relentlessly slain.

"On Sabbath, I preached at two places, where the native Christians are located. I have seldom seen more attentive audiences. Their principal place of worship was on that day reopened for public worship. Windows, doors, sittings, everything breakable had been destroyed at the time of the mutiny. When the native Christians returned, they thought it preferable to meet for a time in one of their own houses for worship. When I was there, it was resolved to recommence the services in the chapel. No window or door had been restored, no sittings had been put in, but the place was well cleaned. Matting was spread on the floor, and the people sat on it. I need not say that I preached in this sanctuary with very peculiar feelings.

The people evidently felt much, as the reoccupancy of their place of worship, looking now so differently from what it had done, vividly reminded them of the scenes through which they had passed since last they had assembled in it, in May, 1857.

"One man sat before me, listening most devoutly to God's word, a native Christian from Fattehpur, in whose narrative I had been deeply interested, and from whom I could scarcely withdraw my eyes, as I spoke. He had suffered much for the name of Christ. He had fled with others, when the mutineers got the upper hand. He fell in with some Sepoys, who had seen him at Fattehpur, and also recognized him as a Christian. They called on him to deny Christ, and made him large promises, but he said he would rather die than deny his Lord and Saviour. On hearing this, they hacked him in a most cruel manner with their swords, and left him as dead. He lay insensible for several hours, and then coming to himself, he crawled to a small village in the neighborhood, where there were low caste Hindus, who pitied him and treated him with the utmost kindness. His hand had been so cut a little above the wrist, that it required only a slight pull to take it off. By the advice of the poor people among whom he had gone, the stump was put into oil, which checked the violent hemorrhage. He was concealed, tended and fed, for some weeks, till he was able to make his way to Allahabad. All about his head, neck and arms, there were the marks of the fearful gashes, the wounds his cruel enemies had inflicted. A few years ago, he was a bigoted Hindu. It has been common to say that persecution would scatter Hindustani Christians like chaff before the storm, but thanks to the grace of God, this is not the only case presented last year, when Hindustani Christians were found ready, not only to suffer, but to die for the sake of the Lord Jesus."[4]

At the beginning of 1858, the mutineers were still in possession of Lucknow and the Province of Oudh. Tantia Topi still carried on a sort of guerrilla warfare in central India. The plan of the military authorities was to crush the rebellion at its centre, which was Lucknow. Until that could be accomplished, there was always a possibility of a recrudescence of sedition in the regions occupied by our missions in the North Western Prov-

[4] *The Missionary Magazine* for July, 1858, quoted in *The Foreign Missionary*, September, 1858, pp. 136-137.

inces. The only feasible thing to do as yet was to preach the gospel in the villages and highways, and to restore the regular service in the churches, and so gather together the scattered forces of the mission.

At Allahabad, by the beginning of April, Mr. Owen was able to fit up temporary quarters in the schoolhouse and to set up a press and with the type, &c, which had been collected by the native Christian workmen, begin to do such job work as could be secured.

In the interim, between January and April, Mr. Owen had been able to pay a visit to Agra, Cawnpore, Fattehpur and Fattehgarh, there to counsel with the missionaries and the native Christians as to the future. In this interim, also, the question of the removal back of the Government offices from Agra to Allahabad, had been decided. Allahabad was henceforth to be the centre of both the civil and military departments of government. Extensive barracks for the accommodation of the troops were being constructed. The boundaries of the station and cantonment were marked out and the whole plot laid out with wide streets and roadways, providing for the present splendid city and its magnificent distances. The missionaries were not disturbed as to their premises and it was therefore possible to undertake the repair and rebuilding of their houses, as soon as funds for the purpose could be obtained.

When Mr. Owen visited the Fattehpur Mission compound, he concluded to advise Mr. Gopinath Nandi to recommence work on a small scale. At Cawnpore, he left money with Heury, one of the catechists, to repair the houses of the four catechists immediately, in order that the natives should see as soon as possible that we have not been driven from the ground.

While there, Mr. Owen visited the scene of the massacre of the Europeans, including the missionaries, who had fled from Fattehgarh. He wrote:

"I drove out to find some of the places, which have obtained such a sad notoriety. No native that I met would tell me the way to the house of murder; they all feigned entire ignorance of its locality and of what had occurred there. At last I got a drummer boy of the Thirty-Fourth Regiment to come with me and to show me the way. He was a bright little fellow, and told me of their recent hard fighting with the Gwalior rebels, and pointed out places where some of the severest struggles took place. The 'slaughter house' had been blown up, and the well in which the bodies were thrown has been filled. A very beautiful monument, 'TO THE MEMORY OF THE WOMEN AND CHILDREN OF H. M. THIRTY-SECOND, WHO WERE MASSACRED NEAR THIS PLACE,' has been erected by twenty men of that regiment, who passed through Cawnpore in November. The well, into which Miss Wheeler threw herself, a few feet distant, has also been covered over. The trees against which the Sepoys dashed the children have been cut down; they were just back of the house, between that and the well. The bark, which was stained with the children's blood, has been taken off, but the trees are lying there still. The 'slaughter house' is in ruins, and one cannot see what it was, but the entrenchment, if such it may be called, is just as it was when Wheeler capitulated."

Mr. Owen mentioned in his journal the great kindness and sympathy he had received from the English officers. The sincerity of such helpful sympathy, on the part of many, has already been described in this history of our missions. There was, however, an attitude on the part of some officials, even in high places, which was a source of sorrow to the missionaries. Mr. Owen wrote:

"Mr. Grant, our Lieutenant Governor, seldom, if ever, goes to Church, and clings to the anti-Christian policy. The missionaries in Benares raised a corps of about four hundred native Christians, for Government service. Mr. Grant declined taking them lest the Hindus and Muhammadans should take offence. The missionaries of Krishnaggar, in Bengal, not long since wished the native Christians to enlist in Government service, and the native Christians themselves desired to do so, but Lord Canning and Mr. Holliday refused to accept them. All we want is that the native Christians have fair play, not to be favoured because they are Christians, not be rejected on that account, but if they are otherwise qualified, they be equally, with Muhammadans and Hindus, eligible to Government service."[5]

At Fattehgarh Messrs. Scott and Fullerton were busy in their endeavor to bring order out of confusion. Mr. Scott wrote thus of their observations and labors:

"Fattehgarh is a total ruin. The whole station may be, not inaptly, compared to an immense graveyard, the monuments of which are crumbling mud walls. It is, so far as everything European is concerned, as perfect a scene of desolation as I have ever looked upon.

"When we came here, we found most of our native Christians already collected. A few have come in since.

"The way was now opened up for native Christian employment among Europeans as servants, watchmen, Government employees, and most of our people have already obtained situations in which they are giving a high degree of satisfaction. Christianity from this time takes a different position politically in India. Caesar now smiles upon her and holds out his hand to welcome her as a faithful ally and friend. Heretofore one of our greatest difficulties was to know what to do with our native Christians; and, in order to find support for them, we were almost compelled to engage, to some extent, in secular work. This necessity has now passed away."[6]

About this time a considerable number of people were added to the church by baptism. Most of them were Begies, one of the lowest castes, but one at least was a Brahmin, who afterwards became a leading evangelist and for some years the pastor of the church in Fattehgarh. "The blood of the martyrs is the seed of the church." That man Mohun Lal, by name, was for long employed by the Rev. Henry R. Wilson as his language teacher, after which he entered the Government service. During the disturbances he had nothing to do, and returning to his home he began to read the New Testament with the desire of finding the truth. This led to his conversion and eventual entry into the ministry of the church.

[5] *Story of a Dedicated Life*, pp. 211-212.
[6] *The Foreign Missionary*, August, 1858, p. 78.

At Fattehpur, Mr. Gopinath Nandi found everything in chaos; their house in ruins and the chapel walls and pillars pulled down. The excessive heat of the summer made it impossible for him to do much work, so that he was asked to go to Allahabad to help in the work of repairing the mission church and the houses in the Christian village; and also in preaching to the Indian congregation on the Sabbath days. In the middle of July, he was able to return to Fattehpur and to repair some of the out offices and a couple of rooms in them for his own residence. He then brought back his family and again began preaching to the people, thanking God for His great mercy in preserving their lives.

At Mainpuri, the work was reopened by Indian workers. Mr. Ullmann had been sent to London on special duty. The School opened with seventy pupils.

At Allahabad, Mr. Munnis having returned, the High School was reopened with two hundred pupils. Mr. Owen continued to carry on the work of printing until it was finally decided to sell the press at a nominal price to the Indian Christians, who were employed in it, from which date they have conducted the business on their own account.

The two Christians who purchased the wreck of the old Mission Press, were Mr. John C. Jordon and Mr. (afterwards Rev.) J. J. Caleb. The latter eventually purchased Mr. Jordon's[7] interest, and gave the Press to his son, E. Caleb, Esq., B. A. Mr Owen was now busily engaged in rewriting his Commentary on the Psalms in Urdu, and in his work as Secretary of the North India Bible and Tract Society, which had been transferred from Agra to Allahabad. "He had much to do in the way of supplying the European soldiers in the

[7] Mr. Jordon was foreman in the Mission press for most of his life. "For more than 60 years, Mr. Jordon probably never missed a day at the press, except during the mutiny. He was held in great regard by all who knew him, and at the funeral young men of the Christian community drew his hearse from his house to the cemetery, where a large company had gathered to join in the burial service."

Northern provinces with Bibles, tracts and other Christian books." On December 20th, 1858, he wrote:

"There has been a revival of religion in one of the Highland regiments, and several of the soldiers have become hopefully converted. In some of the regiments, even on the field of battle, prayer meetings are regularly kept up."

This experience illustrates once more the fact that American missionaries always felt called to labor for the conversion of Europeans as well as of Indians. Their motto was practically that of the late Rev. Dr. John Fordyce, Secretary of the Anglo-Indian Evangelization Society: "The soul of a white man is just as good as that of a black man."

At Fattehgarh, the question was once raised as to whether the site of the Mission premises might not be changed, but in the end of the year 1858, the Mission decided to restore the old mission premises, beginning with the mission houses. Mr. Fullerton built the house at Barkpur and Mr. Scott the one at Rakha. The High School at Farrukhabad was reopened with 294 pupils in attendance.

Thus wonderfully were the missionaries enabled to re-enter the fields so terribly devastated by the storms of hatred and dire persecution. Already the churches and schools were being blessed. A new interest in the work of evangelism had been aroused. The waves of revival among the churches in Britain and America had reached the shores of India, and many, both Indians and Europeans were inquiring the way of life.

It was in the fall of 1858, that during the Annual Meeting of the Lodiana Mission, held in November, in the Church at Lodiana, a call[8] was sent out to the Protestant world to set apart the second week in January, 1860, beginning with Monday the 8th, as a time of special prayer for the outpouring of the Holy Spirit upon all nations. The minute recording this action was printed in broad-sheets and sent to prominent leaders in all Protestant Churches through the world. This movement

[8] See Appendix II.

resulted in the establishment of the *Week of Prayer,* which has been arranged for by the Evangelical Alliance, year by year and observed by Evangelical Churches everywhere. This may be justly regarded as the beginning of a new era in the history of missions in India and the world.

The Farrukhabad mission, notwithstanding their sad losses during the mutiny, had faith to undertake a further extension of their field. They proposed to open two new stations, one at Aligarh and one at Etawah. The welcome news had come that the Rev. J. J. Walsh, now on furlough, with the Rev. Augustus Brodhead and Mrs. Brodhead, new recruits, had sailed from Boston on the 8th of November, 1858. The churches at home were pursuing their work with a new energy. Foreign Missions received a new impetus by reason of the trials and sufferings of the martyrs in India. The missionaries and their Indian helpers consecrated themselves anew.

"A great change too had come over the mind of the Indian public in regard to mission work. Those officers, who had not only disliked missionaries and their work, believing that they were raising obstacles to the government of the people, men who would have prohibited the preaching in the bazars, were now silent. The fact was now clearly proved that the rebellion had been begun among those who had been most carefully guarded against the influence of missionaries and native Christians. It was now generally believed that the mutiny was a Divine judgment on a godless government for their disloyalty to Christ."

The only newspaper published at the seat of the Punjab government had been most unfriendly toward the missionaries. Two or three letters appeared in its columns representing the mutiny as a judgment, when the editor announced to his readers that no more letters of such a character should find a place in his paper.

The *Chronicler* above quoted now wrote saying:

"The spirit of the paper is entirely changed. Its columns

are filled with such letters as it formerly rejected. It now boldly advocates a Christian government, a Christian policy, and Christian missions for India. The Punjab Government has issued a proclamation declaring that all its offices are now open to native Christians."[9]

Another benefit resulting from the Sepoy mutiny was the proof it gave of the sincerity of the Indian Christians. All along during the terrible months of trial and uncertainty, the Indian Christians, whether servants or refugees, exhibited a spirit of helpfulness and loyalty, which did much to correct the notion popularly held that Indian converts were "rice Christians." The way was now open to them to receive the emoluments of Government Service, which at once gave employment and added respectability to them and their families.

[9] Letter of Rev. David Herron quoted in *Foreign Missionary*, January, 1859, p. 247.

CHAPTER XI.

A Mission to the Afghans

THE temporary occupancy of Afghanistan by the British Government 1838-1841 served to call special attention to a new field for missionary endeavor. There were not a few who believed the Afghans to be descendants of the lost tribes of Israel. The Afghans themselves claim the honor of being Beni Israel. This was the special claim of the Durane tribe, which established its rule at Cabul by its revolt against the descendants of Nadir Shah. When the Durani Kings were overthrown and fled to India, taking refuge under British protection at Lodiana, they lived in hope that by some turn of fortune they might be restored to the throne of their fathers.

When the effort of the Indian Government in conjunction with the Khalsa ruler of the Punjab, Maharajah Runjeet Singh, to restore Shah Shuja to his throne, although successful in form yet failed through the incompetency of their protégé, a new barrier was raised against the establishment of a mission in Cabul. The hope of the American Mission at Lodiana to eventually occupy Afghanistan was therefore deferred.

The Church Missionary Society had also a mind to establish a mission to the Afghans and with this in view, they occupied the frontier city of Peshawur at the close of the second Sikh war.

In 1855, Major H. M. Conran, who had been a liberal contributor towards the work of the American Presbyterian Mission, offered to give them the sum of fifteen thousand rupees for the establishment of a mission to the Afghans. The Lodiana Mission, after due correspondence with the Board in New York, accepted this offer.

About this time, the Rev. Isidor Loewenthal, a converted

Jew, joined the Mission. He was highly educated in the schools of Europe and America, having a thorough acquaintance with the oriental cognates of Hebrew. He was offered the honor of undertaking the Afghan Mission. He cheerfully consented to undertake the work for which the money had been given.

The Lodiana Mission, under the leadership of the Rev. Dr. John H. Morrison, selected Rawul Pindi as a suitable station, in which to inaugurate the Afghan work. A number of Afghan refugees were then living there.

Accordingly, Mr. Loewenthal began his work at Rawul Pindi in 1856. It soon became evident that this was not the best place for such pioneer work, because the Pashtu language, the principal language of Afghanistan, was not generally spoken there.

Just then the Church missionaries invited Mr. Loewenthal to come to Peshawur and tarry with them, until he should have acquired the language and felt able to enter Afghanistan. Accordingly, with the consent of his Mission, he took up his abode in Peshawur. Here he gave himself to the acquisition of the Persian language, which was the Court language of the Afghans. The chief difficulty in his way of learning Pashtu was the absence of grammar and dictionary. This added to the difficulty of getting access to the people who ordinarily used it. He succeeded by braving the danger of visiting villages where everybody spoke Pashtu. In his search for Pashtu manuscripts, he was surprised to find volumes, containing "the most profound speculations on the nature of the attributes of the Deity, on the Divine and human agency, which were thumbed by the women of the village."[1]

The most important work to be undertaken seemed to be the translation of the scriptures into Pashtu.

"The first attempt to produce a Pashtu version of the scriptures

[1] *Twenty-third Report of the Lodiana Mission*, p. 43.

had been made by Dr. Leyden, the Professor of Hindustani in the the College of Fort William, Calcutta. In 1811, he had finished a translation of the Gospels of Matthew and Mark, but his death brought this work to a close. The Serampore missionaries then took up the work and, by employing the native translators, which had been in the employ of Dr. Leyden, they carried on the work, and in 1818 brought out an edition of 1000 copies of the New Testament, which was printed in Serampore. 'This edition remained almost entirely in the Depository at Serampore; a few copies found their way into European Libraries, and some doubtless reached Afghanistan through Lohani merchants'."[2]

"At the first establishment of the Lodiana Mission, the missionaries distributed some copies of the Serampore Pashtu version, but with what, or whether with any result, the Great Day only can fully reveal. At the present time (1857) the copies are not numerous.

"As regards the character of this version, while one Afghan will say that the book is a very good one, and the language very good and idiomatic, another has said, that, although containing many Pashtu, Persian and Arabic words, it is such a jumble, that no one can make anything of it. The knowledge of Pashtu possessed by the missionary appointed to labor among the Afghans, is yet too limited for him to venture on the expression of any very decided opinion. Whilst some parts seem to him to be quite faithful to the original, and plainly intelligible, there are, nevertheless, in other parts, mistranslations of such a nature that he would hesitate to put the whole into the hand of the natives. Some gentlemen in Pashawur, who had undertaken to make a new version, state that they have not been able to make much use of the old version. The idea of reprinting this version, therefore, could not well be entertained. But efforts have begun to be made to produce a new translation. The Rev. Robert Clark, on his departure for England, committeed the first eleven chapters of the Gospel of John, in manuscript, to the North India Bible Society, who forthwith ordered an edition of two thousand copies in lithograph, which was also begun. About the same time Captain H. James, Deputy Commissioner of Peshawur, sent them a translation (from the English) of the Gospel of Luke. It is to be feared, however, that both

[2] *Ibid*, p. 45.

of these manuscripts perished in the general wreck, which overtook the Secundra Orphan Press during the mutiny. 'Of the Old Testament, the Serampore missionaries printed the Pentateuch, in 1821, and in 1832, the historical books one thousand copies of each. The want of funds put a stop to further efforts. What has become of these portions of the Old Testament, does not appear; in European libraries a few copies are found; a few copies are also in Peshawur, but the missionary has not yet been able to get a sight of them'."[3]

This interesting account of what had been done to translate the scriptures into the vernacular dialect of the Afghans, illustrates anew the difficult problem of Afghan evangelization. A still further obstacle in the way was the unwillingness of the people to receive Christian books and tracts. In consequence of this attitude, the question was raised as to the need of a Pashtu version of the scriptures. Persian was read and understood by the educated classes and it was thought that the Persian version would be sufficient to meet the present need. Mr. Loewenthal's investigations, however, led him to an entirely different conclusion. He had discovered a considerable literature in Pashtu among the people. Many of the books were original compositions. Numerous translations of various popular Persian and Arabic authors were in existence. He also made known the fact, that at that time nearly all the women were able to read Pashtu, and Pashtu only. The need of a vernacular version of the Scriptures was therefore very evident.

A serious difficulty, however, had to be faced. The vernaculars of Afghanistan differ greatly, so that a man who speaks Pashtu in one quarter can hardly understand the people in another. It was, for this reason, most important that the translations should be made in that dialect which could be understood by at least a considerable number of people. Mr. Loewenthal constantly yearned for an opportunity to travel in Afghanistan. He made earnest appeals to his Mission for

[3] The quotations in this chapter are from Mr. Loewenthal's report, as recorded in the *Twenty-third Annual Report of the Lodiana Mission.*

permission to undertake such a journey, but permission was refused. He, however, set himself to learn the language and became proficient in its use. He also undertook the work of translating the New Testament from the original Greek, in which he was an adept. In this work he was in no way hindered by the Sepoy mutiny. He preached in the bazar and sometimes visited villages in the region near by.

The following extract from one of his letters shows the perilous character of his missionary work.

"My work is nevertheless progressing very slowly. I had planned an expedition into the Yusufzai country, when a sudden attack of the Afghans upon an Assistant Commissioner's camp, in which his tents were burned, five of his servants killed, some horses of his escort carried off, and he himself escaped narrowly with his life, warned me that the time was not yet. Robberies, many connected with murder, are of nightly occurrence in the city, in cantonments, and in the villages, though it is acknowledged by all, natives and Europeans, that there is a great improvement in this respect, in comparison with former years.

"Some thieves, about three weeks ago, dug into my house, ransacked it, and came to the bed where I enjoyed a very sound sleep, but did no harm beyond carrying off what clothes they could find, and some cooking furniture. They also took out a large and costly Persian manuscript, Firdouse's Shah Nama, but not being of a literary turn, they left it outside, where I found it in the morning, together with the trunks they had emptied. They might have done much more mischief, and it is hard to tell why they did not. The Lord is very good."

During his residence in Peshawur, Mr. Loewenthal co-operated with the Church Missionary Society's missionaries in their work there. The Lodiana Mission did not wish to be in any way committed to undertake to maintain a Mission Station at Peshawur. Their hope was that the way would open for them to enter into Afghanistan, and they therefore desired that their missionary should be kept free to enter into that country whenever possible. Accordingly it was arranged that while . . .

"under present circumstances . . . he considers Peshawur as his Station, he should not pledge himself *not* to begin other branches of work at Peshawur, or in any way hamper himself by his proposed co-operation with the English Church Mission at that place; but remain as independent of it as missions of different societies laboring in the same place usually are."[4]

Mr. Loewenthal was a great sufferer from malarial fever and chronic headache, accompanied by insomnia. One wonders at his indefatigable efforts in many directions. He not only translated the New Testament into Pashtu, and thereby sent the Gospel into the interior of his beloved Afghanistan, but he undertook the larger task of translating from the Hebrew the Old Testament. He spoke Persian and Pashtu fluently and made considerable progress in the acquisition of colloquial Kashmiri. These, with all his other varied acquirements, as a polished European and Oriental scholar. pointed him out as one likely to become preeminently distinguished for usefulness in the Mission field. But alas! the brilliant career of this devoted man was suddenly brought to a close on the 27th of April, 1864. He had been suffering from excruciating pain in his head and, as he had often done before, he sought relief by walking in the veranda of his house, or in the garden outside. While thus engaged, he was shot down by his watchman. His death was instantaneous. No one knew why the deed was done, save the watchman, who reported the tragedy, saying that he had mistaken his master for a robber. The watchman was given the benefit of a doubt, but many believed the missionary to have been deliberately murdered. It seems to such men incredible that a servant should not have known his master, who was in the habit of walking about his own house at night.

The death of Mr. Loewenthal led to the abandonment of our mission to the Afghans. The Church Missionary Society having undertaken a similar mission, it seemed to the Lodiana Mission to be wise not to appoint a successor to Mr. Loewenthal. They accordingly presented the library and manuscripts,

[4] *Minutes of the Lodiana Mission*, 1857, p. 22.

which would be of use in the cause of Afghan evangelization, to the Church missionaries in Peshawur. The literary work of Mr. Loewenthal remains as a memorial to his service in the Great Army of the Lord. "He being dead yet speaketh."

The following extract from one of Mr. Loewenthal's reports, at once illustrates his keen observation and profound knowledge of the problems to be solved by the men who would evangelize Afghanistan.

"He who would undertake the glorious task of giving the Afghans the beginning of a real literature, of a Christian literature; who would undertake to translate the Bible for them, would first have to ascertain the most prevalent, the purest, intrinsically and extrinsically the most worthy, the best understood dialect, and not rest satisfied with translating into the language of the frontier. Frontier dialects are always mongrel and inferior.

"An additional task will be his, who shall endeavour to bring the Afghans to Christ, through the instrumentality of religious treaties, or tracts. He will probably find it highly advisable, if not actually necessary, to compose them in the form of verse and rhyme. There seems to be a period in the history of every nation, when prose cannot live, when the distinction between prose and poetry is unknown, and the instructor of a people can only speak to them in measured language, when prose to them is prosy, and rhyme reason. So it is with the Afghans of this day. There are prose works in their language, historical and religious, but while these are merely read by some learned men here and there, the works in verse are extremely popular among all classes, and are recited and sung on the roads and streets by old and young. . . .

"Viewing the peculiar nature of this enterprise, it is impossible to resist the conviction how entirely the work of missions is the work of the Lord. He must appoint the men for it; He must endue them with the needed qualifications; and He must open the door of faith. Standing before the wild range of the Sulaiman mountains, gazing evening after evening, as the sun is setting behind it, on the line of savage, habitationless, precipitous crags standing so distinct against the brilliant sky; seeing, morning after morning the strong sunlight of these latitudes, penetrate one by one, the rugged passes and the jagged clefts, forbidden by man and nature to cross beyond, and knowing that once beyond, he might pass through this vast cradle of nations, from the Khyber to the great commercial entrepot of Yezd, in one direction, and beyond the Oxus as far as Orenberg in another, and be everywhere almost the first to announce the glad tidings of salvation through Jesus Christ,—the missionary is apt to fancy these mountains more and more to be insurmountable barriers; sickness and exhaustion cause him to feel his own weakness and littleness daily more keenly; and he would be tempted to despair, were there not a voice crying in the wilderness, 'Prepare ye the way of the Lord.' . . .

"The peculiar nature of the difficulties with which this Mission, for some time to come, will have to contend, appears to demand two men, at least, of robust health and strong constitution; health and constitutions that have been tried and found of full weight, with juices not dried up in the study and spirits not evaporated by high pressure; let the system be but sound and the theology need not be so profound. They must be able to stand the scorching sun and the stifling simoom as well as intense cold, they must be able to make daily marches of from 25 to 30 miles either on foot, or on camels, as water is scarce; and they could not well travel, except with caravans of merchants, who do not make such long marches. They must be willing to live for weeks and even months, with no other protection from atmospheric influences but the canvas walls and roofs of their tents. They must be willing to forego that prime luxury of Christian civilization, cleanliness, not wash more than once a week, nor be of a sanguinary disposition towards the lower orders of creation; for nothing alienates an Afghan so much, nothing seems to make him more inaccessible, than customs abhorrent from his own, especially if they be harmless, or still more, if they be good and helpful. Let them be able to handle a gun, for often their dinner will depend upon their skill as sportsmen; and the Afghans respect an armed man much more than an unarmed one. Let them possess some knowledge of medicine, and carry with them a good supply of the commonest remedies, and finally to their love of souls and zeal for God, they must add an entire willingness to lay down their lives; and that not merely in that general sense in which missionaries are often said to go forth with their lives in their hands; for having once left the British territory, surrounded as they will be by political fanatics, religious zealots, and the most bloodthirsty robbers, the likelihood, humanely speaking, is small of their ever seeing their friends again."

These words set forth the ideal of the man whom Loewenthal set before himself. He had deliberately entered upon this Mission of a dangerous service. More than once he sought permission to go beyond the border line. His visits to the Peshawur bazar and the nearby villages, were always made in peril of his life. More than one European fell a victim of the fanatic's knife.

Loewenthal lived the life of a martyr.[5] His fellow missionaries erected a memorial tablet over his grave which bears the following inscription:

"To the Memory of the Rev. Isidor Loewenthal, Missionary of the American Presbyterian Mission, who translated the New Testament into Pashtu, and was shot by his chokeydar, April 27th, 1864.

" 'I am not ashamed of the Gospel of Christ, for it is the power of God unto salvation to everyone that believeth.'

"Rom. 1:16."

[5] See Appendix III.

CHAPTER XII.

New Educational Policy: Progress in the Punjab

IN the year 1854, many restrictions upon the work of Christian missions were removed, and a more liberal attitude was manifested by the rulers in India. This attitude was especially notable in the matter of education. Mission schools were now to be aided by generous grants.

The American Baptist missionaries in Burmah had introduced Normal schools at Rangoon and other cities. Grants in aid had been made to these schools, in accordance with the new liberal policy of Government. In his report for 1855-1856, the Chief Commissioner made mention of these grants. A new life and interest had been given to the educational work of missionaries everywhere.

But, in 1858, a reactionary policy was undertaken by the Government in India, under the aegis of Lord Ellenborough, President of the Board of Control of the East India Company and former Governor General of India, and Sir George R. Clark, Under Secretary of the Board of Control. A copy of a letter, dated April 28th, 1858, from Lord Ellenborough, was laid on the table of the House of Lords, which urged a reversal of the educational measures inaugurated in 1854. The letter especially attacked the system of grants-in-aid to mission schools. These were condemned as

"compromising the Government with that which is designated as a system of proselytism and thus endangering the peace of the empire, by exciting the apprehension of the natives that the Government desires, through education, to convert the people.

"To this procedure of giving grants-in-aid to missionaries, the noble writer of the letter chiefly attributes the almost unanimous mutiny of the Bengal army, as well as very extensive indications of a hostile feeling among the people."

In 1855, the convicts at work near the riverside at Rangoon, made a desperate attempt to escape, but were retaken. Such attempts had been made at Pegu and elsewhere in 1853.

Sir George Clark, in his review of the Commissioner's report endeavored to show that these outbreaks were due to the new policy of government in subsidizing mission schools.

The Commissioner had very clearly shown the real cause of these emeutes in his report, but it suited Sir George Clark to omit all mention of this explanation in his memorandum. The cause as set forth in the Chief Commissioner's report was described as follows:

"Under the Burmese Government, criminals were either executed with despatch, or often, even for the most heinous offences, a few weeks' or months' confinement, they were released on payment of a fine, or sometimes by intercession of the Buddhist monks. After the Province became British, and when men were sentenced to imprisonment for terms of seven, ten or more years, they at first never appear to have supposed that this was anything more than a nominal sentence. Their relatives used to apply for their release, as if confident of it being granted. When, however, they saw that these applications were not attended to, despair possessed them, and a general effort was made to escape at the hazard of their lives. For the last two years, the prisoners have, like the community, 'settled,' and general open risings in jails are not heard of."[1]

The letter of Lord Ellenborough, when published, created widespread indignation among Christian people in Britain. A deputation was appointed consisting of prominent persons, connected with various missionary societies, which waited upon Lord Stanley. After being questioned in regard to Lord Ellenborough's letter, his Lordship replied:

[1] *Church Missionary Intelligencer*, September, 1858, quoted in *Foreign Missionary*, November, 1858, p. 201.

"I am bound to say that my feelings are very much in sympathy with those of Lord Ellenborough and Sir George Clark."

This was the spirit of the regime and marked in strong characters the feelings of those who forbade Judson to land on Indian soil at Calcutta; and which most reluctantly permitted the American missionaries to stop in Bombay in 1813. The outbreak of the Sepoy rebellion afforded a new opportunity to voice the antagonism of the enemies of missions.

A paper was prepared by the Rev. John Newton, a pioneer of the Lodiana Mission, dealing with the question of the relation of the missionary work to the Sepoy rebellion. It so completely refutes the claim that the mutiny was in any way due to missions or missionaries, as to entitle it to a place here.

"Men are not wanting—and some too in high places—who have ventured to publish their belief that the discontent of the Sepoys had its origin in efforts made by missionaries and private individuals for their conversion to Christianity. Such an idea finds little favor, indeed, among intelligent Europeans, either in India or elsewhere; yet, since there are some, who, from their ignorance of the subject, or from their hostility to missions, are ready to believe anything however slanderous, against our work, we think it well to bring a few facts to the notice of the Board, which may serve to shut the mouths of such gainsayers.

"It has already been mentioned . . . that some of the Sepoys, who attended the cantonment school (Lodiana), said plainly that the house in which the school was kept, being Government property, would be in danger of being attacked, were it not for the fact that it was occupied by the Mission.

"One of our number was told by some natives at Lodiana, that when the Sepoys from Jalandhar were firing the Mission buildings, they stopped in the midst of their work and refused to go on with it, saying, 'What are we doing this for? Our quarrel is not with the missionaries, but with the Government.'

"At Jalandhar, the children of some of the Sepoys attended the Mission school, both before and after the rebellion commenced; and the company or companies with which the parents of the children were connected, continued loyal, while their comrades mutinied.

"In further illustration of this point it may be mentioned that the Gurkhas, who refused to join the rebels, had some of them been educated by missionaries; and others had their children, both sons and daughters, in Mission schools. This is true of the regiment stationed at Subathu, which was in the Punjab at the time of the outbreak, and did good service to the Government; and especially by the regiment at Dehra, which had recently come from Almorah. This was the corps which first distinguished itself by its fidelity, and which, by its example may have done much towards confirming the wavering minds of some of the Gurkhas at other places."

Testimony like this might be quoted from the experience of every mission in India. The fact, that as soon as the schools, which had been closed during the disturbance, were opened, the old pupils came bringing others until the attendance became greater than before, was sufficient to show that the schools were popular with the people.

The reactionary policy, advocated in Lord Ellenborough's letter to the House of Lords, failed to receive the recognition of the English people. The progressive policy of 1854 was confirmed.

The Queen's proclamation, promulgated in 1858, which guaranteed religious neutrality on the part of the Government, added a further stimulus to the forward movement in education.

Almost immediately the Government began to seek co-operation of the missions for the furthering of educational work, offering grants-in-aid up to one-half the current expenses. The principle of neutrality was maintained by declining to regard the scripture teaching or the prayer service as forming any part of the curriculum of study. Such grants-in-aid were offered, not only to Christian schools, but also to Hindus, Muhammadans and other non-Christian classes. All aided schools were subject to Government inspection and the general oversight of the Directors of Public Instruction in the various Provinces. This wise and generous policy of Government was not intended to interfere in any way with the liberty of denominational schools. Many Christian and non-Christian schools declined to receive any kind of aid from the Government. Many missionaries were hesitant, lest such secular relationship should militate against the spiritual life of their schools. Nor was this fear without foundation. Any system of education, which would dictate the course of study and prescribe text books, which should exclude the basic teachings of religion, subjecting the general management of schools to the will of godless, and even anti-Christian inspectors and directors, was sure to diminish the spiritual life of the school. On the other hand, however, the whole Christian community was dependent upon the course of instruction, prescribed by the educational code, for admission to the degrees necessary to secure employment in the various departments of Government service. Distinctively Christian schools could educate their pupils in accordance with their own ideals, but might be unable to draw non-Christian patronage except from the lowest castes, not to speak of many Christians, who would desire to secure the advantages which the secular schools afford their children. The grant-in-aid system finally adopted opened the way for missionary schools to become widely influential. They gathered thousands of non-Christian youths into their schools where for a long course of years they would receive the secular teaching required by the Government code along with the daily bible lessons and the personal impress of the Christian teacher. For this reason, along with other considerations, the missionaries of the Presbyterian churches fell in with the Government system and so became a prime influence in the education of the masses.

This policy in mission schools naturally led on to the establishment of schools of all grades up to the college in affiliation with the universities. By this arrangement too, missionary educators secured places of influence in the syndicates of the universities, which control the Provincial examination and the granting of academic degrees.

The Mission school building at Lodiana, which had been

destroyed during the mutiny, was rebuilt upon a larger scale. In April 1859, the school was transferred from the Murray Ganj Chapel to the new building. The school before the mutiny had 184 pupils in attendance, but when it became necessary to use the Mission chapel for a school room, there was a considerable falling off. Still later, when two boys were baptized, the number decreased until only 79 names remained on the roll. This was a serious crisis. Strenuous effort was made to boycott the school, but many parents had come to realize the great advantages, which the Mission school was bringing to them.

It was also gratifying to the manager to note the feeling of loyalty among the pupils, who seemed to be pleased to see the courage of their schoolmates in their steadfast confession of faith in Jesus Christ. Many of them were no doubt in sympathy with them, but lacked courage to take the step themselves. The school continued to progress under the superintendence of Mr. Thackwell, and at the close of the year 1861, when he was transferred to Ambala, the number in attendance was 254. The Rev. Adolph Rudolph was now made superintendent, which post he held until the arrival of Rev. Alexander Henry, from America. Mr. Henry entered upon the work with great enthusiasm. The school rapidly increased in numbers. At the end of the year 1863, the whole number of pupils was 380, of whom 245 were Hindus, 121 Muhammadans and 14 Christians. Of these 329 were studying English. The advanced classes were being taught Algebra, Geometry, Natural Philosophy, Chemistry, Astronomy, Evidences of Christianity and History.

The remarkable fact has already been mentioned that the Jalandhar school was not visibly affected by the Sepoy mutiny in the cantonment. The next year, however, being a very unhealthy year, the majority of the pupils were prostrated by malarial fever. In consequence the attendance fell off until the number was only 131. Three years later the number was 300, with higher classes preparing for entrance to college. This school was under the superintendence of the Rev. Goloknath and had become a high school. It was now receiving a liberal grant-in-aid from the government.

The schools at Ambala, Saharanpur and Dehra slowly recovered from the depression due to the outbreak of the Sepoy mutiny. They were quietly feeling their way and looking forward to the time when they should get into closer touch with the higher classes of the Indian people.

The most important advance was made at Lahore, in the Rang Mahal school. The "Rang Mahal" was an old palace, once a theatre for Royal entertainment. It was located in the centre of the city, and had been generously given to the mission for school purposes. The school was somewhat affected by the mutiny, owing to the excitement which then prevailed and the fear lest the mutiny might spread. Perhaps nothing ministered more to the peace and quiet of the city than the spectacle of the missionary walking back and forth to and from the Rang Mahal school, and the attendance of two hundred students. This could not but increase the popular feeling of confidence in the Government in its struggle with rebellion in the Northwest. After the restoration of peace throughout the country, the Rang Mahal school made rapid advance in numbers and influence. Messrs. John Newton and Charles Forman, who began the school in 1849, were both at work there now. Mr. Forman had been in charge continuously as principal and had acquired the confidence of both the Government and the people. He had gathered about him a staff of Bengali Christian teachers, who had been educated in Duff's college, Calcutta. They were competent to teach English classes. Among them were some who distinguished themselves in their profession: Babu Ishan Chandra Mukherji the headmaster, Babu Jadunath Chatterji, Amesh Chandra Ghose, Kali Charan Catterjee, Haresh Chandra Sen, Amarnath Pal, Jogandra Chandra Bose and Nobin Chandra Das. The report for the year 1862 records the fact that in the previous year three young men had been sent up for the entrance examination of the Calcutta university; of whom one passed. Eight more were to be sent for the next year's entrance examination. Besides these, four students had entered the medical college. The Mission school system was now extended throughout the city, so that, in the report for 1864, mention is made of seventeen branch schools. Another class was now sent up for entrance to the Calcutta University, of whom seven passed. A further advance was now to be made. At the next annual meeting of the mission, action was taken to the following effect:

"As it has appeared desirable that there should be an institution in the Mission, at which a higher education should be given, than was aimed at in our other schools, the addition of a college department to the school in Lahore was proposed." This proposal was approved of by the Mission at large, and by the Board in America. Later on the school was affiliated with the University of Calcutta. The first college class was composed of eight students, six of whom had passed entrance from the Rang Mahal school and two from the Jalandhar school. Thus was laid the foundation of the Christian college at Lahore. This was done after careful deliberation. The Government had already established a college in Lahore which would be able to give the same education along secular lines that a Christian college could give. But religious neutrality necessarily excluded religious instruction from all government institutions. The youth in Mission schools had been trained under distinctly Christian influences and, for this reason, it was felt to be a mistaken policy, from the missionary point of view, to pass their graduates on to a college, where there would be no Christian influence whatever. This feeling was intensified when three young men, sons of Indian Christian parents, were now ready to enter a college. This decision of the Mission has been fully justified by the history of this Christian college during more than a half century.

The orphanage and school for boys at Saharanpur continued to provide for the physical and intellectual needs of a considerable number of orphan and homeless boys. These were given such education and training as would fit them to be useful members of society and the church. It was hoped that some of them might become teachers and evangelists in connection with the mission. Eight young men, trained in this institution were already doing excellent work, of whom three were eventually ordained to the ministry. Others were taught mechanical arts and found useful employment in public works.

The girls' orphanage at Lodiana continued to be the only school for Indian Christian girls in the Punjab. It provided for the present education for Christian girls who could attend the classes as day pupils. A few motherless girls came in from other stations. The time soon came, when the local requirements of even the smaller Christian communities obliged the opening of girls' schools at almost every Mission station. Such schools were usually conducted under missionary supervision, the missionaries' wives being in charge.

From the annual report of the Subathu station, for 1863, we learn that a Bazar school for non-Christian girls was carried on with very irregular attendance. At the same time a school for native Christian girls, located on the Mission compound, was taught by Miss C. L. Beatty and Mrs. Janvier. It was a sort of Normal school for the training of girls to be teachers. Grammar, geography, arithmetic, natural science, philosophy and the evidences of Christianity were taught.

At Jalandhar a school for Christian girls was conducted by Mrs. Goloknath. This provided for the need of the Christian community, but a few non-Christian girls were admitted. The attendance rarely exceeded fifteen.

In Lahore a school for non-Christian girls was begun by Mrs. Morrison in 1854. Besides reading in the vernacular, the girls were taught plain needle-work and knitting.

At Ambala a school was opened for Christians girls. It was conducted under the supervision of Mrs. M. M. Carleton.

At Dehra, a girls' school was started in the Mission house

with an attendance of eight pupils. For several years this school was carried on as a day school, under the superintendence of Mrs. David Herron, who, before her marriage, had taught in the Agra Girls' Boarding School. It developed into a boarding school and in 1863, Miss Beatty was transferred from Subathu in order to become principal of this school. From this time onward, the Dehra Christian Girls' School became the leading high school for girls in the Province. It holds its place today and has added a teachers' training department of great importance.[3]

The desire for English education, at this period in mission history, is illustrated by the adult class taught in a night school at Lahore. The class was made up of men, most of them serving in various public offices. The number in this school went as high as one hundred and fifteen. The highest class studied Indian history, grammar and the bible. Once a week a lecture was given by one of the missionaries to the whole school.

The value of Mission school teaching is well described in the following statement made by the late Rev. Goloknath, missionary in charge at Jalandhar.

> "While we have carefully attempted to teach Geography, History and other useful branches, we taught them not for their own sake alone, but for the sake of their subserviency to higher things. Human learning is not the end, but a means by which we hope to prepare these young minds to receive the gospel. The moral benefits, which the Hindu youth derive from the Mission schools are lasting and inestimable in their nature. From a judicious study of Geography, they learn to disbelieve the statements of the Hindu Shastras. From History they learn by example the corruption of human nature, the plan of Providence in the direction of events, the common failure of virtue, and the frequent success of vice. It certainly leads to self-improvement and self-knowledge. It is not our privilege to mention any conversions from among our school boys,

[3] Those who were most prominent as founders and managers of the school were Rev. David Herron and Mrs. Herron, Dr. John S. Woodside and Miss J. Woodside, Miss C. L. Beatty, Miss Mary Pratt, Miss Craig, Miss L. M. Pendleton, Miss S. M. Wherry, Miss E. Donaldson and Miss E. Sleeth.

but it is something to give the Hindu boys a sound knowledge of Christianity. It is something to destroy their prejudice in favor of idolatry and caste. It is something to give them a prepossession in favor of Christ and His religion, before they go out into the world, to exert an influence over the people with whom they are to live."[3]

The Mission schools were not all without definite results in the way of conversions. The reasons why confessions were few may be inferred from the following narrative.

In the Lodiana school there were two young men, who after long trial and waiting decided to be baptized. The trial of their faith was very severe. They loved their parents, and yet felt obliged by their allegiance to God to confess Christ openly as their saviour. The experience of one of them is thus described:

"The poor father then sat down by his son on the edge of the veranda, and by turns used threats and persuasions. 'Come with me to your house, and I will give you sweet-meats to eat and milk to drink.' A wife, young and beautiful, too, he promises, 'and houses and lands.' Then he embraced him with the utmost show of affection, and laid his turban at his son's feet, to show his willingness to be anything, or to do anything for him. But finding him unwilling to yield, he assumed a peremptory tone, saying, 'I am the author of your existence. I am your god. These people have bewitched you; why should you stay with them?' And then he struck his own body with all his might, saying, 'I will kill myself for your sake!' Again 'O! that I had a knife, that in a moment I might put an end to myself. Then you can burn my body and after that, do as you choose.' After succeeding in dragging him a short distance and seating himself by his side, in a despairing tone he made known his intention of remaining until he dies, saying: 'You may kill me or I will kill you.'

"Poor Udhu! His lips are quivering, and his face showing that his heart is rent with anguish, but he wavers not, for he is upheld by Divine power. The miserable father, now becomes fairly crazed from excitement, beats his own head with such violence against the wall, that he seems to become stunned, and

[3] *Lodiana Mission Report*, 1863, pp. 26-27.

presently a native Christian succeeds in leading him quietly away."[4]

A few days later the two young men appeared before the Church congregation to receive baptism. Udhu's father was present and by his violence prevented his son being baptized along with his friends, but a week later, having secured the decision of the magistrate that he was of age and could do as he pleased, he too was baptized.

"The Kingdom of Heaven suffereth violence and the violent take it by force."

[4] Letter "M. R. J." in *Foreign Missionary*, 1858, pp. 174, 205.

CHAPTER XIII.

Unforeseen Losses: New Recruits

THE tragic events in North India had resulted in a depletion of the missionary staff by about one-half. The Punjab Mission was too weakly manned to be able to render any important aid, even of a temporary character. At Fattehgarh, the entire station had been wiped out. Mainpuri was in ruins, and the missionary away on special duty in London. Allahabad had lost two out of three missionaries, not to mention the withdrawal of Messrs. Wray and Hodge. Messrs. Walsh of Mainpuri and Hay of Allahabad, were absent on furlough in America, and Mr. Hay had since withdrawn from the service. Agra had suffered, but not unto death.

At a meeting of a few survivors, it was agreed to send Mr. Williams to Allahabad to take charge of the school work there. Messrs. Fullerton and Scott had been sent from Agra to re-establish Fattehgarh. Earnest representation had been made to the Board in New York, and in answer to the call many volunteers were found ready to fill up the broken ranks.

On the 18th of July, 1859, Rev. J. J. Walsh and Mrs. Walsh reached Allahabad, where they were now stationed. The Rev. Augustus Brodhead and Mrs. Brodhead arrived at the same time and were stationed in Mainpuri. A year later the Rev. B. D. Wyckoff and Mrs. Wyckoff and the Rev. W. F. Johnson and Mrs. Johnson arrived in Allahabad. Mr. Johnson was a younger brother of the martyred missionary, Rev. A. O. Johnson. These recruits were assigned to Allahabad temporarily for language study.

During this year Mr. Brodhead rebuilt the mission house and chapel at Mainpuri. The schoolhouse had remained intact, as has already been explained. The school, which was broken up during the mutiny, had been re-opened by Mr. Fullerton and placed under the supervision of Babu Hulás Roy, its former headmaster. When Mr. Brodhead arrived, there were seventy pupils in attendance. Thus Mainpuri was completely rehabilitated.

Fattehgarh too, as we have already seen, was being rapidly restored, the buildings being rebuilt and the schools reassembled. The Farrukhabad high school rapidly became more prosperous than ever before, having nearly five hundred names on the roll. The members of the church which had been scattered far and wide had returned and at a communion service held on September 17, 1858, sixty-five members were present. The services were held in the school building. A Sunday school was begun. Large congregations, including some eighteen or twenty inquirers, were reported. Scarcely a day passed that some one did not put in an appearance, who had not been heard from before. Among these was a Muhammadan from the city. A man and his wife and three children were baptized by Mr. Scott. These were some of the fruits of the labors of the late brethren, who had been cut off by the mutineers. Thus reinforcements were being raised up within the church itself. By the transfer of three missionaries to Allahabad and the return of Mr. and Mrs. Owen and Mr. Munnis, that station was now strongly manned.

At the annual meeting, the Mission endeavored to so redistribute its forces as to provide for Agra and a new station at Etawah. Accordingly Mr. Owen was transferred to Agra, to take charge of the church there and to pursue his literary work. His books in manuscript having been burned at Allahabad, he was now rewriting his commentaries on the Psalms and Isaiah. Mr. Brodhead was transferred from Mainpuri to Farrukhabad and Mr. Wyckoff was sent to Mainpuri. The missionary to Fattehpur, Rev. Gopinath Nandi, having been ill for a long time, underwent a serious operation as affording the only hope of recovery. The operation proved fatal. This faithful witness before his persecutors during the mutiny met his last enemy in the same spirit of devotion. In his last hour he said: "I am not afraid to die; I can trust that Jesus, whom I have so often preached to others."[1] The Rev. W. F. Johnson was sent to occupy the vacant place at Fattehpur, and became pastor of the church there. On Mr. Ullmann's return from England, he was sent to occupy the new station at Etawah.

Four years after the mutiny, the missionaries were able to make the encouraging statement that the number of Christians in the Northwest Provinces and Oudh had more than doubled.

Owing to ill health, the Rev. Mr. Munnis and his wife and family were transferred from the North India to the Lodiana Mission. Mr. Walsh was obliged to go to America on short furlough, leaving Mrs. Walsh in Allahabad. Mr. Williams, having been obliged to retire from the field, Mr. Owen was recalled from Agra to Allahabad. Thus for awhile, Allahabad, which only recently sèemed so strongly manned, was left without any missionary excepting Mr. Owen. Fortunately there were a number of well qualified Indian assistants; Messrs. John Hari, Yunas Singh, J. J. Caleb and Paul Qaim Khan. The first two of these being licentiates, conducted the church services, while the last two took charge of the midweek prayer-meeting.

In the year 1861, the Rev. Edward Sayre and wife arrived from America and were temporarily located at Fattehgarh. Two years later he was placed in charge of Fattehpur, to take the place of Rev. W. F. Johnson transferred to Allahabad. Mr. Walsh returned to Allahabad, bringing with him his eldest daughter, Miss Marion Walsh.

With the large reinforcements and varied changes above mentioned, including the increase in the number of qualified Indian assistants, the mission had more than recovered the losses caused by the Sepoy rebellion. The schools, orphanages and asylums for the poor and the lepers had all increased in efficiency. The mission press at Allahabad was doing excellent

[1] *History of A. P. Mission*, p. 130.

work in the hands of the Indian proprietors. The work for women had everywhere increased.

At Mainpuri, Mrs. Wyckoff had established ten schools for non-Christian girls, of which a detailed statement will be given later.

At Allahabad, Miss Marion Walsh took charge of the Christian girls' school and carried it on with great zeal and marked success.

The financial stress in America at this time, owing to the Civil War, made it necessary to retrench in some of the mission fields. In consequence, the hope of keeping the Agra station had to be abandoned. The Lodiana Mission fared better by reason of the generous liberality of English friends.

The reinforcements just mentioned were most welcome, but they barely provided for the vacancies made by ill health and the necessary furloughs in the interest of health and the care of children too old to be kept longer in India.

The Rev. Mr. Fullerton had never fully recovered from the suffering and exposure endured during the Sepoy rebellion. It became necessary for him to seek rest and recuperation at Landour in the Himalaya mountains during the hot season. Mr. Scott, with his family, also went to this mountain resort. About this time the Rev. David Herron was bereft of his wife, which obliged him to return to America with his motherless children. By arrangement between the Missions, Mr. Fullerton was placed in charge of the Dehra station. Here he labored with his usual devotion, but failing health obliged him to prepare to return to America.

That journey to the homeland was never made. Mr. Fullerton died at Landour on the 4th of October, 1865. It had been his desire to revisit his native land, and to see his family settled there, but when he felt that the Lord had ordered otherwise, he cheerfully acquiesced. He suffered much during his illness, but no word of complaint or murmuring ever escaped his lips.

Mr. Fullerton was mourned not only by his family and his

brethren of the Mission, but he was also sincerely mourned by the people for whose welfare he had so earnestly labored. Mrs. Fullerton and her children left India for America on the 19th November, 1866.

The depletion of the Lodiana Mission force in 1864 was greater and more tragic than anything that had occurred since the Sepoy mutiny. Mention has already been made of the murder of Rev. Isidor Loewenthal (Chapter XVI). Now another tragedy must be described.

The death of the Rev. Levi Janvier on the 24th of March, 1864, was most unexpected. He had gone from his home in Subathu, in company with his wife and Mr. and Mrs. Carleton of Ambala, to attend the mela at Anandpur, one of the sacred places, especially revered by the Sikhs. As was his custom, he had pitched his tent in a convenient place somewhat away from the great throng of the people attending the mela. During the day he, with Mr. Carleton, had been busy preaching to the crowds, and distributing Christian scriptures and tracts. The ladies too were busy talking to the Indian women. It happened that a Sikh faqir, one of the numerous "holy men" attending such melas, being under the influence of an intoxicant (Indian hemp) became boisterous in his behavior and in consequence was arrested by the European Superintendent of Police, and confined during the day. He was of course furiously enraged and seems to have vowed vengeance against the officer. That evening the superintendent of police, above mentioned, called upon the missionaries at their tent. It was the last day of the mela, and the faqir had been allowed his freedom, and no doubt followed the police superintendent to the tent.

Mr. Janvier proposed that they should celebrate the Lord's supper. Some of the Indian Christians expressed surprise, because it was not Sunday, but he told them it would be appropriate as they were all about to separate on the following morning and go in different directions to their own homes. Accordingly at seven o'clock in the evening they surrounded the communion table in the tent. Mr. Janvier conducted the service and sang the hymn beginning, "Arasta ho, Aimeri jan!" (Be ready, O my soul), a Hindustani hymn usually sung just before a communion service. The service was one of great solemnity, preceded by an address upon the coming of the Lord.

After the service, Mr. Janvier went out of the tent to give some last directions concerning the arrangements for the journey next morning. As he stepped towards a cart to give the order, the fanatic suddenly struck him down with two blows of a club on the head, one of which broke his skull just over the right eye. The fanatic attempted to run away, but was pursued and seized by the servants and native Christians. Mr. Carleton carried his bleeding brother into the tent, where he lay groaning, but quite unconscious, during the whole night. He expired early in the morning. His remains were taken to Hoshyarpur, for a post mortem examination, and then sent on to Lodiana, where arrangements had been made for his burial in the Mission cemetery. A large assembly of missionaries and Indian Christians were ready for the interment, which in that season of the year must be made without delay. There stood men and women with tear-stained faces as they realized they would look upon that face no more which had so often smiled upon them. The pastor was gone whom they always called Padri Sahib (Father). He had baptized many of them, had comforted them in their sorrow, had taught them and their children and had often sympathized with them as he stood beside them at the burial of their loved ones. Old Hindu and Muslim servants and neighbors with grave sad countenance expressed their grief for a sincere friend so suddenly stricken down. The minister with trembling voice recited the sad words "Dust to dust, ashes to ashes" only relieved by the triumphant hope and assurance of the Christian whose Lord and Saviour said, "I am the resurrection and the life; he that believeth in me, though he were dead, yet shall he live."

Mr. Janvier was a man of eminent qualifications for the missionary work. He was distinguished for his great gentleness of spirit. For a generation later, those who had known him, would describe the man of a gentle and forgiving spirit by saying, "Just like Janvier Sahib."[2]

As a scholar, he had a mastery of the Urdu, Hindi and the Punjabi languages. In collaboration with the Rev. John Newton, he compiled the Punjabi-English lexicon and aided in the translation and publication of the Punjabi New Testament and other publications in that language.

Late in this same year another great loss befell the small band of mutiny veterans in the North India Mission. Twenty-four years had elapsed since the Rev. Joseph Owen had arrived in Allahabad. During all these years he had never visited his native land. When his children became too old to permit their remaining in India, his devoted wife undertook the long journey, and placed them among her husband's relatives in America, returning to him again during the course of the terrible struggle of 1857. She had continued to perform the duties of a devoted wife and co-worker in the Mission stations of Allahabad and Agra. "She was a woman of excellent judgment in practical matters, quiet and cheerful in manner, of eminent piety, deeply interested in her husband's work, an ornament to his household, and a stay and support to her husband to the last moment of her life." She died on the 14th of December, 1864. Her social qualities had endeared her to the better class of European residents; and her unostentatious and ever-active efforts to do good among them and to the poor Christian natives. A great assemblage of both classes attended her remains to their last resting place. Although ever happy, death in Christ removed from her friends the bitterness of sorrow, many lamented it as a personal bereavement.

These sore losses by disease and death in no way discouraged the faithful men and women still remaining. By prayer and faith they sought the strength which God alone can give

[2] See Appendix IV.

at such a time. The routine work of the schools, the Mission presses and the Evangelistic preaching went on in city and village with ever increasing vigor and success.

The Indian churches were somewhat depleted by epidemics of malarial fever and smallpox, but continual accretions restored the losses and slowly increased the number of professing Christians.

The increased missionary interest in the Churches in America, led many young men and women to consecrate their lives to the missionary work in foreign fields. The Civil War in America had now practically come to a close and many who had volunteered to serve in the armies of their country, now offered themselves to serve under the banner of Christ in foreign lands. A number of young men in India, who had been serving as teachers, now became preachers of the gospel to their countrymen.

CHAPTER XIV.

The Kapurthala Mission

AMONG the independent native States, west of the Sutlej river, one of the most important is that of Kapurthala. The capital of the same name is situated some twelve miles west of Jalandhar City. The population is predominantly Hindu —including the Sikhs.—It had supplied a considerable strength to the Khalsa reign of Maharajah Runjeet Singh. Dr. John C. Lowrie, in his journal describes a visit which he made to Rajah Fateh Singh of Kapurthala in January, 1835. He said:

"Rajah Fateh Singh is one of the most powerful of the Sikh Chiefs, having a revenue of about seven lac (700,000 rupees). The population of the town of Kapurthala is about ten thousand, chiefly Hindus with some Sikhs. It is a new town, and is apparently increasing with much rapidity. Some of the public buildings are large and not deficient in Hindu taste. The most singular is a temple to Siva, erected for the Hindus by the Chief himself, a Sikh.

"Yesterday, I went to see the Chief, and had much conversation with him and his attendants. . . . I should think it very probable that in a few years a branch of our Mission might be established here under promising prospects. Even now I think the Sirdar could be persuaded to grant his protection, if not his influence in its favor and especially if an English school were undertaken."[1]

In the year 1859, the President of the Lodiana Mission, reported that

"a formal application had been received (June 15)" from Rajah Rundeer Singh of Kapurthala, for a missionary to be stationed at his Capital, with an intimation that all the expenses of the station would be defrayed by him; and with a request that if possible the person appointed might be Mr. Woodside."[2]

---

[1] *Two Years in Upper India*, pp. 153, 154.
[2] *Minutes of the Lodiana Mission*, Prefix, p. 5 (1859).

The Mission carefully considered this request, and being satisfied as to the sincerity of the Rajah's interest in the work of the Mission, consented to the arrangement and permitted Rev. John S. Woodside to undertake the work.

From a letter written to the Board in New York and mentioned in an editorial article in *The Foreign Missionary,* December, 1859, it appears that Mr. Woodside had some time previously been called to Kapurthala to perform the marriage ceremony between the Rajah and a Christian lady, one of the members of the Church, presumably at Dehra, where Mr. Woodside was then stationed. This lady was the daughter of Mr. R. Hodges, and had been educated at Mrs. Fullerton's school in Agra. She was, of course, unwilling to marry even a prince, unless assured that he would be a Christian and that their marriage would be by Christian rites. Mr. Woodside wrote of the Rajah,

> "as having publicly thrown off the distinctive restrictions of caste, and as being looked upon by all his own people as a Christian. His mind is turned to the consideration of Christian truth; and if he may be savingly taught by the Holy Spirit, his example and influence will be of great importance in the extension of the Gospel."[8]

Mr. Woodside added the following words, not altogether encouraging, but expressive of the hope that something substantial would grow out of this new departure:

> "As it is, no such opening for the Gospel has ever before been presented. I look forward with no little anxiety to the future; but I believe God will bring good out of all this, and therefore I am not discouraged."

The Rev. J. S. Woodside and Mrs. Woodside arrived in Kapurthala early in 1860. The Rajah had already begun to support schools in his state. He built a comfortable house for the missionary, and later on provided a schoolhouse and a

[8] *Foreign Missionary,* December, 1859.

beautiful church building with steeple and bell. Later on a medical missionary was added to the mission force. Mr. John Newton, Jr., M. D. was transferred from Lahore and entered upon his work as Medical Missionary at Kapurthala. In the meanwhile, Mr. Woodside busied himself in improving the roadways and in making other public improvements. Regular religious services were held, at which the Rajah and his Christian Rani were devout attendants, the Rajah kneeling with Christians during prayer.

In the second annual report of the missionary at this station, for the year 1861, mention is made of the educational work conducted in three departments: English, Persian Urdu and Punjabi. The attendance in the English classes was 45, in the Urdu classes 120, and in the Punjabi 16, making a total of 181 on the rolls. The study of the Bible was a part of the regular curriculum, portions being committed to memory.

A dispensary and poor house were erected and a fund raised to erect a hospital. The number of patients was about 2,000, while 40 people were receiving aid in the poor house. The work was growing materially, but spiritual results were as yet meager. Two infants were baptized, one of whom was the daughter of the Rajah.

The report of the mission for 1862, written by Dr. John Newton, speaks encouragingly of the spirit of tolerance throughout the State, the prosperity of the school and the medical work and the faithful preaching of the gospel in city and village. The church building was being built under the superintendence of G. R. Dallimore, Esq., architect in the Rajah's employ. The Rajah's two sons, Prince Kharak Singh, the heir-apparent, aged fourteen, and his brother Kanwar Harnam Singh aged eleven, are spoken of as "boys of singular intelligence and promise." These two boys, with their cousin Sirdar Bhagat Singh, a young man of nineteen, formed a class, which was taught for two hours every day by Mr. Woodside at his own house. Of these the report says,—"Few lads, of any rank or any country, could display greater quickness of apprehension or greater love for knowledge for its own sake."

The following year, mention is made of the baptism of a Muhammadan, who had been an inquirer for twelve years. The Rajah had not made confession of his faith by baptism. That he was at heart a Christian seems certain. His open recognition of Christian worship, added to his native support of the missionary work, testifies to his sincerity. In the closing days of December, 1862, a general conference of all Protestant Missions was held in Lahore, covering a period of eight days and closing January 2nd, 1863. The Rajah of Kapurthala was a lay member of that conference. At the opening of the third session the chairman, D. F. McLeod, Esq., C. B. (afterwards Lieutenant-Governor, Punjab) introduced him to the members of Conference, saying that, "He felt sure that the members of the Conference would rejoice with himself, in seeing amongst them the Rajah of Kapurthala."

During the fourth session of Conference, the Rajah having been asked to express his views on the question of Female Education, said:

"He was anxious to see something done in this matter, for there was no doubt, that it was a thing of very great importance to India. The education of females was not forbidden by the religion of the people; but it was disrelished by the *men.* In many high families, especially in the Punjab, women *do* read—chiefly religious books. They are forbidden to learn to *write,*—particularly among the Rajputs; because the jealousy of their husbands makes them afraid of the power this would give them to correspond with others.

"The great difficulty was to know how to get at the females of the country. They were shut up so closely, that it was almost impossible to have access to them. This must be done through the men. He would advise that efforts be made to enlighten the men, as to the advantages to be derived by their wives from education. Christian gentlemen should associate more intimately with natives of the country; and their wives would then have access to the Zenanas.[4] Education must be done in the Zenana. He was certain it would soon be found that the women would become fond of learning. The education given should not be confined solely to reading and writing; but other useful arts should also be taught—such as needlework, knitting, &c, &c. Instances had occurred in the history of India, of ladies of rank having attained much literary distinction. Zeb-un-Nisa Begum, daughter of the Emperor Auranzeb, wrote a poetical work, entitled 'Dewan Makhfi,' which holds the very first rank in Persian poetry. Many other noble ladies had attained a great proficiency in learning. He hoped to see this desire for knowledge increase among his countrymen and countrywomen; and he would do all in his power to encourage this work among his friends and countrymen."[5]

A resolution proposed by T. D. Forsyth, Esq., was unanimously adopted

"expressing their hearty sympathy with His Highness, the Rajah of Kapurthala, in his desire to impart the saving truths of the Gospel to his subjects. They believe that, in doing so, he is disinterestedly seeking the highest welfare of the people God has committed to his charge. They thankfully acknowledge the power and grace of Almighty God, which has enabled him to manifest so much liberality and zeal in the cause of missions, thus setting an example to others, having the authority and influence, worthy of all imitation. The Conference earnestly prays, that his own soul may be sanctified wholly, by the same truths; and, that, with many of his grateful subjects, he may wear an everlasting crown of glory, with our Saviour Jesus in the Kingdom of our common God and Father."

This resolution was seconded by D. F. McLeod, Esq., C. B., in the course of which he testified to the Rajah's Christian conduct, in refusing to make offerings to Hindi shrines at Dharmsala, and his refusing to march on Sunday, and that he had "set up an altar of family devotion, in his own household, at which

[4] Zenanas or women's apartments.
[5] *Report of the Punjab Mission Conference*, 1862-1863, pp. 84, 118.

I and others here present have been privileged to kneel with him."[6]

In December, 1864, the Rev. James H. Orbison, in a letter addressed to the Board in New York, makes mention of his visit to Kapurthala, as follows:

"The large and beautiful church, with lofty spire erected at the Rajah's expense, is nearly finished. It is quite 'a beauty and a joy forever.' I trust, it stands a monument and a preacher of Christianity. It is just opposite the Rajah's new residence, with a broad road running from one to the other. The solemn peals of its great bell, a present from America, are heart stirring. During the time of our visit, the corner stone of an immense building, intended for a Hall of Justice, and other public offices, was laid by the Rajah in the presence of his army and subjects, with reading of the Bible and prayer, and an address by Mr. Morrison, at the request of Mr. Woodside. The Rajah also made an excellent speech on the occasion."[7]

The annual report for the year 1864, confirms the statement of Mr. Orbison concerning the Church building. The missionaries expected only a plain edifice suitable to the needs of a small congregation, but in the hands of an architect it became a very handsome building;

"and will in future years be a source of much comfort to our congregation. We owe our warmest thanks to the Rajah for his enlightened liberality in enabling us to rear this edifice to the glory of the one living and true God. It is due to the Rajah here to state that he has contributed of his substance for the purpose with a willingness, that might well be emulated by professing Christians in works of this kind. We ask the prayers of all our friends throughout the Christian world on behalf of this man. He has lately received one of the highest honors the Crown of England could confer upon him. The Star of India now decorates his breast, teaching by its beautiful motto, that the Light of Heaven—the word of God—is the best guide to man in all the relations of life; but we long to see his

[6] *Idem.*, pp. 125, 126.

[7] *The Foreign Missionary*, April, 1865, p. 267.

inward heart illuminated by the Sun of Righteousness, till not a doubt, nor fear of any kind remains."

During that year the little church at Kapurthala had lost two other friends by death. One was the Rajah's Commander of Artillery Colonel Nabi Bakhsh, a man of really excellent character, honest, and upright in his life. For some years he had been a sincere inquirer concerning the claims of Christ of whom he spoke with great reverence.

One more personage, who had endeared herself to the Mission circle was removed by death. This was the mother of Rajah Rundeer Singh. She had been a great sufferer in her late husband's lifetime. She had been denied her conjugal rights and driven to seek consolation in the only religion she knew. She consequently became very much attached to the religion of the Sikhs, and more than ordinarily zealous for the promotion of the doctrines it inculcated. When Rajah Rundeer Singh ascended the throne, her position was made much better. The Rajah had endeavored to make up to her for the wrongs she formerly suffered, and her attachment to him was proportionately strong.

When the Mission was first commenced at Kapurthala, she was, not unnaturally, alarmed lest those she loved should become converts to the Christian religion. But as she became better acquainted with the missionaries and their wives, these feelings gave way to those of warm friendship and regard. They were thus enabled to hold conversations with her on the subject of religion, and at her own request they had, on more than one occasion, prayed by her sick bed. A few days before her death, she asked one of the missionaries to pray with her as she had formerly done, and during the prayer, she joined most devoutly in the exercise, having her hands folded over her breast and repeating, word for word, after him. On this occasion and subsequently, she listened attentively to the message of salvation which was earnestly pressed home on her. She had several times asked for Christian books; and in other ways had shown an awakening interest in the truth. Her decease was to all the members of the Mission a source of much sorrow.

It was natural that the hearts of the missionaries were filled with hope and a joyous anticipation of a rapid extension of the kingdom of God in this principality. The gospel had been preached faithfully. A great many books were scattered in the villages.

The school at Kapurthala numbered 230 pupils. Even the dismissal of the head Persian teacher, owing to improper conduct, did not make any serious difference in the attendance. Two boys were ready to go up for the entrance examination for the Calcutta University. These splendid results were due to the faithful and efficient work of the Head Master, Babu Nobin Chandra Ghose, and his assistant Babu Shama Charan Ghose, who had been brought from the Duff college, Calcutta.

The Rajah also organized a system of vernacular schools in the larger villages in his state and placed them under the supervision of the missionaries. These village schools were taught by non-Christian teachers. Of course little or no positive Christian influence could be exerted by such schools, but their existence promised something for the literacy of the people.

The Mission opened a school at Phagwara, a town almost as large as Kapurthala, and placed it in charge of a Christian Master, Mr. Joseph R. Kerr, under whose zealous efforts, it made rapid progress. The pupils numbered 90, of whom 30 were studying English. The building for this school was generously given by the Rajah for the use of the school. Mr. Kerr and his family were highly respected both by the Rajah and the people.

Such was the condition of the Mission in the Kapurthala State at the close of the year 1864. From the secular and material standpoint, everything seemed to point to a speedy establishment of the Christian religion as the faith of Kapurthala.

One thing was lacking. There was little evidence of any deep spiritual influence at the bottom of it. The missionaries realized this defect in the work. Their report closes with the following paragraph:

"Pray for the Rajah, pray for his wife, his sons, his daughters, his brothers and his people. Brethren in Christ, pray for us all. We need your prayers at the present time in an especial manner. We feel assured we shall have them, and with them in due time a blessing."

* * * * * * *

One year later the Lodiana Mission reported the practical dissolution of the Kapurthala Mission. The dispensary was made over to the care of the Rajah's principal Hakim (Doctor). The Mission doctor was transferred to Lahore. The apothecary was permitted to leave the service of the Mission and to enter that of the Rajah. Soon after "owing to a series of events, which need not be mentioned" a breach occurred between the Rajah and the missionary in charge, and "as there appeared no likelihood of the removal of the chief cause of the rupture, and as the missionary's position became every day more and more uncomfortable, and his prospects of usefulness more and more restricted, it was resolved that he should for a time withdraw from the station, leaving some of the native assistants to carry on the work, until the Mission should decide as to future arrangements."[8]

This decision led to the Rajah's withdrawal from the work, resulting in his final closing of the schools in the state as Mission schools. A single Christian worker, Mr. George H. Stuart, a Scripture Reader, remained. The Report sadly closes with these words:

---

[8] *Lodiana Mission Report*, 1865.

"It is sad to be obliged to record this unexpected interruption of missionary work at a station once so promising. But it is hoped that the Mission will soon find the way open to resume labours there, and be able to prosecute them without further hindrance. The Lodiana Mission feels a deep interest in the Rajah and his people, and its members will not cease to pray that God, in his mercy, will so overrule these untoward events, that His glory and the good of all concerned may be promoted."[9]

The Rajah closed the church which remained intact during his life and that of his son, who reigned after him. The tall spire, pointing to Heaven, was a silent witness to the Christian faith. The Rajah continued to profess an interest in the Christian religion, but had become helpless to make any outward confession of it.[10]

The long continued and earnest efforts of the missionaries at Kapurthala seemed to have been almost in vain. They consoled themselves with the promises of God to his faithful servants "My word shall not return unto me void."

A few years later, the seed sown brought forth fruit. The heir apparent, Prince Harnam Singh, brother of Rajah Kharak Singh, eldest son of Rajah Rundeer Singh, confessed his faith in the Lord Jesus Christ. At his baptism, the missionary, the late C. W. Forman, D. D. asked him if he realized that by his baptism he was likely to lose his claim to the throne of Kapurthala. Without hesitation he said that he did, and that if such sacrifice were necessary, he was ready to make it.

He lost the earthly crown but he gained a crown of righteousness. His Christian character has been such as to commend him for office in both church and state. He has been a leader among the noblemen of his country, a member of Provincial and National councils, a benefactor to indigent Christian young men seeking a college education, President of the National Christian Association and a Moderator of the General Assembly

[9] *Idem.*

[10] The Rev. J. H. Orbison, accompanied by the author, called upon the Rajah in 1868. He was friendly and expressed his interest in the work of the Mission.

of the Presbyterian Church in India. His family is an honor to him, all of his sons holding important offices in the civil and military service; one lies among the dead on the battlefield in France.

Other children of the State of Kapurthala are honorable members of the church.

After many years, the Mission was permitted by the present enlightened ruler of Kapurthala to resume its work in the capital.

CHAPTER XV.

Medical Missionary Work

IN the original organization of the Mission at Lodiana, medical work had no place as an evangelistic agency. The need of a physician among the members of the Mission staff was felt, notwithstanding the fact that medical men were to be found among the English army surgeons, who were willing to render any aid possible, and that without expense to the Mission. Some of these men were earnest Christians, ready to show their sympathy in a very practical way.

Mention has been made of several men in civil and military service, who had aided the missionaries in the opening up of their work at several stations. The fact that medical aid was practical in India seemed to meet the need of missionaries and their families and so medical missionaries were not yet regarded as necessary to complete the evangelistic forces in India. However, the founders of the Lodiana Mission early realized the need of medicine to relieve the awful suffering among the people. The Rev. John Newton wrote of his early attempt to use medicine as a missionary auxiliary.[1]

"It was my wish after finishing my theological course, to study medicine, and thus become doubly qualified for missionary service, but as the committee wished me to proceed to India with Mr. Wilson as soon as possible after my ordination, the idea of combining the practice of medicine with preaching had to be abandoned. Not knowing, however, how I should be situated with respect to medical advice, I procured a number of medical and surgical books, and a small number of surgical and dental instruments, with a view to any emergency that might arise: and during the voyage out, round the Cape, I endeavoured to obtain from these books as much knowledge, especially of medicine as was practicable. On reaching Calcutta, I obtained a good

[1] *History of the A. P. Mission*, pp. 37, 38.

supply of medicines also. I was able, consequently, in the course of our journey up country, to treat a few sick natives with success, and so also a few mission employees soon after we reached Lodiana. It then happened that a Press Munshi became very ill, and after being treated by the native doctors, with no hope of recovery, he asked me to do something for him. As the case seemed otherwise hopeless, I thought it my duty to do what I could. By the good providence of God, my treatment was successful. The news of this soon spread abroad over the city, and the sick began to flock to my house—so that I soon found myself in the midst of a regular practice of medicine. Difficult cases, of course, I could not undertake; yet it was hard to persuade the natives that if I could cure some diseases, I could not cure all.

"From an English surgeon at Lodiana, I did indeed get some instruction, but not enough to enable me to bear the responsibility which was gathering upon me.

"There was hope of relief, however: for in the year 1842 the Board sent out a regular physician, Dr. Willis Green, to take up the work. But unfortunately, after being at Lodiana only a few months, he came to the conclusion that the climate of India did not suit him; and so he went back to his home in Kentucky. His abandonment of the work was no small disappointment to me."

Soon after this incident, Mr. Newton was sent to Subathu, and there he was able to give up the practice of medicine.

The Rev. Adolph Rudolph, a disciple of the great German evangelist, Father Gossner, who had been sent to India as a medical practitioner, now came to Lodiana. He had considerable experience, and went to work in a systematic way, building a small dispensary and employing a compounder to assist him.

Another missionary, Rev. J. R. Campbell, who had studied medicine for awhile before he came to India, practiced medicine more or less at Saharanpur as long as he lived.

The first regular physician connected with the Lodiana Mission, after Dr. Willis Green, was John Newton, Jr., M. D., a graduate of the medical college in the University of Pennsylvania. He came to India, independent of the Board, in 1858, and became a member of the Mission in 1860. Some account of his work as a medical missionary at Kapurthala has already been given. After leaving the Kapurthala Mission he took charge of the leper asylum at Subathu. He there made a special study of leprosy. He demonstrated the great value of medical work as an auxiliary to village evangelistic work.

The experience of the doctors, who were pioneers in the introduction of European medicines, into India, is graphically described by Dr. John Newton :—

"Within the dense ignorance of this people are imbedded the prejudices of three thousand years, whence it comes, that they look with distrust upon all medical science that is at variance with the precepts of *Bokrat* or *Jalinu.* A man may be unable to read or write, but none the less does he esteem himself competent to decide whether a disease is due to excssive heat, or to excessive cold,—and whether the remedy should, in consequence, be cooling or heating, and if the *Daktar Sahib* persists in prescribing for a fever a remedy, which, according to all the canons of Grecian or Arabian art, should be heating, the veriest boor can see that the Sahib knows nothing of his business! And yet it is patent to all, that the man, who, for weeks, had been shivering with an inveterate ague, suddenly recovered within a day or two after he began to take quinine at the hospital. Moreover, other patients, who had entered the building, had from time to time, gone forth to declare themselves quite cured. Such being the case, the intelligent populace have determined to secure such advantages as may be derived from *Farangi* (European) medicine, without yet running any unnecessary risks. Having exhausted all the resources of all the *hakims* (native doctors) in the town, and found them unavailing, they consent at length to try the Dispensary. By this time, if the patient be not, indeed, *'in articulo mortis,'* his disease, in the vast majority of cases, has at least become obstinately chronic. But having received the medicine, distributed at the Dispensary, he prudently reserves to himself the right to use them as he thinks best. Guided either by his own judgment, or by the advice of a trusted hakim, he either changes the quantity, or else makes such alterations in the time and manner of taking the dose, as Hypochrites himself might approve. Then, if unfortunately a cure does not promptly follow, the failure is published abroad to deter others, not from like manipulation of the doctor's directions, but from trusting themselves in any way to his treatment. Such are some of the causes, which tend to deprive the Dispensary of its legitimate share of influence for good, on the minds of the people."[2]

Dr. Newton began his work at Kapurthala in a dispensary, but at Subathu, where he spent his life, he undertook a large itinerant work among the villages in the hills, and in the plains, during the cold weather. He always carried with him medicine and a few surgical implements to meet minor cases. He was a pioneer in medical work in the villages. He was also a true evangelist, and ever used his medical skill as an auxiliary to his spiritual endeavour. He spent a great deal of time in seeking for a cure for leprosy and at one time thought he had succeeded. Further experience revealed the insufficiency of his remedies. They would alleviate, but did not cure.[3]

The conference of missionaries held in Lahore in 1862, to which reference was made in an earlier chapter, inaugurated a Medical Missionary Association, which has done much to further the work of evangelization through medical service. Indian men and women were now sent to the medical college established in Lahore and trained as assistants, compounders and dressers. The Mission dispensary, thus equipped, became not merely a benevolent institution, but a positive evangelistic agency. Competent catechists and bible women were in daily attendance at the dispensaries to converse with the people, who came for treatment or for medicine. Books and tracts and scripture portions were distributed in the languages read by the people. In this way many printed messages were carried into the villages of that particular district. The opportunity was also used to give valuable instruction in regard to diet and sanitation in the houses and villages.

The dispensaries and improvised wards, the forerunner of

---

[2] *The Foreign Missionary*, 1863, p. 314.

[3] He was experimenting with the now famous *chaulmugra oil*.

the Mission hospitals, obliged the employment of Indians who had little or no knowledge of the duties to be performed. This necessitated the giving of special lessons, so that every medical missionary had a private medical school. When later on medical schools and colleges were established, many of these helpers became students and received fuller training.

In a later chapter, we shall have occasion to chronicle the progress made in introducing the science of the West.

CHAPTER XVI.

Women's Work for Women

THE thought of a special sphere for women, in connection with the foreign missionary work of the Presbyterian Church, was expressed by the fact that almost all of the pioneer missionaries were accompanied by wives. Nor does it appear that these wives regarded themselves merely as companions of their husbands, who would care for them in their home life, but also, by their presence and advice and sympathy, would have a share in their work. We have seen, in the early chapters of this narrative, how many of them had assumed the responsibility of managing girls' schools and orphanages.

The first school for girls, as already noted, was begun by Mrs. James Wilson at Subathu, and carried on by Mrs. Jamieson. Similar schools were undertaken by wives of missionaries at Allahabad, Fattehgarh, Agra, Dehra, Saharanpur, Ambala, Jalandhur, Mainpuri and Kolhapur.

At first the most important schools for girls were the orphanages. Owing to the frequency of famines in various parts of North India, tens of thousands of boys and girls were left homeless orphans. In these orphanages, whether for boys or girls, the wives of the missionaries were the mothers to the homeless children, and they bore a very large part of the labor and responsibility in the conduct of such schools. Here were trained the young women, who became the wives of catechists and ordained ministers and masters in the higher schools established later on.

Facts like these must be remembered when we call the roll of the pioneer missionaries of our Presbyterian Church, or indeed the rolls of other churches, as well.

Another form of service rendered by women in the earlier

years of Missions in India, was the opening of schools for European and Eurasian girls. A considerable number of Europeans, besides the missionaries, had become stranded or domiciled in India. Many were in Government employ; others in business. All of them had families. The children of the well to do were sent home to England in early childhood to be cared for by relatives or to be placed in boarding schools. But the children of the poorer classes of Eurasians were dependent upon the Roman Catholic schools, which were often located in distant cities.

It was therefore evident to all Protestants and especially to Protestant missionaries that suitable schools should be established for their children. It was for reasons like these that a school for this class was begun at Agra by Mrs. Fullerton. That school was a blessing to many families; and, although it was suddenly brought to a close by the ruthless violence of the mutineers, it was in a real sense the pioneer of its sister school, Woodstock, established in 1854 at Mussoorie.

Many schools were also opened for non-Christian girls, and managed by Christian women, generally by the wives of the missionaries. One of the earliest schools for non-Christians was established at Subathu, and in the cantonment bazar. It was begun by Mrs. Jamieson. It held on its way right through the mutiny, notwithstanding numerous panics "caused by remarks made by ignorant and malignant persons." Mrs. Blewitt, a Christian lady, who was staying for some time at Subathu, very kindly assisted in this work.

At Saharanpur, Mrs. Calderwood was very successful in promoting female education. She had as many as fifteen schools, which were taught by Moslem and Hindu priests and pundits. They reported as many as 500 pupils on the rolls.

The schools opened for girls at Lodiana by the missionary wives were taught by Christian teachers, the wives of catechists and Christian workers, native Christian women following the example of the wives of missionaries. In 1866, this work was strengthened by the advent of Miss J. M. Jerrom, an English lady sent to India by the Society for the Promotion of Female Education in the East.

A new impulse had been given to the effort to reach women by the conference held in Lahore in 1862. Efforts were made to reach the wives and female relatives of the many students, or ex-students, of Mission schools. Zenana schools were begun in many places and thus a new era was begun in women's work for women. The initial efforts to educate non-Christian girls were everywhere beset by many difficulties. There was the prejudice born of the caste system. The very touch of a European or even Indian Christian was polluting. Then the suspicion, as to the motives of the missionaries, made the people unwilling to allow their girls to be taught by them. The same obstacles confronted the missionary ladies, who proposed to teach the women in their Zenanas. Still greater difficulties arose when it was proposed to teach the gospel stories. The jealousy of the Hindu and Muslim priests was at once aroused.

Some of the ladies succeeded in gathering together a few girls of the poorer and outcast people and by offering them a reward for attendance, a few pennies, or a piece of colored cloth, some were kept in school until they could at least read and possibly write. Many were taught to sew and to make lace or to embroider, as a part of their school work.

The strongest incentive to further female education was made by the education of the men; so that from about 1860, and onward, the work of educating girls and young women in the Punjab by means of separate schools, usually in the women's apartments, made a good deal of progress.

This subject was well discussed at the conference of 1862. The following items are of special interest:

The Rev. C. W. Forman, the great pioneer of education in the Punjab said:

"I think that those of us, who have the management of

schools, should attempt to reach the females through our pupils. I myself have urged upon my pupils the duty of teaching their wives and sisters; but my success has not been great. I know, however, that one of my pupils has taught his sister to read."

Mr. Forman suggested a conference of European and Indian gentlemen to discuss the question of female education. He further said:

"And why should not all the moral force of the English rulers be brought to bear on this subject? I know that education, begun in this way must of necessity be purely secular; but we would thus introduce the thin edge of the wedge, at least; and the way might be opened afterwards for giving religious instruction also."[1]

Rev. J. L. Hauser of the Methodist Mission, told of a boy in his school thirteen years of age, who was teaching his wife at night all that he had learned during the day.

Rev. Goloknath said:

"We find it exceedingly difficult to persuade the people to send their daughters to our schools. If we wish to educate the females of respectable families, we must carry the work at once into the Zenanas. The work, however, will be easier, when a large part of the male population of the country have received a good education; as this will create in them a desire to have educated wives. They will then endeavor to persuade their fathers to send their daughters to school. Let us try to create this desire in the hearts of our young men, and show the utility of having well-educated wives."

The Rev. Levi Janvier said:[2]

"It is proper to remark how vast the importance of this work of the communication of the Gospel to the women of India; and how great the calamity of their being inaccessible to the blessed message. It is not, merely, that this vast number of souls has as yet remained beyond the reach of the Gospel sound. This of itself were much. The Gospel is to be preached to every creature, and here in this great multitude that have not heard it, and

[1] *Report of the Punjab Mission Conference*, 1862, p. 119.
[2] *Report of the Punjab Mission Conference*, 1862, p. 55.

that, humanly speaking, cannot hear it. But it is much more than this. It is that the women of India have not heard what Jesus has done for them. It is the painful thought, that they have been going on in darkness, while it may be, that many of them, had they fully heard and understood the word, would have received it in the love of it; that while multitudes of men have heard the Gospel only to reject it, she, who was "last at the cross and first at the grave" would have recognized her risen Lord. Who knows? None can tell. But when we do know that nations which perished in sin, would have repented, had they enjoyed the privileges that Jerusalem despised and rejected, we do not risk much in making such a supposition. Certainly when we consider the comparative susceptibility and tenderness of the female mind, its strength of affection, and its quickness to act, when conviction has taken place, especially when we remember to how large an extent the sex, that was first in the transgression has been first also in acknowledging and repenting of it, and in bringing forth fruits meet for repentance, and how much this is the case now in the world, we may well feel pained at heart, to think that the women of India have not at least had an opportunity of hearing the Gospel message. Nor is this all. We have to take into view woman's influence in the family. Had the wives, the daughters, the sisters, of this non-Christian population been fully accessible to the voice of love and mercy, that sounds from calvary, who can tell what an influence they would have exerted on those around them."

This eloquent address of Rev. Levi Janvier, voiced the thought of all missionaries, men and women. Many devoted women, wives of the missionaries for the most part as yet, had accompanied their husbands in their tours among the villages and at the *melas,* used their opportunity to speak to the women who flocked around them, moved by curiosity to see the white women, to inspect their dresses and to hear them speaking their language. Much quiet work was done in this way. Prejudice was disarmed and the Christian faith was commended to the women. Among the lower classes, there was no barrier against their listening to men preaching, except the unwillingness of the priests and also of the men to permit women to be present in a promiscuous assembly. It was sometimes possible for the missionary to preach to crowds of women at the melas and in the courtyards of the low caste villages.

For the higher caste women, the best method of approach was to visit them in their homes. This method is specially practicable in the larger cities. Here Zenana schools were begun in which sewing and fancy embroidery work was taught along with the lesson. Each day some portion of scripture was read and a short prayer was offered. Later on, as we shall see, dispensaries and hospitals for women and children were opened, with lady doctors and nurses in charge.

CHAPTER XVII.

Progress of Education in North India

AS we have seen, the Northwest Provinces had suffered the greatest devastation during the Sepoy mutiny. As soon as the way was cleared and the forces of the Missions were restored, the work of reconstruction was begun. The importance of Christian institutions appeared greater than ever, by reason of their absence, and in reconstruction they were established upon stronger foundations than before.

The mutiny had done much to change the attitude of many Englishmen toward the missionary cause. The attempt to fix the blame of the uprising upon Christian Missions had signally failed. Many Christian men felt that the former attitude of the East India Company toward Mission work was wrong—some regarding the mutiny as a scourge upon their unchristian conduct. The late H. Carre Tucker, Governor-General's Agent and Commissioner of Benares, and afterwards Secretary of the Christian Vernacular Education Society for India, in a letter to the *London Times,* dated November 24th, 1858, wrote:

"Where Government officials most boldly avowed their Christianity, as in Peshawur, Lahore and Benares, there was the least apprehension.

"Mr. Thomason (formerly Lieut. Governor) went further than Lord Dalhousie (late Governor General) and actually abolished every Government school, which any Missionary Society was prepared to take up, making over the schoolhouses to the Missions. I heard him make an excellent speech at Allahabad, to the effect that Government had kept up there a school of about 150 boys at great expense, but that, by transferring it to the American missionaries, double that number of boys were then receiving a better and a Christian education, without any charge to Government. As under the orders from England, a Christian education could not be given in the Government schools, I think that the British public will allow that Mr. Thomason and Lord Dalhousie were right in making way for a more perfect education than they themselves were at liberty to give.

"An English education, no doubt, raises a native's theoretical standard of truth and honesty; but apart from Christian influences, it imparts no motive for acting up to that standard. On the contrary, by removing what little religious sanction previously existed, it cast young India loose at the mercy of every gust of temptation.

"As for the unmixed good of the traditionary policy, we need only turn to the mutiny as its great result.

"In conclusion, I will only add, that on my return to office in India, I shall, God helping me, continue to consider it my privilege, as a Christian man, as well as my bounden duty, to do all I can, in my private capacity to advance the spiritual as well as the intellectual and physical improvement of the natives. I deny the right of any Government to interfere with the judicious exercise of this liberty of private action, to do Christian things in a Christian way."

Encouraged by the sympathy and financial aid of European friends, the missionaries re-established the schools at all the stations, excepting Agra, which they had decided to abandon because of financial stress due to the Civil War in America.

In Farrukhabad, where the violence of the mutineers was greater than in almost any other city, the schools were reopened in 1858, and by June of 1859, they were reported to be more prosperous than ever before, some 500 pupils being under instruction. Similar testimony has been given to the popularity of the Mission schools elsewhere. Many instances of the loyalty of school boys are noted in the annals of the Missions at the time of the mutiny. They not infrequently brought food to the destitute Christian refugees, but also secured refuge for them, for weeks and even months. The following extract from the story of Hulas Roy, head master of the Mission school at Mainpuri, illustrates this.

"In the evening, I set off in the direction of the city, hoping to find some of our school boys, who, I knew, would help us. I had neither hat nor shoes, nor indeed any clothes, except a small piece of cloth about my loins. The villagers had stripped us of everything on the first day of our flight. I had not gone far when I met Cheda, one of our pupils, who gave me a cloth to throw over my shoulders. Another soon joined us, who took the shoes off his own feet and gave them to me; a third gave me a pair of drawers and a fourth, a coat. Cheda now told me that his father had an old house in the city, in which he could conceal us, and that he would see to it that we should want for nothing, if we would put ourselves under his care. We were only too glad to do so, and at night, Cheda conducted us to our place of concealment. It was a dismal old building, with dark damp cellars under it, which had not been occupied for many months, save by bats and spiders, but it was so much the better suited, on that account for our purpose; it was a building which few would think of entering. Here we experienced the greatest kindness from the school boys, for, while they carefully concealed our hiding place from their own parents, they did not hesitate to make it known to their classmates. Dummy Singh and Kurassain, former pupils of the school, but now holding lucrative offices under government, also visited us; and one of them gave us a bedstead and the other bedding. For two months these kind friends watched over us and provided for our wants, even though they knew they did it at the peril of their lives.

"Just after reaching the old house in the city, I asked one of the school boys to try to get me a bible. After searching among the ruins of the European houses, he found one, which was our constant companion during all our subsequent trials, and it was to us a never failing source of comfort.

"With the return of the English, our troubles were at an end."[1]

Mr. Fullerton also notes the fact that Muhinder Singh, who thus befriended Babu Hulas Roy and his family, received from the Government a village worth a thousand dollars a year, as a reward for his heroic conduct. Mr. Fullerton also noticed in his report how valuable this narrative is as showing the influence of Mission schools upon the pupils.

[1] Fullerton's Letter in the *Foreign Missionary*, 1859, pp. 179, 180.

"While other young men were swelling the ranks of the rebels, or joining bands of plunderers, who were swarming like the locusts of Egypt through all parts of the District, these pupils remained in their homes, and, when opportunity offered, imperilled their lives for the protection of their teachers and at no inconsiderable cost to themselves, ministered to the wants of himself and his family. Nor is this an isolated case; I have yet to hear of a pupil of one of our schools, or of any other Mission school, joining the rebels, or of his aiding them in any other way."

The popularity of the Missions among the people was attested in many ways. One was that, notwithstanding the fiery trial of the Christians, resulting in the death of many, the statistics for the decade showed that the number had been more than doubled. When Messrs. Scott and Fullerton were sent from Agra to rebuild the houses and to restore the church and the schools at Fattehgarh, they found nineteen adults there awaiting baptism, one of them a Brahmin.

From this time forth, the educational work of Missions in India, entered upon a new era. Schools for both boys and girls and women in their zenanas were opened in many places.

The report of the Farrukhabad Mission, for 1858-1859, makes mention of a Christian boys' school with 37 pupils; a Christian girls' school with 30 pupils; an English school in the cantonments with 20 pupils, and a village girls' school having an average attendance of 15; a cantonment Bazar school for boys, with 20 scholars and three village schools with 68 pupils.

At the Fattehgarh station (a part of the Farukhabad Mission) there was the high school, already mentioned, which had been conducted for twenty years, under the superintendence of Messrs. Scott, McAuley, Rankin, Irving, Seeley, Ullmann, Campbell and A. O. Johnson. In addition to these there were bazar schools for boys with 86 pupils and a bazar school for girls with 50 pupils.

This remarkable showing was due to the liberality of Maharajah Dulip Singh, the Sikh prince captured by the English during the last Sikh war. It was at Fattehgarh that he was baptized. When he became resident in Britain, he endowed some thirty schools in the Fattehgarh district. Ten of these schools are included in the above statement.

At Mainpuri, the boys' school, which was for a while discontinued, was re-established after the mutiny and placed under the care of Babu Hulas Roy. Here were 125 of his old pupils.

The question of the education of the women of the higher classes was beset by the same difficulties as those already noticed in connection with the opening of such schools in the Punjab. Schools for boys had been in operation in Mainpuri for more than twenty years. At this juncture, Mrs. Wyckoff and her husband, the Rev. B. D. Wyckoff, were transferred to Mainpuri from Allahabad. Mrs. Wyckoff undertook an educational work among the women. She has recorded her experiences in such a pleasing manner we shall present it in her own words:—

"A number of the high caste men of the city had been educated in the Mission School; and when they heard that a new *Padri Sahib* had arrived, they came to call upon him. When they were taking their leave, I thought it would be a good opportunity to put in a plea for the women of their household, and bravely asked if they would not allow them to be taught. I instinctively felt that my question was regarded as being in very bad form; but with a show of politeness they replied: 'It is not our custom, and besides you would find it easier to teach cattle, as our women have no minds, and therefore cannot learn.' I remarked that it is always safe to abandon bad customs for good ones, and that I was sure they would find that their women could learn, if they woud give them a chance.

"An old man of the Brahmin class had accompanied them and overheard the conversation. He lingered behind, and after the rest had gone, he came and asked me if I really wished to see some of the women of the city, and, if so, he thought he could persuade some of his friends to let me visit their families. I told him to see what he could do, and to let me know the result. In a few days, he returned with the good news, that a number of women of high caste were waiting to see me.

"After numerous windings through dirty narrow streets

filled with barking dogs and nude and noisy children we at last reached our destination. Passing through the entrance of a house, built in oriental style, we encountered cows and buffaloes, which, according to native custom, are usually found tethered in the front room of their dwellings. The next door opened into a courtyard. Here were about twenty women and children anxiously awaiting our arrival. Never having seen a white face before, they were thoroughly frightened. The women quickly drew their veils over their faces, and some of the poor things trembled like aspen leaves. I began talking to those near me about their children and they soon lost their timidity, and began drawing closer to me that they might the better examine my white skin, and strange clothing. They now began asking me questions about myself, whether I was married or not, how many children I had, why I did not wear jewelry, &c., &c. Many of the women were profusely decorated with gold and silver ornaments, and I afterwards learned that among the Hindus a husband's love for his wife is estimated by the amount of jewelry he gives her. After awhile, when their fear of me had entirely vanished, I asked them the cause of it. They replied that the men had told them that my only object in coming was to make Christians of them, and to take them to a foreign country. I explained to them the impossibility of my doing either and said that I hoped they would never be afraid of me again. Having been in India so short a time, I had not yet learned the rules of native etiquette, so I said, 'I must now go home' instead of saying 'If you will allow me, I will go.' They no doubt pitied me for my ignorance, but most kindly urged me to stay. Two of the women then went into a room, and brought out trays of nuts and raisins, and various kinds of sweets, which they said I was to take for my children; and then I was generously sprinkled with rose water and showered with rose leaves. Finally, after making me promise to come very soon again, they consented to let me go.

"As I went out I saw a young man of high caste standing near the door. I asked him if he had any work to do. 'No your honour,' he replied, 'I have none.' Then I said 'Come to my house tomorrow morning, and I will give you some slates and books, and we will have a school here for these women and girls; and for every five scholars you have, you will get one rupee a month (nearly fifty cents).

"He did as I said, and after two or three days I went over to see how the school was getting on. I found ten little girls present, but no women. When they heard that I had come, they came flocking in. After the usual salutations and inquiries in regard to health, I asked why none of them came to school, and explained to them the importance of learning to read. There were many excuses made and reasons given why they could not learn, but when I told the widows that they might in time become teachers if they would learn, they at once concluded to do so; as the prospect of being able to support themselves strongly appealed to them.

"The news that a school had been opened for women and girls rapidly spread over the city. The majority of the people laughed at the idea, while a few said it might be a good thing. Before long requests that similar schools might be opened in different parts of the city were brought to me. I replied that if, after investigation, the prospect for a school were favorable, I would open one. In the course of a few months there were six flourishing schools for women and girls in various parts of the city.

"It was not long before similar schools were in demand in neighboring villages. My hands were already pretty full, but the delegates for the villages were so earnest in their entreaties, that I concluded to at least visit them. These visits resulted in the opening of schools in four of the larger villages, within a radius of two to five miles from the Mission house, with an average of fifteen to twenty-five women and girls in each school.

"I now employed a native Christian woman to assist me in the work. This would have been impossible at first owing to the prejudice of the people against native Christians. This also made me hesitate at first, to introduce the bible into the schools, although I regularly taught the truths to the pupils. Pretty soon the teachers began asking for it. I gave them copies of the Gospels bound separately, and soon found, from the questions asked, that some of them were reading the Word with much interest.

"The schools were now in as good working order as one could expect, considering the kind of teachers I was obliged to employ. Every Saturday they came to me for instruction in the art of teaching, but I well knew that their hearts were not in their work, and that they did it merely for the little pay they got for it. I applied to the Government for a grant-in-aid for the schools, and also for a training school for teachers, which I was about to open.

"There were some bright women in the schools, who with special training might become good teachers, and they would not have the same prejudice against teaching their own sex as the present teachers had. I received the grant-in-aid from the Government, and opened the training school with about twelve scholars."

The reader of this interesting experience will understand that this remarkable success was only won by years of persistent effort, often incurring daily excursions into the city, or village, during the hottest season of the year. Her schools once numbered fifteen. They marked an era in the lives of the women in Mainpuri. Such too has been the experience of many other consecrated women, who have given their lives to the cause of the education of India's womanhood.

The progress of education in Mission schools in the North-west Provinces and the Punjab, for the decade 1851-1861, the period of the mutiny, was very remarkable. Notwithstanding the interruption of the work in many places, statistics show that whereas in 1851 there were 5,652 boy's in attendance at Mission schools, there were 10,940 in 1861. Again in 1851 there were only 417 girls in school, but at the end of the decade the number was 1508. The whole Indian Christian population for these two Provinces was 2,032 in 1851: ten years later the number was 5,801.[2]

[2] Dr. Mullins in *The Friend of India* for March, 1863. Statistical Tables of Missions in India, 1861.

CHAPTER XVIII.

Help in Time of Need

WHAT with the exigencies of Civil War in the United States of America, and the consequent depreciation of the paper currency, the burden of responsibility for the support of the Missions in India became very heavy. However, English friends in India came forward and volunteered generous contributions for the support of educational and charitable institutions. Subscription lists were circulated in all the principal stations, which resulted in gifts amounting to $32,245 in gold. This was exclusive of $13,315 contributed by the Rajah of Kapurthala and his brothers for the work at Kapurthala and Jalandhar city. Among the contributors were Sir John Lawrence, Sir Robert Montgomery, Sir Donald McLeod, Sir Herbert Edwards, K. C. B., Lady Edwards, General E. Lake, General McLagan, Colonel C. B. Taylor, Major Hutcheson, Baden-Powel, Esq., Major Anderson, E. L. Brandreth, Esq. and "A. C. S," a man who for nineteen years contributed fifty dollars monthly. The special objects towards which these gifts were contributed were the schools, famine relief, the asylums for the poor and the lepers, orphanages and the Lodiana Mission Press. The largest contributions were for "general purposes" of the Mission. All these contributions were made by friends in the Punjab alone. We have already told of the generous support given for the Mission work in the Northwest Provinces, but no record of these gifts is now extant. No doubt the special interest shown by English men and women in the Punjab was also manifested by English people in that field also.

It is a real pleasure to record the sympathy of Europeans and many Indian friends also, shown by their readiness to aid in the enlightening and civilizing endeavor of the missionaries in

India. Much valuable aid was given in other ways. Doctors rarely ever consented to receive remuneration from missionaries or their families. Advice and aid in the acquisition of property for mission purposes was given gratuitously. Civil engineers frequently gave most valuable help in planning buildings, sometimes superintending the construction of them. Many too, in these early days, were regular in attendance upon divine service on the Lord's Day, and not infrequently were present at house to house Bible readings and prayer meetings. They mingled their prayers with those of the missionaries; and to them belongs the honor of taking part in the great work of evangelizing the people of India.

Men there were who not only were indifferent to the missionary work, but were often strongly antagonistic. Of some of these mention has already been made; but it must not be supposed that they represented the great body of earnest Christian people in Britain, who inaugurated and have continued to support the missionary cause in India and elsewhere.

We have now arrived at a period, when, at the close of the Civil War in America, large reinforcements came to the help of the men and women, who had been carrying heavy burdens during the five years of warfare in the homeland.

It was in the closing days of 1864 that Rev. Samuel H. Kellogg and Rev. Joseph H. Myers, with their wives, sailed from Boston for Calcutta. A year later, Rev. James Alexander and Mrs. Alexander sailed for India. Rev. S. H. Kellogg and Rev. J. M. Alexander were sent to the Northwest Provinces; Mr. Kellogg being appointed to Farrukhabad and Mr. Alexander to Allahabad. The Rev. Mr. Myers and Mrs. Myers were sent to Lodiana. The coming of these strong young men and their gifted wives, was most timely.

The third Synod of India met in Ambala in November, 1865. Of the members present at this Synod, one had been in India thirty-one years; one twenty-seven years; two twenty-six years; one twenty-five years; one twenty-two years; one seventeen years and the remaining members from fifteen years to a few months. Twelve churches were represented in the Synod.

Although the Indian ministers, catechists, teachers and colporteurs now numbered one hundred and twenty, the burden of the churches and the evangelistic work and the management of the schools and orphanages bore very heavily upon this small band of workers. Six of these veterans had passed the limit of the average working life of a missionary in India, which was about twenty years. Two years later two ministers were lost to the service: Rev. J. L. Scott and his family left India owing to failure of health; and the Rev. Ishwari Das,[1] lately appointed to take full charge of the Fattehpur station, fell a victim of disease.

A strong appeal for reinforcements was sent from the Synod of India, at the meeting above mentioned, addressed to the theological seminaries at Princeton and Allegheny in America.

In response to this call, four missionaries sailed from Boston on the 18th of October, 1867: the Rev. Elwood Morris Wherry and Mrs. Wherry, the Rev. Charles Beatty Newton and the Rev. Francis Heyl. The good ship Zephyr, after an uneventful voyage of five months and two days, arrived in Calcutta on March 20, 1868.

Mr. Wherry and his wife were appointed to Rawul Pindi in the Punjab; Mr. Newton to Lahore and Mr. Heyl to Mainpuri. During the same years Mrs. Walsh and two daughters sailed for India. In November, 1867, Rev. J. F. Ullmann returned to India from England and was stationed at Farrukhabad.

Encouraged by these accessions to the missionary force, Rev.

---

[1] Ishwari Das was one of the orphan children made over to the Rev. H. R. Wilson by Dr. Madden at Fattehpur. He was associated with the Christian village at Rakha for most of his life. He accompanied Mr. Wilson to America, and spent some time in that country. He was the author of several books, for one of which, his *Lectures on Theology*, he received the prize offered by a learned Bengal civilian for the best work on Theology. He also took the prize offered for the best essay on French Education. In every way Ishwari Das sought to be useful to his own people, and was in consequence greatly loved and respected by his countrymen.[2]

[2] Mrs. Holcomb in *History of A. P. Mission*, p. 133.

C. W. Forman and the Rev. J. H. Orbison ventured to take their wives and families to America for a well-earned furlough. In the North India Mission, the Rev. B. D. Wyckoff was obliged to take his family to America, on account of ill health. The Rev. Theodore S. Wyncoop came out the same year. He was stationed in Allahabad.

Thus we see how it was that, notwithstanding substantial reinforcements, the Missions were still practically marking time. The accessions merely availed to fill up the gaps caused by disease and death. If all those remaining should continue in life and health, the plans then being carried out might eventuate in substantial success.

This was the situation at the beginning of the year 1869. During the course of this year serious epidemics of cholera and malarial fever broke out in the early summer and spread over North India and the Punjab with terrible mortality. The country had scarcely recovered from the devastation caused by the famine of 1866. Food was still selling at a high price and the poor were maintaining a bare existence, many families having scarcely one full meal a day and that of the poorest quality. Under such conditions, millions fell victims to disease. The vast majority had no medical help whatever. Even in the native Christian communities, many deaths were reported in spite of medical treatment. A number of deaths occurred in missionary families.

> "Parents are yet weeping for their children because they are not; widows and orphans are still mourning the loss of husbands and fathers; and the whole Mission, afflicted with them in their affliction, feel saddened and weakened by the removal of loved and honoured fellow-workers from their posts of labour and usefulness."[3]

The most serious calamity that befell the Missions at this time was the sudden death of three of the strongest men in the Lodiana Mission. The Rev. J. H. Orbison, who had just re-

[3] *Lodiana Mission Report*, 1869.

turned to America with his wife and children, seemingly strong and in the prime of life, suddenly died. He had rendered nineteen years of service in the mission field.

Soon after this sad event, the Rev. Alexander Henry, principtal of the Mission college in Lahore, after six years' service was stricken down by Asiatic cholera. A few months later, the Rev. Joseph H. Myers died at Lodiana, a victim of malaria and dysentery. Thus three stations were bereft of their strong men. To add to this depletion of missionary forces, two of the older missionaries, the Rev. John Newton, Sr. and the Rev. William Calderwood were obliged to go on furlough on account of the illness of their wives.

As a result of this reduction of the Mission force, Rawul Pindi was left with a young man in charge, who had scarcely a single year's experience in the work. Lahore had lost the principal of the college and high school, and was soon to lose its senior missionary, leaving two young men in charge. At Lodiana the situation was no less grave. Rev. Mr. Bergen was in America on furlough and Mr. Rudolph was in ill health and had been ordered to go home on long furlough. He was to leave early in the year and had expected Mr. Myers to take charge of the Press. Mr. Myers' death seemed to paralyze the work of the station, especially as, by an unfortunate accident, Mrs. Myers was incapacitated for service in the girls' orphanage for months to come.

At Saharanpur, Mr. Calderwood's absence on furlough would leave no American missionary to take charge of the boys' orphanage and the boys' high school in the city.

In the presence of such serious depletion, the only prospective help from America was the possible return of Rev. Mr. Forman to Lahore, and of Mr. Bergen with Mrs. Bergen to Lodiana. The Rev. Reese Thackwell was also expected to return within the next year. Notwithstanding these prospective accessions, the problem of making satisfactory adjustment of missionary forces, so as to meet all the requirements of the various institutions, was beset with serious difficulties. After long discussion the following disposition of the members of the Mission staff was made:

The Rev. E. M. Wherry was transferred from Rawul Pindi to Lodiana to take charge of the Press; Mr. Thackwell to take his place on arrival, at Rawul Pindi. The Rev. C. W. Forman was appointed principal of the college and superintendent of the Rang Mahal high school and its branches in Lahore. The Rev. W. J. P. Morrison and Miss Morrison were transferred from Lahore to Ambala. The Rev. Alexander Peebles Kelso, who came out to India from America with Mr. Forman, was appointed to take charge of the educational work at Saharanpur.

The retirement of Miss C. L. Beatty from the Christian girls' school at Dehra Dun was a serious loss to the school and to the cause of the education of women in India. Her death occurred a few weeks after her arrival at home in America.[4]

The Rev. David Herron and his wife took charge of the girls' school.

The most serious loss to the cause of education was the necessity for suspending the Mission college at Lahore for want of men to carry it on efficiently. Sixteen years later it was again reopened. Of this, notice will be taken in a later chapter.

---

[4] The following notice of Miss Beatty's work appeared in the *Annual Report of the Lodiana Mission* for 1870, pp. 24-25:

"Miss Beatty joined the Dehra Girls' School in the spring of 1863. She then took charge of the Educational Department and continued in charge of it till the end of that year, when on Mr. Herron's leaving the country, after the death of Mrs. Herron, the entire charge of the school then numbering 44 pupils, was committed to her. The charge was a weighty and responsible one: but she proved herself fully equal to it. Her experience as a teacher, her decision of character, and her administrative ability fitted her in no common degree for the work. Her heart was in it, and she gave herself wholly to it. She lived in the same house and sat at the same table with the children, and had them under her eye and influence continually. Their progress in learning, their cultivated manners, their prompt obedience and their order and good conduct were proofs of her ability and devotion that all could see, and evidence of a success which is seldom attained in so short a time. . . . There are many in this land who 'arise up and call her blessed.'"

CHAPTER XIX.

Theological Education

IN the early days of Missions in India, it was natural that almost every convert became a prospective candidate for the work of teaching and preaching. In order to give the necessary training, some one at each principal station would undertake to train these candidates, giving some kind of systematic instruction in bible knowledge. To this he would add a knowledge of the creed, the church order and the doctrine and practice of his denomination. This laudable effort involved a great deal of labor, not to say inconvenience. The many and varied duties of his calling and his forced absence from home, consumed so much of his time as to oblige him frequently to leave the teaching in abeyance. In consequence both teacher and pupil were discouraged by the slow progress made. Nevertheless patience and perseverance were rewarded by the growth and efficiency of the Indian workers. It was such effort as this that enabled a number of young men to prepare themselves for the work of the ministry. Among these were the Rev. Goloknath, Rev. Guru Das Moitra, Rev. Kali Charan Chatterjee, Rev. Jogandra Chandra Bose, Rev. William Basten, Rev. Puran Chand Uppal, Rev. Kanwar Sain, Rev. T. W. J. Wylie, Rev. Gilbert McMasters, Rev. Ishwari Das, Rev. Gopinath Nandi, Rev. J. J. Caleb, Rev. Pundit Mohun Lal and the Rev. Nabi Bakhsh.

Now that candidates for the ministry increased, the need for a theological school became imperative.

In the year 1870, effort was made by the Lodiana Mission to secure the establishment of a theological seminary under the auspices of the Synod of India. The Synod met in Allahabad in November, 1871. The proposal to establish a theological school was taken up and after some discussion it was decided to open such a school in Allahabad, early in the following year. The Rev. Augustus Brodhead and the Rev. Theodore S. Wynkoop were appointed to take charge of this work. A canvass of the Presbyteries and Missions disclosed the fact that twenty-five candidates for the ministry were prepared to attend the theological school. The school was opened on the 15th of April, 1872. After an address, Dr. Brodhead, the acting principal, formally declared the school to be open.

The Rev. T. S. Wynkoop was chosen secretary of the faculty and authorized to act as Librarian. Additional instructors were appointed. The subjects to be taught, as prescribed by the Synod, were Bible Geography, Biblical History, Jewish Antiquities, Systematic Theology, including the Sacraments, Chrisian Economics, Church order and the Evangelistic and Pastoral work of the Church. The instructors were expected to give lectures for short periods of two or three months each on special subjects. The Rev. Dr. J. H. Morrison gave a series of lectures on Muhammedanism and Muhammedan Controversy. The Rev. Kali Charan Chatterji lectured on the Evidence of Christianity. The Rev. J. J. Caleb gave lectures on the Confession of Faith. Other instructors taught the Urdu and Hindi languages.

During the winter vacation, the Rev. Samuel H. Kellogg, D. D. returned from America and took his place as principal of the seminary. A suitable compound, separate from the Jumna Mission premises, was enclosed and thirteen houses were erected for student accommodation.

The first session of study had been sufficient to determine the limitations of the students, so that when the second session began only sixteen names were entered on the roll, of which three were new. This lapse of twelve names was not entirely due to the unfitness of the candidates, but in part to the expense of travel to and fro, and the fact that one year's course was all that was necessary for certain men already advanced in years.

During the second session, two important changes were found to be necessary. The first was that the plan for non-resident instructors had to be given up, because of the distance, long journeys having to be made in the intense heat of an Indian summer, and the consequent menace to health and life. The second change made was in the interest of the health and life of the resident professors: the change of the time of opening the session in April, the beginning of the hot season. It was determined to open the sessions thereafter in October and let the school run throughout the cold season. These changes were approved by the Synod. The faculty now consisted of the following teachers: the Rev. Samuel H. Kellogg, D.D. principal; the Rev. Dr. Augustus Brodhead, the Rev. Theodore S. Wynkoop and the Rev. J. J. Caleb.

The third session of the seminary opened October 15th, 1874. The attendance was now found to be only thirteen, due no doubt to the difficulty of parting with the services of the students during the touring season among the villages. The class completed the course of study toward the end of the winter session, but before the final examination could be taken, an epidemic of cholera in the city obliged the dismissal of the students to their homes. Certificates were given to those who had completed a three year course of study. Most of these were licensed by their Presbyteries to preach, and some of them were ordained as pastors or evangelists.

Owing to the paucity of candidates for the ministry, the Synod ruled that, unless as many as twelve students could be assembled, the seminary should be temporarily closed. The required number of students not being available, the seminary was not reopened. One cannot but question the wisdom of this course. The candidates available had to be taught by individuals in pre-seminary days, which meant either very defective training, or, if effective, it was done at a great expense of brain and nerve by the individual missionaries with whom the student labored.

The apparent failure of this enterprise, was in no sense due to failure on the part of the honored men who served as professors and instructors in the seminary. It was due remotely to the want of educational facilities in the churches and missions. The constituency was spiritually weak. Christian parents were more ambitious to secure lucrative posts for their sons in secular employment than to see them trained for the spiritual work of the church. The theological seminary was suspended for several years. The work done had not been in vain. It had produced some strong men for the pastorate and evangelistic work. It had also accentuated the need of a thoroughly equipped Indian ministry and the possibility of an educated pastorate had been demonstrated.

CHAPTER XX.

The Kolhapur Mission

KOLHAPUR is a native principality, which occupies a territory of about 8,000 square miles, in what is known as the southern Maratha Country. The population numbers about four millions, being Hindus of all casts, Muhammedans and outcastes.

In the year 1852, the American Board of Commissioners of Foreign Missions, sent the Rev. Royal Gould Wilder to begin missionary work in the city of Kolhapur, the capital of the state of the same name. Here, as we have frequently noted before, the key to the hearts of the people was the school. Mr. Wilder established a school for boys, while Mrs. Wilder opened a school for girls. The Royal family was friendly toward them and approved of their plans for educating the people. The schools were conducted after the manner of the Mission schools of that day. Most of the teachers were non-Christians. Christian school readers were used, but bible lessons were taught by the missionary in charge.

Some years later, the American board, being dissatisfied with the paucity of conversions in India, sent their secretary, Rev. R. Anderson to visit the various stations occupied by their missionaries, with a view to a possible change of policy and a more aggressive method of evangelism. As a result of Dr. Anderson's study and report, it was determined to close all schools, excepting those needed for Christian children and those having Christian teachers.

This radical change of policy was not approved by some of the missionaries. Among these was Mr. Wilder, who wrote a learned volume as a protest against the somewhat autocratic ruling of his secretary and the board.

Mr. Wilder appealed to the home church, through the prudential committee, and secured permission to re-open the schools at Kolhapur. The old teachers and most of the scholars returned. Among the pupils was a nephew of the Maharajah and three others from the palace. A site was purchased for a church and a building was erected. Mr. Wilder's health gave way under the great stress of the work. By the advice of his physician he and his wife sailed from Bombay for America the day after the mutiny of the native army broke out, although they did not learn this fact until some weeks later. Their European neighbors in Kolhapur were killed and three English officers were murdered in their homes.

The rest of the Europeans took refuge with the Resident, who was guarded by a regiment which did not mutiny. Later the mutineers were overcome and nearly all slain, the leaders being blown from cannons located on the Mission compound.[1]

During Mr. Wilder's absence the Kolhapur Mission was closed out, and the church was sold to some Muhammadans, who converted it into a Mosque.

The result of Mr. Wilder's controversy with his Board was the severance of his connection with it. Personal friends in his Presbytery undertook to support him and his family in an Independent Mission. They went back to Kolhapur in 1861. Through the favor of the Maharajah, Mr. Wilder secured property adjoining the old church and in spite of the efforts of the Muslims, who protested against his building so near them, he erected new buildings for church and school. He had protested to Sir Bartle Frere, the Governor of Bombay, against the conduct of the Resident of Kolhapur, who would do nothing to replace his property which had been sold in his absence and for which he held a deed. The Governor of Bombay compensated him for all his losses.

For ten years Mr. Wilder carried on his Independent Mission work.

---

[1] *Western India News*, Vol. II., No. 3.

"He took a prominent part in the agitation carried on for reform in the Indian educational system and in memorializing Government to establish the present educational system. In a letter from Sir Bartle Frere to Mr. Wilder, which was later published in the Missionary Review, it was stated that Mr. Wilder had done more for the existing system of education in the Bombay Presidency than any other person."[2]

During these ten years, 3,300 pupils were in attendance in the schools under the influence of Mr. and Mrs. Wilder. Of these 500 were girls. Mr. Wilder preached in 2,165 villages and left a bible or a gospel in each village.

"Previous to 1869, thirty-two adults and nineteen children had been received into the Kolhapur Church. In 1870 there were twenty-one communicant members, and six baptized children."

The nominal adherents were enough to reconcile these divergent reports.

The city of Kolhapur then had a population of about 45,000. The ruling family was descended from the great Shivaji, the founder of the Maratha Kingdom. Kolhapur was an ideal centre for a new Mission. The Maratha Brahmins were the strongest element in the population. Along with them many people representing other classes—Khatris, Vaish, Sudras, Muslims and depressed classes, were to be found in the capital city. The gospel message, if once accepted here would naturally spread out through family relationships into the outlying towns and villages.

Years of faithful service in city and village resulted in removing much of the prejudice against Christian Missions in many Hindu communities. Hundreds of young men had entered the schools, and gone forth into the world as living witnesses, testifying to the pure lives and the kindly helpfulness of the missionaries. But the field was too great to be cared for without a larger staff and the means of financing the extension

[2] *Western India News*, Vol. IV.

of the work. As in all such Independent Missions, the limitations of age emphasized the necessity of making arrangements for the continuance of the work in the future.

Wherefore Mr. Wilder approached the secretaries of the American Presbyterian Board in New York, with a view to make over to them the Kolhapur Mission. In the year 1870 the Mission was placed under the care of that Board and henceforth was to be known as *"The American Presbyterian Mission in Western India."*

Toward the close of 1870, the Rev. Galen W. Seiler was sent to Kolhapur to be associated with Dr. Wilder. In December, 1872, the Rev. William Pratt Barker and Mrs. Barker, the Rev. James Johnson Hull, Rev. Joseph Patterson Graham and Miss Mary Bunnell joined the Mission. Miss Bunnell soon after was married to Mr. Graham.

Mr. Barker had been an experienced missionary of the American Board at Ahmadnugger, who, after ten years' service, was obliged to resign his place because of ill health. After a few years in America, he seemed to have fully regained his health, when he applied to be sent to India under the Presbyterian Board. In January, 1873, he was sent to Ratnagiri to open a new station there.

Ratnagiri is a city on the seacoast, 125 miles south of Bombay. It has a population of 12,000, of which about one-third are Muhammadans. The main source of wealth is fish, oysters and mussels. The cocoanut trees furnish a means of livelihood to many people.

Mr. and Mrs. Barker were obliged to return to America after three years' service, with no hope of return. Their place was filled by Rev. Galen Wilkins Seiler, transferred from Kolhapur.

In 1875, the veteran Missionaries Dr. and Mrs. Wilder were obliged to retire from the Mission work, which they had loved so well and served so faithfully. On arrival in America, Dr. Wilder founded the *The Missionary Review of the World,* which has become one of the most important Missionary magazines in the world.[8]

Miss Annie McGinnis arrived from America in December, 1874, and was married to Rev. Mr. Hull. After Mrs. Wilder's departure for America, Mrs. Hull took charge of the girls' school in Kolhapur. The Mission was further strengthened by the arrival of the Rev. Joseph Milliken Goheen and Mrs. Goheen, who were appointed to Kolhapur.

Mrs. Goheen was in very delicate health when she arrived in India and could do but little beyond setting before the Indians the example of a true Christian. After a wearysome illness she entered into rest on January 17, 1878.

Miss Amanda B. McGinnis arrived in Kolhapur December, 1876. She was appointed to assist Mrs. Hull in the Kolhapur girls' school, where she taught until May, 1879, when she became the wife of Rev. J. M. Goheen.

Panhala, a small town of 3,000 inhabitants, is situated twelve miles north of Kolhapur. It is the site of a large fortress built upon a spur of the mountain.

The Mission occupied this town at first as a sanitarium. It is some 3,000 feet above the sea. In 1875, it was made a Mission station and ever since has been regularly occupied. The Rev. J. P. Graham and his wife were the pioneer missionaries.

Later on a new station was occupied at Sangli, a city of 15,000 inhabitants situated in a fertile plain 30 miles east of Kolhapur. This was a strong Brahmin town, but permission was given to build Mission houses on premises near the city.

In January, 1879, the Rev. George H. Ferris and Mrs. Ferris joined the Mission. In the same year Mr. Graham was transferred from Panhala to Ratnagiri. He had gathered a Chris-

[8] Dr. Wilder's literary work in Indian was considerable. He wrote in Marathi *Scientific Errors of Hinduism;* a Commentary on Matthew and Luke, as a Theological class book. He wrote a work on Arithmetic, and translated into Marathi the following books: *Jane, the Young Cottager, The Shepherd of Salisbury Plain, The School Boy* and *Theological Class Book.* All these were published by the Bombay Book and Tract Society.

tian community of several families and a church of a dozen or more members. Mr. and Mrs. Ferris, after the rainy season in 1880 were sent to Panhala.

In December, 1880, Miss Esther E. Patton arrived from America and went to Kolhapur. Soon after, she was sent to Panhala, where she engaged in teaching and in visiting the women in the district.

Kolhapur was again strengthened by the arrival from America of the Rev. L. B. Telford and his wife. In 1879 Mr. Hull's health failing, he returned to America. He had secured the respect and affection of the people, who greatly sorrowed because they should see his face no more. He died in March, 1881. Mrs. Hull returned to Kolhapur with her children in December of the same year, and resumed her work in the Kolhapur girls' school.

The educational work at Kolhapur had advanced very considerably. In addition to Mrs. Wilder's girls' school for high and low caste girls, there were now two girls' schools and a Christian school for boys and girls. An English high school was started after Mr. Seiler's arrival in 1870, which was attended for awhile by nearly 50 students. Afterwards, on the making of a rule requiring attendance at the Sunday preaching service, the numbers dwindled down to 15. In February, 1875 the school was suspended.

In the report of 1884, it was stated that there were in all 12 boys' schools and five girls' schools in the Mission, in all of which were taught the Lord's Prayer, the Ten Commandments, Elementary and Shorter Catechism, the Summary of Christian Doctrine, and Bible portions. A night school for teaching English was conducted in Kolhapur. Since the Mission began up to 1884, nearly 4,000 boys and girls had been taught in the English and vernacular schools, the large majority of whom were of the Maratha caste. Several high and low caste pupils had been baptized and many of all classes were made more liberal minded by long attendance in these schools. The total number in attendance in 1884 was 660 boys and 100 girls.

During the famine of 1876-1877 an orphanage for boys and girls was opened. The orphans were carefully instructed and brought up as Christian children. Most of them were baptized and in due course were made communicant members of the church. Poor and crippled Christians were provided for by the missionaries and Indian Christians. At Ratnagiri many lepers were cared for. A hospital for lepers was built by a benevolent Parsee at a cost of 27,000 rupees, providing accommodation for 100 lepers. This institution was financed by annual grants made by the Government.

The efforts of the missionaries in this field, during their first quarter-century may be regarded as seed-sowing. At the close there were only two organized congregations, having on their roll, 84 communicants, of whom two were lay-preachers, two Bible women and twelve teachers. Sunday schools for Christians and non-Christians were carried on, with an average attendance of about 400. A Presbytery was organized in December, 1872, composed of six ordained ministers, none of whom were natives.

Meagre as these results may seem, the way had been prepared for great work and a plenteous harvest in the future.

CHAPTER XXI.

Progress in Publication Work

THE impetus given to missionary endeavor at the great Conference of 1862 held in Lahore, was perhaps most distinctly illustrated by the advance made in literary and publication work in the Punjab. For more than a quarter century, the Lodiana Book Depot had been the centre from which was sent out literature in the various vernaculars of North India for missionary use.

In the meanwhile, several other societies had undertaken to support Missions in the Punjab. The American United Presbyterians began work in Sialkot. At the same time, the Church of Scotland undertook work in the same place. The Church Missionary Society had established itself in Kotgarh, Amritsar and Peshawur. The English Baptists were long established in Delhi. But none of these Missions undertook to set up presses for themselves, but depended upon the Lodiana Press and its book depot, which was largely financed by the American Bible and Tract Societies. Some of these Missions, realizing their obligation, persuaded their societies to make grants of money to aid the work at Lodiana.

After the Lahore conference, the Church missionaries and many distinguished laymen united to establish a Bible and Tract Society at Lahore, which should become branches of the British and Foreign Bible Society and the London Religious Tract Society respectively. At first these English societies were conducted as a single institution, known as the Punjab Bible and Tract Society, having its own committees and a common depot in Lahore.[1]

---

[1] *Resolved:*

(1) That a Bible and Tract Society be formed to work, as far as possible, in connection with the Lodiana Press.

Besides publishing scriptures and tracts and books in the Urdu and Punjabi languages, they carried a considerable stock of English books, most of which were published by the London Religious Tract Society. The printing of vernacular publications, was done at the Lodiana Mission Press. They also placed on their shelves a good supply of the Lodiana publications.

When we consider the primitive means of transportation then possible, we can understand the boon thus bestowed upon the missionaries in the Northwestern Provinces of India.

There were at this time in North India four centres of publication for vernacular literature: the Lodiana Mission Press, the Mission Press at Allahabad, the London Mission Press at Mirzapur and the Punjab Bible and Tract Society, Lahore. The printing presses at Lodiana and Allahabad were the property of the American Presbyterian Mission, but as has already been noted the press at Allahabad had been turned over to Indian Christians. Nearly all of these presses were eventually taken over by Indian Christians, who were thus enabled to undertake a very important part of the responsibility resting on the shoulders of the missionaries. Each of these institutions sought to meet the special needs of the Missions with which they were connected, instead of working towards an ideal broad enough to provide for every possible exigency. This was an entirely natural course to pursue, but the growth of the work due to the rapid increase of general knowledge, due to the educational work of the Government and the Missions, and also to the growth of the Christian community in numbers and intelligence, opened up new spheres of literary influence de-

---

(2) That the Lieutenant Governor (Sir Robert Montgomery) be asked to be a patron.
(3) That the following be a Committee for this object:—
Chairman,
Donald McLeod, Esq.
Members,

Sir Herbert Edwards, K. C. B.	R. N. Cust, Esq.
Colonel Lake, C. B.	Edward Princep, Esq.
Colonel Maclagen	T. D. Forsyth, Esq.
Dr. Farquhar	J. G. Mellvill, Esq.

The Chaplains Lahore, Mean Meer and Amritsar.
Report of the Punjab Mission Conference, 1862, p. 345.

manding a new and varied form of literature. Books were needed in the vernacular languages, especially in Urdu and Hindi, for young people, for boys and girls, for the homes, and, for the reading community in general; works on biography, history, fiction and general knowledge. Such a programme could only be carried out by united effort for the establishment of an institution which could minister to the needs of all.

A paper was prepared for the Lahore Conference of Missions by the Rev. J. H. Budden of the London Missionary Society, Almorah, and read by the Rev. J. Barton of the Church Missionary Society, Amritsar.[2] This paper urged upon the publication societies the need of a change both as to the matter and the form of the books and tracts then being issued. In regard to publication for non-Christian readers, it was urged that, instead of the bald western prosaic style, so commonly found in the translations and even in the original writings of European missionaries, effort should be made to orientalize such works, both as to language and method of expression.

"European forms of expression, modes of thought, and style of reasoning, are probably as strange and unintelligible, if not repulsive, to the natives of India as theirs are to Europeans. . . . Therefore the translation of the standard works of English or American divines (whether apologetic, didactic or expository) and of English treatises, and the employment of English forms of expression, and illustration, and modes of reasoning in original work such as tracts, sermons, and commentaries, &c,—although the language may be the purest and most correct vernacular,—still fail, it is to be feared, to convey to the minds of the readers, (if readers they find) the thought that was in the mind of the original writer or translator."

These statements as to what should be done in order to produce a readable and attractive vernacular literature, were a just criticism of much that had been written in the past.

Another point noted in this paper was the controversial character of much of the literature written for non-Christian

[2] *Report of the Punjab Mission Conference,* 1862, p. 268.

readers. The learned critic's remarks are so pertinent to present day conditions in India that I shall quote them in full.

"The question arises as to how far, in the present circumstances of India, it is needful or desirable, for the vernacular Christian literature prepared by missionaries, to be at all of the nature of a direct assault upon Hinduism or Muhammadanism. Such works have already been prepared to meet a felt want, and it is hoped they are doing good service. But other most potent influences are now at work throughout the country, the direct bearing of which, on both Hinduism and Muhammadanism, is plainly destructive, and it becomes a serious question, whether all available missionary effort, and vernacular Christian literature among the rest, should not now have a directly constructive tendency; and whether even then, it will be able to keep pace with the process of dissolution going on so rapidly all around us. God is in his providence destroying both Hinduism and Muhammadanism for us, apart from all direct Missionary effort to that end. Would it not then be better, that all vernacular Christian literature, intended for non-Christians, should take no direct notice of Hinduism or Muhammadanism as systems of religion, but tactily to assume it, as a settled point, that they fail to meet the demands of the times, and the wants of man's nature; and then occupy itself in showing in all possible variety of ways that these can only be met by the Gospel of Christ."

The Lahore Conference took up the question of the typographical preparation of books. One writer said,—

"Instead of the flowery title page, the limp cover and the running oblique gloss of a genuine native work, we have had the stiffly formal straight lines, the rigid binding and the cut-and-dried appearances which a severe Anglo-Saxon taste has conventionally taught us to deem beautiful."

Another criticism along this line was made by the Rev. C. W. Forman of Lahore. He said,—

"On receiving an Urdu book, one of the first things which strikes the recipient is the European style of binding; the next is the name on the book in Roman letters. He opens the book and finds in the back part of it an English title page. It has been printed with Arabic and Persian *type,* which he can with difficulty read; whilst diacritical marks, which he does not at all understand, are scattered over its pages. Moreover, the title of the work is repeated at the head of each page, which every native reads as a part of the text, thus obscuring the meaning. If our object had been to deter the people from reading our books, we could scarcely have devised means more likely to succeed. I would have our books made so much like their own, that no one could distinguish them by the style in which they are got up. They would thus be much more attractive; and besides some, who are now ashamed to be seen with a Christian book in their hands (because every passer-by can see at a glance what is a Christian book) would then read them without fear of being called Christians."[8]

The inspiration received at the Lahore Conference led to increased activity in the production of Christian literature at the Lodiana Mission Press, then conducted under the superintendence of the Rev. Adolph Rudolph.

At the close of the year 1863 he wrote in his report:

"At the commencement of the year, it was feared that the ever increasing demand for vernacular publications would eventually become too great to be met by the limited means at our disposal. The subsequent formation of the Punjab Bible and Tract Societies, however, lead us to hope that the work carried on at this press, so necessary an auxiliary to the Missionary, either when at his station or when out itinerating, will be supported to the full extent of the requirements of this region."

At Lodiana, the scriptures were published at the expense of the American Bible Society. Tracts were published at the expense of the American Tract Society or of the Lodiana Mission.

During the year 1863, the Punjab Bible Society published 3,000 copies of the Psalms in the Punjabi language. During the next year that Society published 6,000 copies of the Gospels of Matthew, Mark and John. The following year, the New Testament was published in Urdu (2,000 copies) and also 2,000

[8] *Report of the Punjab Mission Conference*, 1862, p. 268 *et al.*

copies of the Gospel of Luke. Thus the Punjab Bible Society became established as a permanent factor in the work of evangelization in India.

During the same period the Punjab Tract Society published 20,000 tracts in the Urdu and Punjabi languages.

The publications of the American Tract Society for this same period amounted to 101,000 tracts and books in Urdu, Hindi, and Punjabi for the year 1863, and 194,000 copies for the year 1864. In addition to these the Lodiana Mission issued from the press 122,000 publications in these three languages.

The literary work of these Societies was largely accomplished by the missionaries of the Lodiana Mission. The entire New Testament in Punjabi was revised, indeed practically retranslated by Rev. John Newton, Sr. The entire Bible was published in three volumes in Persian Urdu (Lithographed) at the expense of the American Bible Society.

In the North India Mission, the work of the North India Bible Society, whose office and depot were transferred from Agra to Allahabad, soon after the Indian mutiny, was carried on independently of the Mission. The Mission Press was operated under Indian Christian management, but was still doing most of the printing for the societies. The North India Tract Society was conducted as an auxiliary of the London Religious Tract Society. The Presbyterian missionaries were actively interested in both of these Societies, and to their active aid as authors and managers, their success has been largely due. The literary work of Rev. J. L. Scott, D. D.; Rev. J. F. Ullmann; Rev. Joseph Owen, D. D.; Rev. Augustus Brodhead, D. D.; Rev. W. F. Johnson, D. D.; Rev. Samuel H. Kellogg, D. D.; Rev. E. P. Newton, Rev. E. M. Wherry, D. D. and the Rev. J. J. Lucas, D. D. have had much to do with the revision of the scriptures in the Urdu and Hindi languages, and the creation of a large portion of the hundreds of volumes of book and tract literature published during the half century succeeding the cataclysm of 1857.

CHAPTER XXII.

Occupation of Bundelkand

BUNDELKAND is a large territory south of the Jumna river extending into rugged regions generally known as Rajputana. Its people are Hindus, who for generations occupied the lands as farmers and herders. They were a bold warlike people who would flock together as vassals of their chiefs when any occasion arose. After the Muhammadan conquest of the Northwestern provinces and the establishment of the Mogul Sultans in Delhi, Agra and Allahabad, every effort was made to reduce these tribes to submission, but their success was only partial. Numerous tribal chiefs maintained their practical independence. Later on, when the Marathas had established themselves in Western India, Bundelkand became subject to the Hindu marauders, and the towns of Gwalior and Jhansi were made strongholds, whose chiefs were powerful rulers among the Marathas. The citadel at each town was built upon a rocky hill, almost impregnable except to heavy artillery. The chief of Gwalior is known in history as Maharajah Jayali Scindia, who abandoned his former capital at Ujjian to secure a better and more central site at Gwalior, with fort built on a hilltop 300 feet high. Here he became one of the most powerful chiefs of central India.

The missionary records show that this principality was visited more than once by Rev. James Wilson and Rev. Joseph Owen of Allahabad. Mr. Wilson wrote as follows:

"We visited Kalpi, Hamirpur, Banda, and other villages on the way. At each of the larger places we stopped several days, in the smaller places generally only one day. At Kalpi and at Banda we had interesting discussions with a Pundit or learned Hindu, and a Maulvie or learned Mussalman. These were such as to give us pleasing evidences that Christianity is making steady and distinct advances in this country. We distributed all the books and tracts which we took with us, and two porter's loads besides, which the Rev. Mr. P. sent from Cawnpore at our request."[1]

Some years later, in response to a request prepared by an English gentleman at Banda, Dr. Owen recommended to the Mission at Allahabad the opening up of a Mission in that territory under native management. In 1853, two Christians, Paul Qaim Khan and Melancthan Catechist were sent to Banda to open a school. The school was begun and rapidly grew in favor so that within one year the head master, Mr. Paul Qaim Khan, reported 144 boys enrolled. A year later, a suitable building was erected and paid for by English gentlemen, who were interested in the missionary project.

This work so auspiciously begun was rudely terminated by the Indian mutiny of 1857 and never again undertaken by the American Mission. Occasional visits were undertaken by evangelists and Bible Colporteurs sent from Agra.

Plans were perfected for the occupation of Gwalior as a station in 1873. The first missionary to occupy this station was Rev. Joseph Warren, who had returned to India after an absence of nearly 17 years. His experience of sixteen years between 1838 and 1854 had specially qualified him for the responsible work of inaügurating the Mission in a new field. Dr. and Mrs. Warren were transferred from Fattehgarh to Morar, the cantonment at Gwalior. Here they opened schools for boys and girls, and in due course a church was built.

"At the time of his going to Morar, a regiment of Scotch Highlanders was garrisoned there, and they (mostly Presbyterians) were soon after Dr. Warren's arrival deprived of their Chaplain. It was at once arranged that Dr. Warren should act as Presbyterian Chaplain at Morar, which arrangement not only provided him with an important and congenial sphere of usefulness, but gave him a standing in the British cantonment,

[1] *In the Heart of India*, p. 3.

which was advantageous, and furnished him with pecuniary aid for his missionary work."[2]

Mrs. Warren was bereft of her husband in the year 1878. Not long afterward, the cantonment was abandoned. This left the missionary's widow alone. Many of her friends advised her to move over to the city. The Maharajah favored the change, but Mrs. Warren chose to remain alone. Friends urged her to go lest she be attacked by lawless people. She only smiled saying she had a troop of angels to guard her. Here she wrought alone with her Indian workers. When 22 years had passed she returned for a rest to America. After a short furlough, she returned to India in 1901 only to die and be buried beside her husband in the English cemetery at Morar.

"At the funeral of the lamented Missionary, His Highness the Maharajah Sir Madho Rao Scindia, was not only in attendance, but in preparation for the obsequies everything had been done at his command which could attest the high esteem in which Mrs. Warren had ever been held by him. One of his gun carriages drawn by four horses carried the deceased to the grave, and forming a part of the cortege which followed was his own carriage containing himself, his English physician, whose attention to Mrs. Warren during her illness had been unremitting and most kind. Mrs. Warren had known the Maharajah from his infancy, and he had been accustomed to speak of her as "Mother."[3]

The work so auspiciously begun by Dr. and Mrs. Warren, has been carried on by several others. Conspicuous among these were Rev. Dr. Henry Forman, whose educational work has so commended him to the Maharajah Scindia that he has become superintendent of schools through the state.

On agricultural lines the North India Mission has permitted Mr. Samuel Higginbottom, Principal of the Agriculture Institute, Allahabad, to direct the introduction of modern methods of agriculture throughout the state. A lay missionary, W.

[2] *In the Heart of India*, p. 13.

[3] Mrs. Holcomb in *The Heart of India*, p. 14.

Griffin, Esq. has accepted from him the office of mechanical engineer. Such methods of missionary work are not altogether new in India, but the demonstration of the gospel and the plow has commended itself to many who once were skeptical.

The question of establishing a Mission at Jhansi had often been considered. For awhile the missionary at Etawah, Rev. J. F. Ullmann, had sent his entire village force to preach in Bundelkand. They occupied as centres of touring circuits four principal towns: Jhansi, Kalpi, Orai and Kunch. For three years these workers labored under the leadership of the Rev. Nabi Bakhsh, a convert from Islam. Two hundred and sixteen towns and villages were visited and great numbers of gospels and Christian books were scattered among the people. Among those who were brought into the Christian church was a Brahmin priest Devidas, who received at baptism the name Prabhudas, and who became a distinguished evangelist.

Sometime in the eighties, the British decided to return the fort at Gwalior to the Maharajah Scindia and to transfer the cantonment from Morar to Jhansi. This city had become a railway center on the India Midland Railway, where four lines of railway cross. Naturally Jhansi was chosen as the site for a new cantonment. The Jhansi fort too was suited to take the place of the Gwalior fortress.

The time had come when Jhansi should be chosen as a station in connection with the North Indian Mission. The Rev. James F. Holcomb, D. D. and his gifted wife were transferred from Allahabad to Jhansi. At the same time Rev. Nabi Bakhsh[4] was transferred from Etawah to be the assistant evangelist in a district where he had laboured for three years before. Soon

[4] The story of Nabi Bakhsh illustrates the wonders of Divine Providence. Kidnapped when a child of eight he was carried from his home in Lucknow to Rampur. After brutal treatment by his captors, his slave seized an opportunity, when his Master was away from home, to flee for freedom. After travelling nearly fifty miles he reached Bareilly, where an English magistrate took charge of him and most kindly arranged for his further journey to the Presbyterian orphanage at Fattehgarh. Here he was cared for and educated by Rev. J. L. Scott, the Missionary in charge. Later on when he had confessed his faith in Jesus as his Saviour, he was trained for the ministry and in due course he was ordained. Mrs. Holcomb in *The Heart of India*, p. 151.

after arrival in Jhansi, the new cantonment was established there. A regiment of Scotch Presbyterians were billeted there and Mr. Holcomb was asked to officiate instead of the chaplain. Thus, as in many other stations in India, the missionary was enabled to minister to Europeans and so by spiritual gifts to make return for temporal and financial aid. A commodious dwelling house was purchased and suitable houses were erected for the Indian workers. In due course a site was secured for a church and public reading room. Schools for boys and girls have been opened and thus by the teaching of the Bible and the preaching of the gospel the good news of salvation has been spread among the people. A considerable community of believers has been created. Jhansi has become one of the great centers of moral and spiritual influence in Bundelkand.

CHAPTER XXIII.

Preaching in Towns and Villages

THE method of work for village evangelization had undergone a considerable change. The older pioneer missionaries undertook extensive journeys, exploring the country, scattering books and tracts, stopping at the larger towns and cities for several days to preach in the streets as they had opportunity. These journeys accomplished an important work in the way of calling the attention of a wide circle to the purpose and character of the missionary work. Large cities were chosen to become central stations for smaller areas. But such work was always more or less desultory and therefore unsatisfactory. The time had now come for a more thorough organization of this work. The field was contracted, so that a more thorough canvass of the villages could be undertaken. In the interest of efficiency, it was important that the more promising villages should be visited frequently, and so by intensifying the work a personal touch might become possible. Converts and a second generation of Christian young men and women were now ready to enter upon evangelistic and school work in the smaller centers. Small village communities of Christians were now begun. At first there might be but a single person like Nicodemus who would seek the spiritual help of the missionary. Then his wife or a neighbor would confess their faith. By and by a company of six or more would agree to be baptized, when more or less regular services would be held for the public worship of God.

The village of Ghorawaha in the Hoshyarpur district affords a good illustration. The Rev. Kali Charan Chatterji had frequently visited this Muhammadan village. In this village he found a remarkable man, a *faqir,* or mendicant, Gamu Shah by name, who had eight disciples. Gamu Shah had discarded the Quran and accepted the New Testament instead. He taught his followers that Jesus was Divine and their mediator and Lord. His teaching was defective on many points, but antogonistic to Islam. Mr. Chatterji expounded the scriptures to them and prayed with them.

A year later, twelve of the disciples of Gamu Shah were baptized. They were all Muhammadans of the Rajput class, belonging to five different families, two of which were head men in the village. They became Christians by the advice of their leader although he did not then receive baptism. Mr. Chatterji's description of the man and his history is so interesting, it is best to give it in his own words:

"The movement toward Christianity amongst these people has been neither sudden nor impulsive. They first commenced their inquiry after the truth five years ago, being directed to do so by their own religious teacher. The name of this interesting man is Gamu Shah. He is of Hindustani[1] extraction, about five feet ten inches in height, of dark complexion, and of a very quiet and thoughtful disposition. His mind seems to have long worked on the subject of religion. While yet a boy, he was a lover of truth. Dissatisfied with orthodox Muhammadanism, he sought for salvation and peace in the instruction of a Faqir by name Sultan Shah, and soon became one of his most distinguished pupils. I saw Sultan Shah twelve years ago. He was a brother of the Chief of Amanu, a village in the Kapurthala territory, and in early life left home and domestic comforts for the life of a faqir. He lived partly in Amanu and partly in Ghorawaha. To all outsiders he appeared to be a madman, going about with a coloured beard, and a rod decorated with a bunch of keys and birds' feathers, and speaking words without meaning. He pretended to be an incarnation of the Imam Mehdi,[2] and also called himself the messenger of Jesus Christ. The rod in his hand he called 'the scepter of Jesus'; of the two keys suspended on it, one he called the key of Heaven

[1] In the Punjab the term *Hindustani* applies to the people of the Northwest provinces.

[2] The *Mehdi* is the last of twelve Imams recognized by Shiah Muslims who will be revealed (they say) in the last age of the world.

and the other the key of Hell; and the feathers indicated that his soul would fly to Heaven after his death. He ate and drank with Christians, and invariably sought their intercourse and society. He was a constant visitor at Mr. Goloknath's in Jalandhar, and probably at Mr. Woodside's also.[3] But under this feigned madness, Gamu Shah assures me, he cherished a belief in Christ and Christianity. This belief he had learned from his own murshid, or leader, one Rustum Shah, a wandering dervish who, during the latter part of his life, settled down in Amanu at the earnest request of his disciple, Sultan Shah, who furnished him with a *takya*[4] and contributed to his support. No one knows the antecedents of this man, for he never discovered them to any one. To the bold and curious, who ventured to question him about them, his invariable reply was that he came from the *Nila Mahal* (the blue palace), by which he probably meant the sky. Gamu Shah now thinks he was probably a Hindustani and a Christian. All of his disciples thought him to have been endowed with miraculous and prophetic powers.

"On the death of this man, Gamu Shah took his master's place and collected a large number of disciples. Unlike most *faqirs* in this country, Gamu Shah neither drank *bhang* (hemp) nor smoked *charas* (a secretion from the flowers of hemp), nor did he keep a *takya*. He lived inside the village in a decent little house with his family, consisting of a wife and four children. In this place, sitting under the cool shade of a *bakayan* tree,[5] Gamu Shah expounded the mysteries of his faith to the most advanced of his pupils, which consisted of the following cardinal doctrines.

"1. God is the creator of Heaven and Earth, but man, his creature, was polluted and 'Hell deserving on account of sin.'

"2. Muhammad is not the prophet of God, nor the Quran His word.

"3. Christ is the only true Saviour of men, the Son and Spirit of God.

The Bible (the Tauret, Zabur and the Injil)[6] is from God and the only repository of His will."

---

[3] Rev. John S. Woodside then resident in Kapurthala. See Chapter XX.

[4] In Muslim countries a *takya* is a sort of retreat in which a faqir or monk may rest.

[5] Oleander.

[6] The Law, the Psalms and the Gospel.

These precious truths were taught in an imperfect and indistinct manner, as Gamu Shah had never seen a copy of the Christian Scriptures, but had acquired his knowledge from the oral and incidental remarks of his master. And along with these truths, many crude and imaginary ideas of creation, judgment, heaven and hell were inculcated. He strictly enjoined on all his followers to cultivate the acquaintance of Christian missionaries, and to learn from them more about Jesus and His salvation.

"We came across these interesting people in the course of our itineration in the winter of 1869, and were not a little surprised to find them ready to accept the Sonship and Divinity of Christ, the great stumbling blocks and rocks of offence to the believers of the Muhammadan faith. On inquiry, we soon discovered that Gamu Shah was the source of enlightenment on these points. We then visited him and persuaded him to accept a copy of the New Testament. The intercourse thus opened, a regular communication was kept up with him and his disciples. We frequently visited them in their village and invited them over to our house in Hoshyarpur. Making the ground prepared by the faqir the basis of instruction, we endeavored to build them up in the knowledge and faith of Christ. The consequence of these humble labours, with the Divine blessing, has been the conversions mentioned above."

The first of these men was baptized on the 23rd of December, after an interesting and impressive service in the presence of three hundred spectators.

The next baptisms, three in number, took place on the 27th of January, when a large number of spectators were present. These four baptisms aroused the feelings of the whole village. The Rajputs are a manly race, proud of the honour and purity of their blood. The conversion of their brethren to Christianity was regarded as a slur upon the whole community, and a determination was made at once to remove it, either by bringing the apostates back to their former faith, or by extirpating them from the village. With this object in view, they first of all attacked the Catechist placed there for the instruction of the converts, beating him mercilessly, and turned him out of the village. The injury thus offered was patiently borne and passed by with a spirit of Christian forgiveness. But this, instead of doing any good, only emboldened the perpetrators of the deed. They interpreted it as a mark of helpless weakness, and commenced persecution of the converts themselves. Not to mention the abuse, taunts and ridicule to which they were almost hourly exposed, their opponents cast them out of society, excluded them from the use of public wells, forbade them the houses of their neighbors, and put a stop even to their buying and selling in the bazars. The common mechanics such as the blacksmiths and carpenters and even the barbers were prohibited from doing their work. The sweeper and the water-carrier were forcibly withdrawn from rendering them the most necessary services, on pain of excommunication, if they did not obey. These persecutions were of the severest form and a source of very great trial and annoyance to the converts. But they bore them with remarkable cheerfulness and fortitude. Their enemies, however, were not satisfied. They collected upwards of fifty maulvies from different parts of the country. The converts were arraigned before their tribunal and asked to give a reason for their faith. Ghulam Gauns, the boldest and strongest man among them, stood before the whole assembly and unreservedly witnessed for Christ. He said he had renounced Muhammadanism and believed in Christianity;

"1. Because there is no salvation in Muhammadanism. The Quran itself says: 'There is no intercession in the Day of Judgment' (Sura Baqr, sipira 3, verse 954) Muhammad could not save, as he himself was a sinner, (see Sura i Fatah v. 2).

"2. There is no testimony about Muhammad in any of the previous books.

"3. The Tauret, Zabur, and the Injil testify, 'There is no other name given under heaven whereby a man could be saved, except the name of Jesus.'

"4. How do you prove Muhammad's apostleship, since it is expressly said in the Quran:

" 'Answer, Signs are in the power of God alone, and I am no more than a public preacher,' (Sura, the Spider, v. 49) and again:

"Nothing hinders us from sending thee with miracles except that the former nations have charged them with imposture" (Sura Saba v. 44).

These points were written on a paper and given to the maulvies, with a declaration that if they were satisfactorily answered, the Christians would return to their former faith.

The maulvies kept the paper for three days and returned it without a reply. On the fourth day, the converts were sent for again. This time no reasoning was used, but love, threats, worldly honour and promises of wealth and aggrandizement were employed to bring them back. But all this was to no purpose. The brethren had grace given them to withstand these temptations, as they had on the first occasion boldly confessed the Saviour's name.

The maulvies then proposed a public discussion with the missionary of the station, who was living in the village at the time. Considering the circumstances of time and the place, and the wishes of the converts and the inquirers, it was thought best to accept the challenge. A controversy was held for two days on the village common. It was a grand occasion and a most noble opportunity was afforded for witnessing in behalf of Christ. Upwards of eight thousand people were present on each day. Most of these were illiterate and too far removed from the scene of controversy to be profited by it. The few intelligent men, who sat near, alone entered into the merits of the discussion. The details are too long to be given here, but they have already been placed before the public by means of the mission periodical, the *Nur Afshan.* I would only remark here that the Maulvie Fateh Muhammad,[7] who headed the controversy on the opposite side, frustrated his own purpose by attempting to accomplish too much. In his anxiety to expose

[7] Fateh Muhammad was a native of Kasur, but usually resided at Lahore. He was a Wahabi and was celebrated for his enmity against Christianity.

the Christian religion, and to put it to contempt and ridicule, he spoke of Christ and God in the vilest and most blasphemous terms. The moral effect of his discourse was most ruinous to his cause. Prejudiced and opposed though most of his hearers were to the Christian faith, their better feelings revolted against the filth and abuse that seemed to be his only element and delight at the moment. He also distorted and misrepresented facts and passages of scripture in such a manner as to attribute to the Christian's God such actions as one would be ashamed of in men. On these being contradicted, he persevered in his statements, but was soon proved to have been false before the assembled people, by a simple reference to the book.

With this the discussion ended, and the result was favorable to the work of God. The converts felt an additional assurance of being in the right, and the enquirers were strengthened also. One of them immediately came forward and received baptism. Exasperated at this, the maulvie resorted to most exceptional measures. He instigated the people to quarrel and fight with the Christians and to use violence on their persons, and so far forgot himself as to preach the merits of martyrdom and the duty of killing all apostates from the faith of Islam.

The effect of this preaching upon the already excited multitude was serious, perhaps more so than he had calculated. Infuriated with rage, they ran to pull down the tents of the missionary and to burn them up. Some of them assaulted the missionary's wife and children the next day, while they were passing by an adjacent village, and would have inflicted serious injury had not friendly aid arrived in time. Others were heard to declare on oath that they would kill the new converts on the arrival of the first opportunity. The whole village was put in a state of fanatical frenzy and excitement.

"It was our desire from the commencement to avoid, if possible, any reference to the civil authorities in connection with this subject. But when affairs came to this critical pass, forbearance appeared no longer desirable or wise; so, after prayerful consideration, the whole matter was brought to the notice of the Government, with an application for the protection of the converts, and the prevention of worse complications.

"The magistrate of the District at once instituted an enquiry, the result of which was the apprehension and trial of Mirza Fateh Muhammad, the author and abettor of all the mischief. The trial of this man, which was conducted by the State, created a great sensation in the Muhammadan community at the time. But those who knew the facts of the case never sympathized with him. They knew well that Fateh Muhammad had himself to blame for all the ignominy and shame that came upon him. He was charged under four different sections of the Penal Code, and the charges were sustained with such strong evidence, given by Hindus and Muhammadans as well as by Christians, that there was no loophole left for escape. Most probably he would have been convicted and severely punished; but as the case originated with us, and we were so intimately connected with it, we felt it our duty to try to save the man, at least to give up all our claims against him. With this in view, we applied to Government in the maulvie's behalf. Our application was granted, and Mirza Fateh Muhammad was discharged, though not acquitted."

This case, thus decided, at once illustrated the forgiving spirit of the Christians and vindicated the intervention of the civil authorities, who, to prevent future trouble and persecution, placed in the village a police guard and at the same time bound over the leading members of the opposition by personal recognizances to keep the peace. Thus, peace was restored in the village and Christian community. The interest in the word of God increased among the inquirers and shortly after three more members were added to the church, one of whom was the head man of the village and another still more important being Gamu Shah himself. Three months later, four more converts were baptized. Thus, notwithstanding fierce persecution, a little Christian community sprung up in a bigoted Muslim village.

This movement acquired a special interest from the fact that it occurred in an agricultural district and in a Muslim village. It was hoped that it might spread far and wide, but this hope was not realized. Some additions have been made from the village itself and from a few neighboring villages. The church continues to grow, but it has never been characterized by a strong spiritual life. A few of the younger generation have become teachers and preachers, one a professor in the Saharanpur theological seminary and a writer of some notoriety.

Mention has been made of the persecution of Christian converts by prohibiting them from drawing water from the public wells. This form of boycott becomes exceedingly oppressive when a convert has the option of drawing water from a well used by outcasts, whose filthy habits pollute the water, or of smuggling water from the forbidden wells, with the possibility of a violent assault and a merciless beating. In the case of private wells, there is no redress, but in the case of public wells, which are provided by the Government and from which many castes of both Hindus and Muhammadans may and do continually draw water, the boycott against Christians becomes invidious and open to objection.

The missionaries and Indian Christians made a test case at Ghorawaha with the result that the English magistrate ordered that:—

> "Christians should continue to use such public wells as they had been in possession of within three months of their conversion, until the party desiring to exclude them from those wells, shall obtain a decision of a competent Civil Court adjudging them to be entitled to such exclusive possession."[8]

This decision brought relief to Ghorawaha, but the Muhammadans at Hoshyarpur, where Christians had been using public wells without objection, under the instigation of the Ghorawaha Muslims, secured from Lahore a *fatwa* (decision) prohibiting Muslims from using water from wells used by Christians. Many Hindus fell in with this anti-Christian movement. The Maulvies passed a sentence of excommunication against any

[8] Act X of 1872, see 532.

Muhammadan who would draw water from a well used by a Christian. The effect was that the public wells were left in the hands of the Christians and a few courageous men, who defied the Maulvies and pundits.

It was not long before both Hindus and Muslims began to see how foolish this sort of thing was. They had long drunk from these wells without any loss of caste or religion, and now they were only being forced into a senseless opposition to Christian neighbors, whereupon some two hundred Hindus drew up a protest against the Muhammadan agitators, saying they would prefer to draw water with Christians rather than with Muhammadans. Some Muhammadans also united with the Hindus in this protest, and by this united protestation the magistrate was pleased to commend the liberal stand of the non-Christians, which led to general use of public wells by Hindus, Muslims and Christians.

To give entire assurance to the weak, ignorant and prejudiced Muhammadans three distinct fatwas were secured from learned Maulvies to the effect that it was lawful for a Muhammadan to eat and drink with Christians and that it was also lawful for a Muhammadan to drink water from a Christian well. Even the famous Maulvie, Fateh Muhammad affixed his name to the fatwa permitting Christians and Muslims to eat and drink together.

Among the varied methods of work for village evangelization during the seventies and the early eighties, a few are characteristic. The Rev. John Newton, M. D. spent most of his missionary life in village work. His home was in Subathu in the lower slopes of the Himalaya mountains. On all sides were villages, inhabited by Hill men, while at the foot of the hills, and on the fertile plains beyond are some scores of towns and villages, affording an almost ideal field. In the winter months, Dr. Newton travelled throughout the towns and villages on the plains lying along the hills. In the summer he visited villages in the hills, travelling as far as Kotgarh and Ani, fifty or sixty miles beyond Simla. He carried with him besides scriptures and tracts in Hindi and Punjabi, a supply of medicine, wherewith he might minister to poor people who had no medical relief in times of sickness. This was an extension of the medical work carried on at his dispensary and leper asylum in Subathu.

Perhaps we can get a better insight as to the methods of this devoted missionary's work, if we go out with him for a day or two and see him at work. He tells the story in his diary entry of February 17, 1874. He was at Ramgarh, a village nine miles east of Lodiana which had contributed a number of families to enlarge the Christian church at Lodiana:

"Having a succession of visitors at my tent nearly all day, I did not go into the village at all, though close at hand, but showed and explained my pictures and preached for some hours. I find that these pictures are greatly admired, and never fail to attract a crowd. They are large lithographs, about eighteen inches long by twelve or fourteen inches wide, printed in colours rather more gaudy than is consistent with the most refined tastes. But they are all the better for that, for not only do the people of this country generally admire these brilliant tints, but they are, in consequence, better seen at a distance. When at Lodiana the other day, I had a large portofolio made for the picture, which is easily carried under the arm. I also provided myself with a box of tacks and a small hammer, which can be carried in the pocket. I have only now to fasten a few of the pictures with tacks to the wall, to collect an audience at once, all eager to learn their meaning. I have at present twelve or thirteen of the large pictures. All but four of them are illustrations of Bible narratives, either in parables like that of the Prodigal Son, or of historical incidents like the story of Naaman, the leper. Besides the pictures, I have also a few broadsheets. One of these contains the Ten Commandments; others various texts beautifully illuminated in blue and gold, and printed in the different vernaculars, in large characters. I find it a good plan to hang up one or more of these above the pictures, making it the text or key-note both of the illustrations and of the discourse."

On the 27th February, he wrote the following in Rupar, a

town of some ten thousand inhabitants situated at the head works of the great Sirhind Canal.

"Rupar has been occupied as a sub-station by the Missionaries at Lodiana, who are at present represented here by a Catechist and a Scripture Reader. They could not have found in all this region a more important centre for Missionary operations. One of the first things I did was to visit these brethren. The wife of the Catechist, I found very ill; nor is she any better yet. Her illness has constituted the only drawback to the pleasure of our intercourse.

"It is peculiarly refreshing to meet with Christians, above all such sincere Christians as these, after having spent some weeks among Hindus and Muhammadans alone. In addition to these, I have had the pleasure of meeting several others, native Christian preachers and colporteurs, from Lodiana and Santok Majara, who are passing through Rupar on their way to the great Spring Mela at Anandpur.

"The most interesting event in my experience here has been my visit to a large and flourishing Anglo-vernacular school. I have carried out, on a larger scale than before, a plan which I hope to execute frequently hereafter. When I first visited the school, the boys were clamorous for books. They were eager also to see the pictures, of which they had got a glimpse. I told them there were but two ways in which they could get books: either they must pay the usual price, or if any were unable to buy, each of them might earn a book as a prize by committing to memory and reciting to me the Ten Commandments. I then showed them some of the books, which I was willing to give them as prizes. To all who were willing to accept these conditions, I offered to give at once copies of the Broad Sheet containing the Ten Commandments in Persian Urdu. About twenty-five eagerly accepted the offer. I then appointed a time for the examination and left them.

"The day following, at the hour fixed for the examination, which was before the usual hour for opening the school, I returned with a large assortment of books and the portfolio of pictures. The whole school, including the teachers, had voluntarily assembled. The teachers, to my surprise, displayed a friendly spirit, entering heartily into the undertaking and assisting greatly by keeping order among the boys during the examination. Twenty-two boys had prepared themselves, and recited the whole of the Ten Commandments unabridged, most of them with remarkable accuracy. Meanwhile I kept a record of their names and gave marks to each, in order to be able to adjust the prizes according to merit."

After a brief examination as to the content and purpose of the Law of God, Dr. Newton distributed the prizes, much to the delight of the fortunate boys.

Another extract from the journal of the Rev. E. P. Newton of Lodiana (1875) gives a fair account of the work and experience of the village preacher, illustrating his method of work. It also shows something of his success as well as his ofttimes disappointment:

"At Morinda there seemed to be rather more than usual interest in Christianity, and we spent some days there.

"The Ram Dasis[9] earnestly requested us to establish a School for them, as their boys were not allowed to enter the Government school. On returning home, I consulted with the other Missionaries at the Station on the subject. It was decided to begin such a school, and a teacher was sent out, who began the work with about thirty pupils. In June I went to Morinda to spend a short time and to look after the school. I felt encouraged by what I saw. Although the number of pupils was not as large as it had been, owing to the baptism of a man and his wife, belonging to the Ramdasi community, the interest in the school seemed to be maintained in the minds of many. There were several persons in town, who appeared to be sincere inquirers. I spent about two weeks there.

"In November I went out again with my wife and spent seventeen days at Khamanon, a village of good size about seven miles from Morinda. The people were all Sikh landlords, who showed the utmost friendliness. From this point I daily visited the neighboring villages within a distance of two or three miles and was generally well received.

"In the village of Samrala, I went one morning to preach in front of a little shop. While thus engaged, a Hindu cloth merchant stopped and listened to what I was saying, and presently at my request sat down. He told me he had copies of

[9] A sect of the Sikhs, followers of a Guru named Ram Das, and of a low caste, chamars tanners and weavers.

the New Testament and the Ten Commandments. On my asking him some questions, he told me to follow him to his part of the village, where he could converse with more freedom. I did so, and on the road he said he believed in Christ, but did not wish to talk of these things before the people who were present where we had been sitting. He took me to a shop on the other side of the village, where we sat down and had some further conversation. He presently sent for a Brahmin, who, he said, also believed, and who had in fact led him to accept Christ. He said that he and this Brahmin and two or three others, including the man in whose shop we were sitting, were in the habit of listening to the reading of Christian books. I talked also to the Brahmin and tried to show him that it was his duty to receive baptism and confess his faith publicly. He said he believed in Christ, but could not see the necessity of being baptized. God cares not, he urged, for what is external, but only for what is in the heart. So long as we have the right faith, where is the use of baptism."

This experience of Mr. Newton might be duplicated by almost every village preacher. Sometimes it is a solitary man, who, living in his own house, reads a portion of the scripture, which he jealously conceals. In other places there are a few men, who even openly confess themselves believers, but who do not break their caste and so are not disturbed by their relatives until by and by conscience drives them to confess their faith in baptism, when they are confronted with the loss of all things for Christ's sake.

It was in Rawul Pindi that an old man came to the missionary, led by a little girl, for he was blind. He told a pathetic story of how he had stopped at the door of the school in the cantonment, a school in the bazar, to listen to the bible teacher, when he taught his classes. He had come to believe in the Saviour of whom the bible teacher spoke, but blind and poor as he was, he hesitated to ask for baptism. But now he had come to ask the missionary to baptize him. "Last night," he said, "I was awaked in my dream by a voice calling and urging me to flee for safety. I awoke to see flames leaping up about my bed and heard the voice saying, 'Why sleep amid the flames! Rise! fly!' I then awoke from from sleep to find it was only a dream.

But soon I slept again and the dream was repeated, and again I awoke, trembling with fear. Missionary, I know what this dream means for me. I am an old man, my legs are dangling in the grave and I have been disobedient to my Saviour. I wish now to confess him publicly in baptism." The following Sabbath, the old blind man witnessed a good confession and his name was entered upon the roll of the church.

A week passed and the old man did not appear in the church. The elders sought him out and found him lying helpless in the veranda of an old house because the people would not allow the little girl to lead him about. His daughter refused to cook for him, and his stalwart sons would not help him! The elders arranged for him temporarily and persuaded the daughter to care for him, giving a small monthly allowance for his support that he might not go about begging. He was a true believer and daily urged his relatives to give up idolatry and to become followers of Christ. He was the first of his caste to be baptized in Rawul Pindi, but soon after a number were baptized and the movement extended to relatives in other parts of the province.

The writer of these annals was once called up at midnight in Lodiana to baptize a Hindu girl of seventeen years, who lay dying in the Mission hospital. On arrival I was introduced to her father, who proved to be a pupil of mine many years before in Rawul Pindi. I was glad to see him again and asked him if he was willing his daughter should be baptized. He said, "Yes, I am because she wishes it. The fact is we are all Christians. We have not been baptized, but we confess ourselves believers. We read the Bible daily."

I then questioned the daughter as to her knowledge and faith in Christ. She said she had been taught by the ladies for years. Her replies to my questions were clear and her confession of her faith and experience was most satisfactory. Her mother, father and a sister besides the hospital staff were present at the baptism. After the baptism, the girl asked me some questions as to what she should eat and wear, and whether she might take part in the marriage customs connected with her sister's wedding. Poor girl, she was far gone in consumption and only lived a few days when she was called to meet her Lord and Saviour.

Many incidents of a like character might be given, but these illustrate how the seed sown often brings forth fruit years after it has been sown. Many a soul enters into the kingdom who is unknown to the worker who brought it into saving relation to the Saviour of men.

The first half century of missionary work, as conducted by the Presbyterian church in India, bore comparatively little fruit in the villages. The work of education was as yet almost entirely limited to the large cities occupied as Mission Stations. From these centers the work of evangelization, as we have seen, was carried on by long tours in the village localities, made by the missionaries and their native assistants. In a few of the larger villages, Indian evangelists were located permanently, who, following the example of the missionaries, would travel among the villages in their circuit. All of these itinerant missionaries and workers were well supplied with scriptures and tracts in the vernacular languages, which they distributed by sale and gift. Medicine was also given out to many suffering from the more ordinary ailments, malarial fever, diarrhoea, dysentery, &c.

During the famines, many missionaries took charge of relief centers or camps, and supervised the distribution of food to the starving, or the payment of money to the refugees employed on public works.

In many places they gathered together children, whose parents had died or deserted them. After the famines were past, every effort was made to return such children to their parents if they could be found. For those left homeless, the orphanages provided for bodily wants, and, as soon as they were old enough, they were taught in the schools for boys and girls.

Previous to the year 1881, but few converts dwelt in their native villages, excepting those living in Ghorawaha and Morinda. Such converts were ostracized from their homes and found a refuge in the Mission compound. Thus sprung up the native Christian villages as a sort of suburb near to the Mission compound. By this arrangement, such converts were trained and many of them became preachers, teachers, colporteurs, assistants in hospitals and dispensaries, compositors in printing presses, book-binders, bible women and domestic servants. Comparatively few Christians were as yet engaged in Government employ. A few were employed as carpenters, shoemakers, weavers and other forms of handicraft.

CHAPTER XXIV.

Two New Religious Sects

1. The Kuka Sect

AS early as 1863, mention had been made in the Lodiana Mission Report of a new sect of Sikhs. The founder of this sect was a carpenter, Ram Singh by name, who lived in a small village near Lodiana called Bhaini, but who also had a shop in the city near the Mission church. It is said he was often seen in the church during preaching services. He was a man of little learning, beyond his ability to read and write the sacred character of his religion, the Gurmukhi.

By and by he closed his shop and set up as a religious teacher (Guru) in his native village. He laid hold of a prophecy in one of the sacred books of the Sikhs, to the effect that a new incarnation of the Deity should arise in the east at a place called Sambal Muradabad, who should bring deliverance. Crowds began to flock to his village, numbering thousands. Questioned as to the ground of their faith, they would mention old predictions recorded in their sacred books. New prophecies were invented. The fact that these prophecies were baseless, or that they were full of contradictions counted for little. The disciples had no mind to examine into the merits of such claims. The peculiarity of the sect was that they were heard to utter groans frequently, and so the name was given them as Kukas, or Groaners.

The movement professed to be religious, but it was more of a political character. The disciples were taught a kind of military drill, which was practiced at Bhaini until they began to be suspected to be a political party. They then became reticent and suspicious of all inquiry as to their faith and practice. They desired to have people believe there was nothing peculiar in the new sect. Nevertheless the Kukas were busy making disciples for their Guru. They were known by their head dress, which was the ordinary Sikh turban worn at a different angle, something like a felt hat sitting crosswise on the head.

The attitude of the Kukas toward the gospel was antagonistic, as their attitude toward the English Government was distinctly unfriendly. Christianity is the faith of the conquerers of their country.

Little mention is made of the Kukas in the Mission reports, but in the report for 1867, we find a brief note. The Christian preachers, as usual, visited the Anandpur Mela. They reported that "Although disturbances were expected on account of the new sect, the Kukas, our native brethren were permitted to labour among the people while the mela lasted."

The Kukas seem to have become a reform sect and therefore more interested in their own co-religionists than in opposing the work of Christians. The statement of the Rev. K. C. Chatterji, in his report for 1870, would lead us to believe they had much sympathy with the teaching of the missionaries. He said that "In almost all our discussions, we had the sympathy and support of the Kukas, against other sects of the Sikhs, who held many doctrines analogous to those of Christianity." It may be that Guru Ram Singh[1] had accepted some of the lessons he heard in the Mission church near by his shop in Lodiana. It is certain that he sought to reform Sikhism and to restore it to its original character as a pure monotheism, free from idolatry and caste. Unfortunately he did not try to free it from the militant spirit of Guru Gobind Singh. His folowers carried the almost universal *lathi,* a bamboo stick, six feet in length and often bound with iron or brass. The drill which was practiced somewhat surreptitiously suggests a militant spirit. When crowds of these men gathered at the melas the police watched them with some solicitude.

In the year 1871, a band of these fanatics assaulted a petty

[1] The title of the Kuka reformer.

sardar (nobleman) wounding some of his servants and taking with them his guns and horses. Pushing on to another town they robbed and killed a nobleman and one or two of his servants, carrying away his guns and horses. The marauders added to their numbers, as they went, until several hundred men, partially armed, proposed to attack the Rajah of Patiala. Their plan was to proceed to Ambala, after they had captured Patiala, with his arms and munitions, to attack the English troops.

They were now in open rebellion, crying "Khalsa raj Karega": *the Sikh regimé shall rule!* The news of this rising had reached the Deputy Commissioner at Lodiana and also the Rajah of Patiala. Gathering together the Lodiana police and the Rajah's forces, the Deputy Commissioner attacked the Kuka mob and took some 300 prisoners. Believing these to be but a part of a rebel army, the Deputy Commissioner blew away from a cannon's mouth about forty men. The following day, the Commissioner came from Ambala and, after further investigation, caused sixteen more to be blown away.

These transactions occurred within the territory of the Patiala state, accounting for the rapid course of justice. The sentences were made by the Rajah himself, but with the approval of the English deputy commissioner.[2]

This retribution was terrible; but the Sepoy mutiny was still fresh in memory and men remembered its brutal tragedies. The government of India disapproved of the act of the Deputy Commissioner and dismissed him from this office.[3]

The Kuka rebellion was suppressed. Ram Singh the Guru and some of his principal followers were deported to Rangoon in Burmah, where they remained during their lifetime. The Rajah of Patiala refused to allow the Kukas to hold any public meetings within his territory, nor could more than five persons assemble at any one time for any sort of meeting.

---

[2] At this time the Patiala Rajah had not power of life and death over his subjects; but had to receive sanction from the Commissioner at Ambala.

[3] This officer had assumed the prerogatives of his superior officer and for this reason he was dismissed from office. The Commissioner was within his power.

This rising caused great anxiety in Lodiana, because it had been reported that the city was to be attacked. The police patrolled the streets night and day. The missionaries were all away from home. The ladies were alone. For their protection, the police set a special guard.

No further trouble came from the attempt of the Kukas to expel the English and restore the Khalsa Raj. The following cold season one of the Indian preachers reported his reception in a Kuka village:

"While preaching in a village near Maler-Kotla, a numbardar[4] of a Kuka village accompanied by several men came and listened attentively to the preaching. After the discourse was concluded he brought oxen and men to remove the tent, and that same night almost forcibly constrained the preacher to go with them to their village. Arriving there, they assembled the people to hear the Gospel preached, and during the discourse the numbardar broke his *mala* (rosary) and declared that he was no longer a Kuka, but determined to be a follower of Jesus, and also urged the villagers to do the same. They constrained the preacher to remain with them two days."

The Kukas still exist as a small sect of the Sikhs, having a shrine at Bhaini in memory of Guru Ram Singh. So long as he lived as a state prisoner in Rangoon, he was visited from time to time by devoted followers, who would bring back letters of counsel and encouragement to sundry members of his cult. These were usually captured and read by the police. Nothing was found to incriminate them, wherefore the letters were returned. Whatever ambition there had been in the mind of Ram Singh to pose as a political leader seems to have died out and the aged Guru was satisfied to become a martyr to his faith. In 1874, the Rev. A. Rudolph of Lodiana made a tour in company with his Indian assistants, passing through the region in which the Kuka disturbances had occurred. He found that the people generally deprecated the outrage, and that most of those who

[4] A *numbardar* is a chief of a village and chairman of the village Board or Panchayat.

had been members of the Kuka sect now disclaimed all connection with it, and the few that still adhered showed no ill will towards the preachers. In the town where the Kuka rebels had been arrested, Mr. Rudolph met with much kindness. On one occasion, a Kuka family, which had lost several members in the outbreak, constrained the Indian preachers to stay and receive a meal at their hands. "The impression that Mr. Rudolph received was that those sad occurrences two years previously had no permanent effect in casting new obstacles in the way of propagating the Gospel."[5]

2. THE SAT SANGI SECT took its rise about the same time as that of the Kukas. The founder was one Hakim Singh a shopkeeper in the village of Rampur in the Patiala state. He had a friend in a neighboring village, a contractor on the Sirhind Canal, who was taken ill with a fatal disease. Some time before his death, he called for Hakim Singh and told him he was about to die and that he was dying in the faith of Jesus Christ, whom he believed to be none other than the *Nishkalank Autar,* the sinless incarnation of the Deity, who was foretold in some of the sacred books of the Sikhs. He then produced a book from beneath his pillow, called the *Upadeshpatri* (the *Instructor*) published in the sacred character at the mission press in Lodiana. This book was a popular work in poetry, treating of the duty of men to their rulers and of homage to God. It told of sin and the way of salvation, closing with an account of the second coming of Christ on earth to judge the world.

"Take this book," said the dying man, "and have it read to you, and if you want to learn more about this Incarnation of God, inquire of the missionaries at Lodiana."

Hakim Singh took the book and had it read to him. He then procured a New Testament and had that also read to him. He then distributed the grain in his shop among the poor in his village and made over his farm to his son and gave himself up to the life of a Guru. He began to gather about him disciples

[5] *Lodiana Mission Report,* 1874, pp. 4, 5.

to whom he taught the faith of Jesus, the sinless Incarnation of God, who was soon to come to judge the world. Not till sometime early in 1871, did the missionaries receive any knowledge of this man or of his sect. Early one morning a tall Sikh and his son, a lad of ten or twelve years, came to the house of the superintendent of the Press. They said they had been sent from Rampur by their Guru, Hakim Singh, to get some copies of the New Testament in the sacred character, Gurmukhi, and also some copies of the "Instructor." They moreover had money wherewith to pay for the books.

On inquiry as to what they wished to do with the books, they said there were many disciples of Hakim Singh, and that those who came in from distant villages were given a copy of the New Testament for use in that village, where the people would come together to hear the book read.

A few days later, two men came for more books. They had been instructed to stop with the Christians and to eat whatever was set before them. This they did. The next day, before leaving, they invited the missionary to visit them in their village.

A few weeks later, the Rev. John Newton, M.D. of Subathu, and Rev. E. M. Wherry of Lodiana, paid a visit to Rampur. They found that Hakim Singh had already secured the recognition of the village, where everyone called him the "Sant" or Saint. The following account of this visit was given at the time:

"We were led through the narrow lanes of the village, comprising some 5,000 inhabitants, until we reached an adobe building, one story high, with a courtyard, about twenty-five yards square. Entering through a strong wooden doorway, we passed through a long stable into the courtyard. On the right hand were the living rooms of the family. On the left was a commodious veranda with a platform two feet above the ground, where the Guru or Saint sat upon a bedstead. He was almost naked. A hooka or Indian pipe with a long stem stood near by. In front of him men and a few women sat crowded together, reverently listening to the reading of the 24th, 25th and 26th chapters of the Gospel of St. Matthew. The reader was a boy about fifteen years of age, who read very fluently. Every few minutes the Guru would ejaculate wildly, 'Yes, Yes! He is coming. Did you not see the stars falling last night? Hip, Hip, Sh-h-h-huh!' With this the Saint underwent strong contortions, causing his entrails to twist and move as if they were living creatures trying to escape! Then another ejaculation of 'Hip—Hip—Sh-h-h-huh'!"

The people prostrated themselves with murmurings. The reading went on until the chapters were ended. It was a strange sight. Closer observation showed us that the great majority of the devotees were Sikhs, many of them gray headed; a few were Hindus, one or two Brahmins and some men of low caste. There was evidently great enthusiasm among the hearers. The courtyard was jammed full.

After the service was over, we greeted the Guru and were received very kindly and given seats near by. We were asked to speak, which we did, emphasizing the atoning work which Christ wrought through his suffering and death on the cross.

We spent a week in this village preaching every day there and in nearby villages. The people listened to us respectfully but some of them said; "Yes, but he has come already!" On enquiry we learned that many believed that the Saint, inside the four walls of his own house was a reincarnation of Jesus Christ! They expressed themselves as confident that he would soon come forth from his seclusion and manifest his Divine power and authority. In regard to his teaching, we learned that he antagonized caste among his followers; that he refused to allow offerings to be made to the spirits of the dead and that he refused to allow the ashes of the dead to be carried to the Ganges river. These reforms were all to conform his disciples to Christian custom.

* * * * * * *

A year later when next we visited Rampur, a great change had come over the new community. The Kuka rising had brought the Sat Sangis under suspicion. The police had interviewed the Sant and some of his followers. They satisfied themselves that the *Sant* had no political ambition. Nevertheless the law prohibiting assemblies of more than five people at a time tended to greatly lessen the enthusiasm of the people.

When the missionary at a meeting in private alone with the Guru reproached him for allowing his followers to think he was Christ, he said he had never taught such a doctrine, but when he learned that some of the people had such a belief, he winked at it for the time being, expecting to correct their faith. For the present he said he could not antagonize the error without losing his followers. We had reason to believe he did correct the error, explaining that he was sent to prepare the people for the coming one.

The missionaries tried to get him to permit his disciples to be baptized and so openly to profess themselves to be followers of Christ. To this he replied that spiritual baptism was sufficient and that water baptism was not needed.

It became clear to us that the Sant did not wish to cut loose entirely from the Indian community, although he uniformly treated Christians with deference. He encouraged his followers to observe worship on the Lord's day. The manner of worship was a simple reading of a portion of the gospel, all sitting in a circle. Then after meditation all prostrated themselves with their hands extended, palms upward. This was to signify their expectation that they would receive the blessings they asked in prayer. The disciples usually made offerings to the Sant whenever they visited him.

After his death, the disciples for awhile seemed to regard the place where he had sat as sacred, but did not erect any temple there. Some of the Sat Sangis occasionally call on the missionaries. A few of them declared themselves Christians. Some who lived in the Nabha state were persecuted as Christians and were obliged to either leave the state or re-enter the fold of the Sikh faith.

The hope of the missionaries was not realized, but important results can be traced to the teaching of Hakim Singh, Guru and Saint. Among these were the following:

1. The name of Jesus was widely proclaimed as the Sinless Incarnation of God and the Saviour of sinful men. Many members of the "True Companionship" (Sat sangi) died in the hope of salvation through Jesus Christ.

2. A school established in Rampur, was taught for nineteen years by one of the readers of the Sant. Two young men taught in that school confessed their faith as Christians. Both of these were poisoned, one of whom died, the other, the now famous Sadhu Sundar Singh, evangelist, recovered and still lives to proclaim the gospel in many principal cities of India and in regions abroad; in India and in foreign lands.

3. The witnessing of other members of this community has no doubt done much to publish the gospel in the Sikh states of Patiala and Nabha and in the Montgomery district, whither many of this sect emigrated.

"The fact of this movement is interesting, as it shows the secret power of the Gospel working out the destruction of old ideas and institutions in the country. People are fond of speaking of the rise of reformatory sects among the Hindus as the result of English education of a secular kind. Here we have a case of a like reformatory sect in a Rajah's territory, where few could speak or read a word of English, showing that it is due entirely to the power of the word of God read and heard in the vernacular[6] language of the people."

[6] *Lodiana Mission Report*, 1870-1871, p. 9.

CHAPTER XXV.

Church Organization

THE primary purpose of missionary work is the propagation of the gospel of Jesus Christ. This postulates the organization of churches wherever companies of believers may be found.

The first baptism in the Lodiana Mission took place in 1837. The first church session was established at about the same time, and the first church of Lodiana was organized, consisting of five members; the wives of the missionaries and three Indian Christians.[1]

In a similar manner churches were organized at Subathu, Ambala, Jalandhar, Lahore, Rawul Pindi, Allahabad, Fattehgarh, Fattehpur, Mainpuri, Agra, Etawah, Hoshyarpur and Firozpur. As soon as possible such organizations were completed by the ordination of ruling elders and deacons. The missionaries performed the pastoral duties, until such time as made possible the installment of Indian pastors. Church buildings were usually built at the expense of the Missions; one at each station. In some stations the main hall of the schoolhouse was used for divine services on the Lord's day.

The next stage in the development of the visible church was the organization of the Presbytery, whereby a number of churches were united to promote the highest interest of each by the strengthening of the spiritual life, by the orderly discipline of the members and the ministry, and the furthering of the work of evangelization.

The first Presbyteries consisted of the missionaries at the stations, but as soon as Indian ministers and elders were ordained, they became members of Presbytery.

[1] These first converts were Messrs. Goloknath, J. B. Lewis and William Basten.

Our Missions in India

In the year 1841, the General Assembly, in the United States of America, adopted a resolution recognizing the three Presbyteries of Lodiana, Allahabad and Farrukhabad, and also constituted them, "The Synod of Northern India." The first meeting of this Synod was held at Fattehgarh in 1845.

In the year 1868, the Presbytery of Lodiana was divided so as to form two Presbyteries. The dividing line was the Sutlej river. The new Presbytery was called the Presbytery of Lahore, to which was added the district of Firozp. To the four Presbyteries in Northern India was added the Presbytery of Kolhapur in the year 1872, at which time the old and new school Presbyterian churches were reunited in America.

The name of the Synod was then changed by dropping the word "Northern" making it *The Synod of India.*

In the original constitution of the Lodiana Mission there were several members of the Reformed Presbyterian Church of America, who were affiliated with the Mission, occupying the separate stations of Saharanpur, Dehra and Rurki. In 1841, the Reformed Presbyterian missionaries organized the Saharanpur Presbytery, but in 1884, all the members of this Presbytery united with the Presbytery of Lodiana, excepting two ministers and one elder, who perpetuated the Saharanpur Presbytery.

At the meeting of the Synod of India, December 8th, 1884, the membership was as follows, indicating the growth of the church during the first half century of its existence:

ALLAHABAD PRESBYTERY:

Rev. W. F. Johnson, Rev. Thomas Tracy, Rev. J. F. Holcomb, Rev. J. J. Caleb, Rev. J. C. R. Ewing, Rev. E. Nabi Bakhsh, *Ministers;* Malcolm Lewis and Daya Ran, *Elders.*

FARRUKHABAD PRESBYTERY:

Rev. J. S. Woodside, Rev. J. J. Lucas, Rev. G. A. Seeley, Rev. Mohun Lal, Rev. G. W. Pollock, Rev. Rajaram Chitambar, Rev. J. M. Alexander, *Ministers;* J. F. Houston, T. Scott, Baldeo Parshad, Sukh Pal and Dharm Singh, *Elders.*

LAHORE PRESBYTERY:

Rev. John Newton, Rev. C. W. Forman, Rev. J. F. Ullmann,

Rev. Goloknath, Rev. K. C. Chatterji, Rev. B. D. Wyckoff, Rev. F. J. Newton, Rev. P. C. Uppal, Rev. J. C. Bose, Rev. Abdullah, Rev. R. Morrison, Rev. Isa Charan, *Ministers;* David Abdullah, R. C. Das and Gamu Shah, *Elders.*

LODIANA PRESBYTERY:

Rev. A. Rudolph, Rev. E. M. Wherry, Rev. J. B. Dales, Rev. W. Basten, Rev. Matthias, Rev. Ahmad Shah, Rev. J. M. McComb, Rev. H. C. Velte, Rev. Sundar Lal, Rev. W. J. P. Morrison, Rev. A. P. Kelso, Rev. R. Thackwell, Rev. C. B. Newton, Rev. G. McMaster, Rev. T. W. J. Wylie, Rev. Kanwar Sain, Rev. M. M. Carleton, and Rev. E. P. Newton, *Ministers;* R. K. Bannerji, Jaimal Singh, Joseph Kerr and K. B. Sircar, *Elders.*

KOLHAPUR PRESBYTERY:

Rev. R. G. Wilder, Rev. G. W. Seiler, Rev. J. M. Goheen, Rev. G. H. Ferris, and Rev. L. B. Tedford, *Ministers.*

This Synod was on the same footing as those of the home Synods, so that cases appealable to the General Assembly in America might be carried up through the Synod of India. After two or more such appeals had been considered by the Assembly, it was decided to make the Synod of India the final court of appeal for all Indian members. It was in fact almost impossible for the General Assembly, or even a Judicial Commission to properly adjudicate such cases in America.

Not only so, but the personal presence of an appellant obliged an expense too heavy to be borne by him. Moreover such cases were likely to create unpleasant relations between the Indian and foreign members of the church.

The Synod did much to secure regularity and uniformity of procedure, carefulness in keeping the records of business, and promptness in carrying out the program of Presbyterial business.

When the Presbyteries grew in strength and the Indian membership became equal in number, and sometimes greater in number than the American membership, much dissatisfaction grew up in the church. As an Indian democracy, the inequality between American and Indian members was too clear to escape observation. Two proposals were made to solve the problem.

One proposal was to sever the Presbyterial relation of the foreign missionaries from the Indian Presbyteries, and so make the latter entirely independent, foreign missionaries being permitted to sit as consultative members.

The second proposal was that foreign missionaries be allowed to unite with the Indian and American churches, having full powers as ministers in the courts of the Indian church and yet retain full connection with their home presbyteries and be amenable to them in case of discipline.

Neither of these proposals was practicable. To eliminate the foreign missionaries from the Indian Presbyteries would practically dissolve most of the Church sessions and many of the Presbyteries. In some of the Presbyteries, there were as yet no Indian pastors. In any case the sessions and presbyteries would be too weak to do effective work. To be sure the foreign missionaries might sit as corresponding or consultative members, but such a plan would certainly become irksome to both Indian and foreign constituents. The second proposal was condemned by the fact of its being contrary to presbyterial law and usage to permit a minister to belong to two presbyteries at the same time.

One other plan was possible, but for the time being was held to be inexpedient. This was that foreign missionaries be permitted to withdraw from their home presbyteries and to unite with their Indian brethren to form an independent Indian church. This plan involved the separation of the Synod of India from the parent church in America. This plan eventually had realization, when many Presbyterian denominations united to form the Presbyterian church in India.

In the meanwhile, the Synod of India continued as a Synod of the General Assembly of the Presbyterian church in the United States of America. It achieved the translation into the Hindustani language of the *Confession of Faith,* the *Form of Church Government,* the *Westminster Larger and Shorter Catechisms,* including the *Apostles' Creed.* To these was added a hymn book, compiled by a special committee, which has run through several editions.

The question as to the reopening of the theological seminary within the bounds of the Synod was brought before the Synod at its meeting held in Saharanpur in 1883. Eight years had elapsed since the closing of the seminary in Allahabad. A committee of three, consisting of the Rev. K. C. Chatterji, Rev. J. J. Lucas and Elder Malcolm Lewis, was appointed to consider and report upon this matter. They were to report specially as to the probable number of students available, the best place in which to establish the school and to discover some way of providing for its support. As the outcome of this committee's work and the deliberation of the Synod, it was resolved to establish the theological seminary at Saharanpur. A board of directors was appointed, consisting of two members from each presbytery, ten in all, with instruction to take all necessary steps for the inauguration of the seminary. The Rev. E. M. Wherry and the Rev. J. C. R. Ewing were appointed professors. Suitable buildings were erected for the accommodation of the students, with class rooms, both for the students admitted to the regular course of theological study and also for a preparatory class with a course of study covering two years.

Early in the next year the seminary was formally opened. The ambition of the new regime was to present to the students a course of study such as would make them fit for the pastorate and evangelistic work of the Indian church. Special stress was laid on the spiritual life. Close attention was given to Bible study. Theology was made a systematic study of the doctrinal teaching of the sacred scriptures. Church history and also secular history, in so far as it touched upon the history of the Bible, were taught, so as to enable the Indian student to understand the historic setting of scripture narrative. Regular evangelistic work was carried on at stated periods in city and village in order to make the work of the seminary practical.

One great difficulty in the work of teaching was the want of suitable text books in the Urdu language. This obliged teaching by lectures, or at least the outlines of lectures, to be written out slowly by men unaccustomed to taking notes in a lecture hall. This also led the professors to write text books, most of which are still used in this and other theological seminaries. Among these were a *Greek Urdu Lexicon* of the Greek Testament, by Rev. J. C. R. Ewing, D. D. an *Outline of Ancient History,* and a *Manual of Islam,* and a *Compend of Church History,* written by Rev. E. M. Wherry, D. D. Along the same line, text books on *Genesis* and *Exodus* and *Commentaries on Leviticus* and the *Epistles of Paul to the Corinthians* were written by Rev. J. J. Lucas, D. D. An *exegetical commentary* on the *Acts of the Apostles* was written by Professor B. B. Roy. The same author has written excellent booklets on the teachings of various phases of Hindu thought and life. Rev. H. C. Velte, D. D., has contributed two valuable works on *Biblical Introduction;* and Rev. Dr. W. F. Johnson has given the Indian Church a profound work on *Systematic Theology,* along with *Commentaries on the Minor Prophets.* This literary work has contributed much to further the cause of theological training and has also added much to the volume of religious literature, suited not only to the needs of the ministry but also for the general reader.

The Saharanpur theological seminary has continued to send out a number of men annually, who have entered the service of the church as evangelists and pastors. Some of these have distinguished themselves as pastors and superintendents of home missions. Not a few have been successful as authors and translators. In almost all of our Presbyteries they outnumber the foreign missionaries and are nearly always a majority on important committees. There is no institution within the bounds of the Missions which ministers so much to the advancement of the church.

An important annex to the seminary is the training school for the wives of the students, founded by Mrs. Wherry and Mrs. Ewing. The purpose of this school is to teach the wives of those, who are being trained for village work, so that they may be worthy helpmeets, capable of promoting the work of evangelism among the village women, who are almost entirely illiterate. This school has been continued through the years gone by and is still a very important institution. It has always been conducted by the wives of the professors, aided by Indian and American ladies. Along with it is a school for the children of the married students.

Through the beneficence of two consecrated laymen in America[2] the Taylor Memorial and the Severance hall have been built, providing commodious classrooms for both men and women and a library for the seminary.

The advance of English education in India has made it possible for young men to receive their theological education in English. Several men have received training for the highest places in the Indian church.

[2] Mrs. Livingstone Taylor of Cleveland, Ohio, and Mr. Louis Severance of New York City.

CHAPTER XXVI.

Evolution of a United Church

EARLY in the history of organized Presbyterianism in India, the thought of uniting the many denominations of Presbyterian name began to move the leading men to consider the question of bringing these bodies together so as to form a single Presbyterian organization.

"The subject of a closer union of Presbyterian churches in India was first brought prominently forward in 1863 by a pamphlet written by Mr. J. T. Maclagan, an elder of the Church of Scotland and later Secretary of the Foreign Mission Committee of that Church. The matter was taken up definitely by American Presbyterians at the triennial meeting of the Synod of North India in 1865. A Committee was appointed to correspond with different Presbyterian bodies in India to ascertain their thought on this subject. This Committee—Messrs. John H. Morrison, J. J. Walsh and James L. Scott—reported to the next Synod meeting held in Saharanpur in 1868 that the proposal for a closer union among Presbyterians had been cordially approved, but that several of those who replied to the circular saw many practical difficulties in the way. The Synod reappointed the Committee, except that instead of Rev. James L. Scott, gone on furlough, Rev. Samuel H. Kellogg, D.D. was named."

This committee issued a new circular, addressing the representatives of the various Presbyterian churches in India, asking them to secure from their Presbyteries the appointment of one representative from each Presbytery "to continue this correspondence and endeavour to induce other bodies of Presbyterians to appoint similar Committees to confer either by letter, or to arrange a meeting among themselves for conference, as to what are the practical difficulties in the way of a United Presbyterian General Assembly for India, how those difficulties may be overcome, and on what terms such union could be accomplished."[1] It was understood that the results of this correspondence would not commit the bodies represented to any action. Each Presbytery was asked to say whether it approved of a special general conference for a fuller discussion of the question of union.

After further correspondence a conference was called to meet at Allahabad on the 5th January, 1871.

This conference met in the Katra Church, Allahabad, at 12 o'clock on the day appointed and continued in session for two days. The discussion was in general on the following two points:

1. The means to be employed to secure definite opinion of the different churches as to the advisability of forming a general organization for the Presbyterian Church in India.
2. In the event of this general organization for the Presbyterian church in India, being formed, what would be its relationship to the Mission Boards of the different Home Churches?

The Rev. Dr. J. H. Morrison presided at all the sessions of this conference. When the scheme had been approved by the conference, the Moderator was asked "to prepare a minute, setting forth the scheme to be presented to the different Presbyterian organizations in India, which would embody the views of this conference on the proposed general organization of the Presbyterian Church in India." The moderator, Dr. Morrison, drew up a formal statement as to the plan for a general Presbyterian organization for India, particularly emphasizing the benefits it would bestow upon the Indian people. He said,

"The effect of such an organization would be, that all the advantages, derived by our Home Churches from their General Assemblies, and of which we are practically in a great measure deprived by reason of our distance from them, would be enjoyed by Presbyterian Churches in India through their own General Assembly."[2]

[1] *Presbyterian Union*, p. 9.
[2] *Presbyterian Union*, p. 18.

The conference appointed a committee of correspondence as follows:—Rev. Dr. J. H. Morrison, Rev. J. J. Walsh, Dr. Valentine, Rev. Dr. Murray Mitchel and Rev. J. Williamson.

The conference adjourned to meet again in Allahabad on November 16, 1871, at the time of the meeting of the Synod of India (the name of the Synod having been changed by the General Assembly of the Presbyterian Church, U. S. A.).

The conference again met in Allahabad according to the adjournment. Besides the members of the Synod of India who were present, representatives of the Church of Scotland, the United Presbyterian Church of Scotland, the Free Church of Scotland, and the Irish Presbyterian Church were present. Rev. Dr. Murray Mitchell was elected chairman.

The question of Union was again discussed and the following resolutions passed:

"1. That, while the Conference is fully convinced of the exceeding desirableness of a corporation union embracing all Presbyterians in India, it yet sees certain practical difficulties in the way of its immediate accomplishment.

"2. That for the present and with a view to the realization of this union in due time, the conference recommended that a general convention of Presbyterian ministers and elders be held from time to time, as may hereafter be determined, for the purpose of consultation and cooperation in all that pertains to the extension of the Kingdom of Christ in India; and that, as a means of securing this object, a meeting of ministers and elders be held at the time and place of the proposed General Missionary Conference for all India.

"3. The Conference is fully persuaded that a corporate union of those who hold the same principles of Church government would not retard, but would really hasten the coming of the blessed day when over the whole earth there shall visibly be one fold under one shepherd."[3]

At the time appointed (December 30, 1873) forty-two members of the All-India Conference of Missions meeting in Allahabad came together to consider the matter of the union of

[3] *Presbyterian Union*, pp. 21-22.

Presbyterian bodies in India. The Rev. Dr. Wilson of Bombay was elected chairman. After much discussion, it became evident that the way was not yet open to realize the ideal of one Presbyterian church of India. The Americans were ready. Their church organization was more complete than that of any other Presbyterian church in India. Not one of the Scotch churches had cared for a Synod. Very few of their churches had native pastors, and the number of ministers was so small that without European membership even a Presbytery was impossible of realization. Union of some kind was believed to be exceedingly important and every conference insisted upon persistent effort to further the eventual organic union of the churches. To this end the Allahabad conference of 1872 passed the following resolutions:

"1. That in the present circumstances of the several Presbyterian bodies here represented, it is most desirable, that, without reference to any organic union, they should be as speedily as possible consociated together for consultation and cooperation in furtherance of the common work in which they are engaged in this great Gentile country, such a consociation being declarative of the agreement which existed between the different Presbyterian Churches in India.

"2. That the Committees and Boards in Europe and America, who are represented in India, by these Presbyterian bodies, be informed of the opinion of said bodies with reference to the formation of a Presbyterian consociation, which shall in no degree compromise the position which these bodies at present occupy in connection with their respective Churches and Church Courts."

"3. "That for the purpose of formally founding the proposed consociation, a meeting to be convened by the Rev. J. H. Morrison, D.D. shall be held at Allahabad next cold season at which representatives of the different Presbyteries and Classes of India shall be invited to attend."[4]

As authorized by this resolution, Dr. Morrison named November 26, 1873 as the date for the next conference. At this

[4] *Presbyterian Union*, p. 24.

conference the idea of organic union of Presbyterian churches in India was practically abandoned as impracticable, at least for the present. Although the way towards organic union of Presbyterian churches in India seemed to be closed for awhile at least, the appointment of a committee to correspond with the home assemblies and Boards of Foreign Missions, in regard to a confederation of churches, gave assurance that the ideal of a united Presbyterianism had not been given up. The meeting of the convention of the confederation according to the arrangement made at the conference held in Allahabad in November, 1873, was called to meet in Allahabad on the 4th Thursday of December, 1875. The Rev. Dr. Morrison, chairman, and the Rev. J. Williamson, secretary of the conference of 1873, were asked to serve in the same offices for the conference on Presbyterian Alliance. The members delegated to attend this meeting were:

"The Rev. Messrs. J. H. Morrison, E. M. Wherry, S. H. Kellogg, A. Brodhead, J. F. Holcomb, F. Heyl and J. J. Caleb, ministers; and Munshi Paul, Ruling Elder of the American Presbyterian Church; the Rev. T. W. J. Wylie of the Reformed Presbyterian Church of America; Rev. J. Williamson, minister, and Messrs. R. Simson, A. Anthony, and J. Clark, Ruling Elders, of the Church of Scotland; Rev. W. Stevenson, of the Free Church of Scotland; Rev. W. Martin, and Dr. Sommerville, of the U. P. Church of Scotland; Dr. J. Scudder, of the Reformed Church in America."[5]

The secretary having read the deliverance of the General Assembly of the Church of Scotland, members of the Free Church of Scotland and of the U. P. Church of Scotland made verbal statements, showing the agreement of their churches with the proposed confederation. Dr. Morrison reported the action of the General Assembly of the American Presbyterian Church; and Dr. John Scudder reported the action of the Reformed Church of America. All these churches commended the plan of a Federate Union, but enjoined their representatives to do noth-

[5] *Proceedings of the Conference on Presbyterian Alliance.*

ing affecting the authority of their churches in the homeland, without first presenting the proposals to them for approval. After full discussion the following action, in agreement with the sentiments of the home churches, was adopted.

1. That the name of the proposed Presbyterian organization should be the "Presbyterian Alliance of India."

2. That the Churches, which hold the word of God as contained in the scriptures of the Old and New Testaments, to be the only Rule of Faith and Practice, and whose system of doctrine and general principles of Church polity are common to the standards of the Presbyterian Churches in Europe and America, be eligible as members of the Alliance.

3. That the Alliance should meet in council ordinarily once in three years.

4. That the Council shall consist of delegates appointed by the Ecclesiastical bodies forming the Alliance, the ratio of representation to be one Minister and one Ruling Elder for every six members of Presbytery or body corresponding thereto, it being understood, that when a Presbytery or body corresponding thereto had fewer than six members, that they appoint one Minister and one Ruling Elder.

5. That the officers of the Council shall be a Moderator and a Clerk.

6. That the objects of the Alliance shall be—

(a) To promote mutual sympathy and the sense of unity among the Presbyterian Churches in India.

(b) To arrange for co-operation and mutual help.

(c) To promote the stability and self-support of the Native Churches, and to encourage them in direct labour for the evangelization of India.

7. That the *powers* of the Alliance shall be limited to the carrying out of the above specified objects, and to the adjudication of such questions as may be referred to it by the Supreme Courts of the mother Churches; further than this, they shall be merely consultative and advisory.

8. That the several Presbyteries, and Ecclesiastical bodies corresponding thereto, be made acquainted, through their Clerks, with the basis of alliance approved of by this meeting, and that they be invited, after obtaining the sanction of the Supreme Courts of the mother Churches, to become members of the

Alliance by appointing delegates to its next Council, or by otherwise signifying their adhesion thereto.

9. That the Chairman and Secretary draw up a letter to the Home Churches, setting forth the desirability of such an organization as the "Presbyterian Alliance of India."

10. That the Chairman send copies of all the documents which bear upon the question of the Indian Presbyterian Alliance to the President of the Presbyterian Council which is to meet at Edinburgh in July, 1876 and that he request the Committee of business to be good enough to make arrangements for giving the Rev. Dr. John Scudder of the Reformed Church of America, the Rev. Dr. Brodhead of the American Presbyterian Church, and the Rev. W. Martin, U. P. Church of Scotland, an opportunity of explaining to the Council the position in which the Presbyterian Churches in India stand.[6]

The Alliance then arranged for collecting statistics of all Presbyterian churches in India, and, at the suggestion of the late Dr. Wilson of Bombay, a Committee was appointed to consider ways and means to establish a periodical for Presbyterian and Missionary Intelligence, consisting of the American Presbyterian missionaries resident in Allahabad, the Rev. J. J. Caleb, the Rev. J. Williamson and Messrs. Anthony and Simson. This committee was authorized to take such action as might be regarded advisable.

It was agreed that the first meeting of the Council of the Alliance should be held at Allahabad on the 19th December, 1877.

This organization of the Indian Presbyterian Alliance served a most valuable purpose in the interest of Presbyterian Union in India. Many churches had lost interest because they could not see a practical solution of difficulties. The apathy on the part of some churches in the home lands sometimes approached an open antagonism. All were discouraged by the slow progress made. Conference after conference seemed to be helpless. Finally the suggestion of a federal union in the interest of co-

[6] *Proceedings of Conference*, Allahabad, 1875, pp. 4, 6.

operation and sympathy seemed to provide for our need. Enthusiasm characterized the meetings. Members felt that they received much help from the conferences. Many began to realize a new strength in union. In a way the churches realized a new dignity due to the Alliance taking the place of an assembly. And yet they more than ever realized the need of an assembly. They began to work up union endeavor to further education, especially in theological education. They even thought the home churches might constitute the alliance as a sort of high court to decide questions and disputes, especially where Indians were concerned. But in this they had a sad disappointment. The home assemblies decided that such assembly would be anomalous and so the hope died. More and more the need was felt and soon they turned back to the original thought of an Independent Indian Presbyterian Church.

Accordingly, at the fifth Council, Dr. J. W. Youngson gave notice as follows:—

"That whereas there is nothing in doctrine, polity or worship to keep the Presbyterian Churches in India apart, and

"Whereas the interest of Christianity more especially from a missionary point of view, would be advanced by their union, it is resolved to appoint as a Committee of the Alliance the Committee of the Indian Presbyteries on union, to formulate a basis of union, on the basis of the resolutions of this Council, and to send it down to the various Presbyteries and bodies corresponding thereto for approval and transmission to the Home authorities for their sanction."

The work of the Council of the Presbyterian Alliance had culminated in a definite scheme of union. The proceedings had been printed and were placed before the Presbyteries or bodies corresponding thereto in order that they might take action for approval, amendment or rejection, such action to be reported to the next (the sixth) Council of the Alliance. "The arrangements for the meeting of the Council were left in the hands of the Moderator (K. S. Macdonald) and the Clerk (J. M. Hamilton)."[7]

These bright hopes of a speedy consummation of the union of Presbyterians were again doomed to be deferred. Some Presbyteries, when confronted with the responsibility of severing their connection with the home churches, hesitated and finally concluded that the time had not come when they could venture on so serious a change. They could not reject a proposal so true to their ideal, but they could wait.

Other Presbyteries could not get the consent of the Home Assemblies, who were afraid their children in this land could not grow up without the nourishment provided by the mother church. Still others were held back by financial interests which would be affected by their withdrawal from the home assembly. These reasons and others not mentioned caused so much delay as to discourage those responsible on this side and so it came to pass that the sixth Council of the Presbyterian Alliance was not called to meet for eleven years!

In this interim, the churches in the Madras Presidency had taken action in the interests of Presbyterian union. It seemed wise to form a Synod to be composed of the Scottish Presbyterian churches and the classes of the Reformed Church of America. This church was called the *South India Presbyterian Church*. This union had demonstrated the feasibility as well as the advantages of any union of Indian Presbyteries. It was a great stimulus to the larger movement toward the union of all Presbyterian churches in India.

When therefore a few representatives of the Presbyterian Alliance met, at a conference of Christian workers in Mussoorie in 1900, and the question was asked, why the Alliance seemed to have become moribund, some one suggested that measures should be taken to restore the union movement. A meeting was called for the next morning, when a letter was addressed to the Rev. Dr. Macdonald, Convenor of the Fifth

[7] *Proceedings of Council Alliance*, p. 25.

Council, asking him to call another council meeting to assemble at Allahabad in February, 1901.

In February the sixth Council meeting was held in the Jumna Mission church. The two questions proposed for discussion were those apparently settled eleven years before:

(1) Is organic union of Indian Presbyterian Churches desirable? and (2) Is organic union now practicable? We quote from the Minutes:

> "Although there had been no meetings, it was soon found that the sentiment in favor of union had gained much strength in the interval. It was realized that organic union was not only desirable, but also practicable, and a Committee was appointed to draw up a synopsis of doctrine and to complete the work of formulating in detail the basis of the proposed union of the Churches."

The Committee on Synopsis of Doctrine met in Dehra Dun on the 28th-30th of September, 1901. They had before them the Confession of Faith, and Constitution and Canons of the South Indian Presbyterian Church. Taking this as a working basis, the committee went over the Confession of Faith article by article, making note of changes suggested in order to adapt it to the purposes of the proposed united church and as a definite proposition resolved to present the following synopsis to the Seventh Council of the Presbyterian Alliance.

The Committee on Synopsis of Doctrine then printed its report and sent copies down to the Clerks of Presbyteries and to members of the committee for criticism and amendment. The synopsis of the replies received from the Presbyteries were considered by the Committee, in consultation with the committee for completing the basis, at Allahabad on the 9th, 10th and 11th of December, and was modified somewhat further.

Printed reports of the work of the Committee on Synopsis of Faith, Rev. Dr. Fraser Campbell, Convenor; and the report of the committee for completing the basis of union, Rev. Dr.

Kali Charan Chatterji, Convener; were presented to the Seventh Council of the Alliance which was held at Allahabad on the 11th, 12th, 13th and 14th December, 1902. The Seventh Council accepted the Basis of Union presented by its committee tentatively, and appointed a special meeting, to be held one year later, when all the replies of Presbyteries in India and of the mother churches in the home lands could be considered.

This meeting, held in 1903, had before it in printed form the results of the work of the Committee of the Alliance and also of the various assemblies in the home land. Out of this the Alliance was able to formulate, in a complete form, the Confession of Faith, the Constitution and Canons of the United Church. The name finally adopted was *The Presbyterian Church in India.*

A representative Council was called to meet at Allahabad in December, 1903, Rev. James Gray, D. D. Moderator. This Council completed the work of organizing the new church.

A Provisional General Assembly was arranged for in 1904. The Eighth Alliance Council meeting met in the Jumna Presbyterian Church, Allahabad, on the 15th December. Rev. Dr. D. Mackichan was elected Moderator. Rev. Dr. K. C. Chatterji, Vice Moderator, and Rev. Dr. J. A. Graham, Clerk. Final reports of business committees were presented. After instructing the delegates appointed by Presbyteries to meet at 8 A. M. December 19th for the purpose of constituting a Provisional General Assembly, the Council adjourned *sine die.* The work of the Indian Presbyterian Alliance was now finished. On the morning of December 19th at 8 A. M. the delegates to General Assembly met in the Jumna Presbyterian Church, Allahabad.

After a devotional service conducted by the Rev. Dr. K. C. Chatterji the Assembly was constituted. The Rev. K. C. Chatterji, D.D. was elected Moderator; the Rev. J. A. Graham was elected Clerk. The various Committees of Assembly were announced. The Moderator addressed the Assembly and closed the session with the benediction.

The consummation of the union of nine Presbyterian bodies to form a single Presbyterian church in India was in a very special sense an accomplishment of our American Missions in India. The first promotor of such a union was Rev. Dr. John H. Morrison, who for twenty-five years labored in season and out of season for Presbyterian union. He especially desired to see the Indian churches occupy a place of independence. While two important bodies, the American United Presbyterian and the Welsh Presbyterian churches were at that time unable to come in, yet one, the Welsh Presbyterian church, was able to unite in 1919. It is hoped that the remaining unit may yet join up.

A later and larger union of Protestant churches has been accomplished. The Synod of Madras, which came into the Presbyterian church in India on the understanding they might withdraw in order to unite with the Congregational churches to form the South India United Church, was permitted to withdraw in 1908 in order to consummate that union. And later, when the possibility of a union of the Bombay Synod with the West India Congregational Church to form a West India United Church, was suggested, the Presbyterian church in India proposed a larger union of all Presbyterian and Congregational churches to unite with the South India United Church to form one United Church of India. At present writing this union seems near at hand.[8] Most of the missionaries are connected with this Indian church and are in a position to place it upon a solid basis. The result is that our missionary work is on the way to become a part of the work of the United Church in India.

[8] On the 30th day of December, 1924, the organic union between the Presbyterian Church in India and the Congregation Church of Western India was consummated. The name of the united body is THE UNITED CHURCH OF INDIA (NORTH). This Church is in doctrine and polity a sister to the South India United Church. E. M. W.

CHAPTER XXVII.

Co-operation of Missions and the Church

IN the early days of the Mission, Dr. John C. Lowrie advised the missionaries to form a Presbytery as the official body which should transact all business relating to the evangelization of the non-Christian people. His purpose was to interest every elder and ordained minister of the Indian church in the work of the missionaries. But as yet there was no organized Presbytery. Not until three years had passed (1837) was any effort made to organize one. The need was keenly felt, but two ministers could not legally act. There should be at least three. It so happened that among the recruits lately arrived one was a minister of the Reformed Church (Covenanter), Rev. J. R. Campbell. He was asked to unite with them to constitute the Presbytery of Lodiana.

Three missionaries had come out as teachers and were unordained: Jesse M. Jamieson, William S. Rogers and Joseph Porter. These men were now, after the usual examinations, ordained to the ministry. The Presbytery thus constituted consisted of the following members: Rev. John Newton, Rev. James Wilson, Rev. James R. Campbell and the three newly ordained ministers above mentioned.

"The whole thing," says Mr. Newton, "was of course irregular; but the anomalous position in which the missionaries were placed seemed to them to justify it: and the principle of it has since been recognized by the proposed alliance of different Presbyterian bodies occupying the same Mission field, for certain ecclesiastical purposes.

"The matter was soon after brought to the notice of the General Assembly (in America); and, while the Assembly disapproved the measure, it gave informal validity to it, by acknowledging the three brethren — Jamieson, Rogers and

Porter as truly ordained ministers, and directing them, with the original two in its connection, to constitute the Presbytery of Lodiana."[1]

It was not until ten years later that an Indian minister, the Rev. Goloknath was added to this Presbytery. In this interim, a few ruling elders were ordained and so became eligible to be representatives of their church in the Presbytery.

The Reformed Presbyterian (then Covenanter) Church missionaries organized their own Presbytery, known as the Presbytery of Saharanpur. The American missionaries of both of these Presbyteries constituted the Lodiana Mission. Under such circumstances, it was difficult to work out a scheme whereby all the work done by the Mission could be undertaken by the Presbytery. Morever, the fact that the Mission, as a finance committee of the board in America, had from the beginning transacted all the business of both the Mission and the Indian churches, excepting the purely ecclesiastical affairs of the congregations and the discipline of the members, tended more and more to exalt the Mission above the Presbyteries. This state of things eventually created a spirit of dissatisfaction among the Indian ministers and elders. The question arose as to some way out of this embarrassing situation. The first plan proposed was made by Rev. John Newton, the senior member of the Mission. It was that the Mission be dissolved and that all business be transacted by the Presbyteries. A committee was appointed, consisting of Rev. John Newton, Rev. E. M. Wherry and Rev. A. P. Kelso, "to draw up a definite plan for conducting Mission business through the Presbyteries with a view to dissolving the Mission, and to present it at the next annual meeting."[2]

The deliberations of this committee resulted in a definite conclusion: (1) That the Mission should not be dissolved, because many matters could not be wisely managed by the Presbyteries: e. g. the conducting of business relating to the woman's work

---

[1] *History of the A. P. Mission*, India, pp. 67, 68.
[2] *Minutes of the Lodiana Mission*, 1877, p. 30.

in zenana and girls' schools, the union work of the two Presbyterian churches and the problems growing out of correspondence with Government, and all questions of inter-Mission co-operation, (2) The Committee recomnended a gradual commitment of Mission work to the Presbyteries. The first department of work to be committed to the Presbytery was that of evangelistic service in the sphere of the preaching of the gospel, the formation of churches, the appointment of pastors and evangelists, and the general work relating to church life.

If the Presbyteries should be unable to collect from the churches the money necessary to carry on the work of evangelization, they might appeal to the Foreign Mission Board in America through the Mission; but, in such case, the Mission should be entitled to inspect the work done and also to receive reports for transmission to the Board.

"According to this view, the Mission would be a medium of communication between the Presbyteries and the Board in regard to any agents the Board might be expected to furnish, and any pecuniary grants the Presbyteries might be constrained to ask; and the Mission, as the Board's representative, would at the same time keep an eye upon the work done at the Board's expense, so as to know whether such work was entitled to continued support or not.[3] Besides this work in co-operation with the Presbyteries, the Mission should have the entire control of the work of Missionary ladies, of Mission day-schools, and of all Missionary institutions of wider territorial interest than the bounds of any one Presbytery, being supported independently of Presbyterial funds, such as the Press, Orphanages, and Christian Boarding Schools; that is, until the Synod might be prepared to take the management of them."[4]

This scheme and program was formally presented to the Presbyteries and to the Board in New York.

In due course the Mission received the Board's approval of

[3] *Minutes Annual Meeting*, 1880, p. 24.
[4] *Idem.*

the plan. Accordingly the following action was recorded in the minutes of the Mission:[5]

"The Committee appointed to report on the transfer of Mission work to Presbyteries, reported as follows:—

"That they recommend the transfer to be made according to the plan approved by the Mission at the Annual Meeting held in January, 1880, and that the President be instructed to inform the Presbyteries within the bounds of the Mission, that the Board has expressed its acquiescence in the measure proposed, and that therefore the Presbyteries are now at liberty to take up the Mission work proposed to be made over to them in the plan above referred to."[6]

This plan of procedure was duly laid before the Presbyteries, which had expressed a willingness to undertake to carry on the direct work of evangelization. To enable the Indian members to understand the proposal better, the minute of the Mission was translated into the vernacular language.

A year or two passed without any definite action being taken by the Presbyteries. The chief reason alleged was insufficient financial support and a lack of men with a burning zeal to direct and carry on the movement. At the annual meeting in 1886, the whole question was reconsidered and as a result it was abandoned! However, the labor and discussion were not altogether without fruitage. The Presbyteries were anxious that some more practical scheme for definite home missionary work might be undertaken.

The missionaries also felt that their policy of excluding the Indian Ministers and Elders from the councils of the Mission was defective in that it failed to develop the practical interest of the Indian church in the great work of evangelism.

A Committee on *Ecclesiastical* Relations was appointed to consider this subject anew and to report at the next Annual Meeting (1891), the Rev. Robert Morrison being chairman. This Committee after considerable discussion concluded that the time

[5] *Minutes Punjab Mission*, 1882, p. 27.
[6] *Minutes Annual Meeting*, 1882, p. 29.

had not yet come when the Mission could safely commit to the Presbyteries the management of funds contributed by the American churches. They therefore proposed the following:

"That the Missions give over to the Presbyteries the entire control of all native ministers, licentiates and colporteurs; the Mission yet to continue giving them their salaries; and that the Presbyteries determine the location of men in the places where work is to be taken up and the kind of work to be done. It shall supervise the work, hear reports concerning it, and be the body responsible for the efficiency of the work. Its recommendations shall, unless possibly in very exceptional cases and for strong reasons, always be the determining factor with the Mission in its continuing or discontinuing of salaries."

In addition to this, the Committee recommended that Indian ministers, nominated by a two-thirds vote of the Mission, should be appointed as full members of the Mission, "this appointment to membership in the Mission having no connection with, or reference to their salaries. Those thus appointed would cease to be employees of the Mission, but would have direct connection with the Board."

These proposals were unacceptable to the Indians, to the Board, and to the Mission. They, however, served to keep the question of Presbytery and Mission alive, while they voiced the willingness of many missionaries to sacrifice much of the policy of the past, in order to get into closer fellowship with their Indian brethren.

As a result of correspondence with the Board, the Rev. Dr. Gillespie, Secretary for India, suggested that the Mission in the Punjab might allot to each of the Presbyteries a field to be evangelized by the Presbytery; to this object the churches should be urged to contribute annually a definite sum for mission work, to be administered by a committee of the Presbytery. To this work of the Presbytery, the Board would grant a sum, at the rate of three rupees for every rupee contributed by the churches. This proposal was accepted by both the Mission and the Presbyteries connected with the Lodiana Mission.

To the Lodiana Presbytery was allotted a large district, which was named *The Thenesar Home Mission Field.* The headquarters in this field was the town of Thenesar, one of the holy places of the Hindu people. In this district had been fought some of the decisive battles of the centuries past. In Thenesar were holy tanks in which thousands of devotees bathed to wash away their sins.

The Rev. Talibuddin, B.A., a graduate of Forman Christian College and also a graduate of the Saharanpur Theological Seminary, was made superintendent. A school was opened and a band of preachers was appointed to work in the surrounding villages.

To the Lahore Presbytery was allotted a field in the Lahore and Kasur Tahsils,[7] with headquarters in Lahore. Here the organization was about the same as that in the Thenesar field.

These home missions became a permanent feature of the village work of the Missions and the Indian church. The amount of the Board's grant was to be decreased by eight annas (per rupee), every five years, so that by the year 1923, the grants would cease and thenceforward the Home Mission would be conducted at the expense of the Indian church.

In the year 1920, the Lodiana Presbytery voluntarily withdrew from this connection with the Mission and the Board and after a vote of thanks to the Board of Foreign Missions for the aid given in past years, they resolved to assume the entire expense of their Home Mission work. Pledges were taken from representatives of the churches and societies and the total budget was subscribed on the spot. It was delightful to see the enthusiasm of the Indian members, realizing the blessed privilege of an independent sphere of work in the evangelization of their countrymen. Practically similar plans were adopted in other Presbyteries in North India. The interest of the churches

[7] A tahsil is a sub-district—a township.

in the work of evangelization constantly increased, so that in addition to the Home Mission work, they planned to undertake a special work among non-Christians in their own cities, towns and neighborhoods.

To promote the evangelistic spirit among the churches, conventions and special revival meetings were held once a year, as soon as convenient after the Week of Prayer, a campaign was arranged, which should include the whole Christian community. The men, women and youngs boys and girls were divided into bands and trained for the expedition. The mode of procedure was to assemble in the church or meeting place for a short prayer service. A good supply of books, scripture portions and tracts printed in the vernacular languages was given to each band. The bands thus armed would proceed to the quarter in the town assigned and approach the people in their shops or their homes, offer their books for sale or a tract or leaflet to those who would not buy. Some would raise a hymn or spiritual song. The women would visit the women. At certain points open air preaching would be started and kept up during most of the day. Some parties would go to the villages within a radius of five miles and conduct meetings for all who would hear. In the evening the parties would return and report to the leaders. Thus the entire week would be spent, resulting in many testimonies, some open confessions and some inquirers, who would agree to join a class with the expectation of being baptized. This awakening of the Indian Christians to their responsibility for the conversion of their non-Christian neighbors marks a new era in Indian evangelism. From this date onward the foreign missionary is no longer the voice of one crying in the wilderness. As he tours through the country, he visits numerous villages, where he finds small groups of Christians who unite with him in work and worship.

The Presbyterial work of Missions underwent some changes, due to the union of Presbyterian denominations in India to form the Presbyterian church in India (Chapter XXV). This union has given the people a wider vision and has promoted the spirit of independence. The church is now an Indian church and in a large sense the Home Mission is their own Mission. The older missionaries retained their membership in the Indian church, but many of the younger men retained their Presbyterial relation with the American churches and would only become consultative members of the Indian Presbyteries. This attitude of some of the younger missionaries was resented by the educated Indians, who deprecated such aloofness as signifying a want of confidence and unwillingness to co-operate with them on terms of equality.

They realized that such a policy must eventuate in the entire withdrawal of the foreign element, whose counsel and practical wisdom they needed. The result was an increasing antagonism to the missionary policy showing itself in the unwillingness of educated young men to take service in the Mission unless they should be placed on the same footing as the missionaries.

The intensity of the feeling of educated Indians is well expressed in a letter written by an elder in the Presbyterian church, Allahabad, to a Secretary of the Board of Foreign Missions. Writing on behalf of a number of members of the Presbyterian Church in India on the relation of the Mission to the church, he said:

"The present policy of isolating the Mission and the Church and keeping them apart from each other, has resulted in such friction and misunderstanding as practically to paralyze all Mission work and to retard the growth of the Church in India.

"There is not a single Mission station in India which does not bear testimony to this unfortunate state of things, and Missionaries and Indian Christians are at one in regretting it. It is further a cause of offence to the non-Christians, who see in it the failure of practical Christianity. We appreciate the motive which dictated the present policy—a desire not to pauperize the Indian Church, and hinder its development by putting the Mission in the place of the Church. By an irony of fate it has been perverted from its true ends and has succeeded in achieving what it set out to avert, viz: the hindering of the growth of the Church.

"It is a case where attendant events seem to be too great for 'policy,' and have provided it with a setting which has given it a very different meaning from what it was meant for. The outstanding menace of the world today is the possibility of a conflict between Asia and Europe, or the East and the West,—a conflict between the white and the yellow races. The religion of Christ, in theory, is the solvent of this racial strife, but, in practice, it will be dependent on the institutions of Christianty and their presentation as these are to be met with in life. Any presentation of Christ, or any expression of the Christian life in institutions which are rooted in a narrow individualism, will only intensify this racial strife, fail to furnish the Christian corrective, play into the hands of the enemy, and hasten on the day of destruction. This is just what we venture to think has happened with the present policy of isolating the Mission and the Church from each other. It has preached 'self help' and 'self determination' to the Indian Church, but has failed to observe a just balance, by forgetting that in life there is such a thing also as 'other help' and 'other determination.' The response in the Indian Church to this teaching has been a fierce resentment against the foreign missionary and foreign missions, and a determination to have as little to do with them as possible, and so to boycott him and his work. This policy has made Mission work of all grades a by-word and reproach and has practically emtpied our theological classes and has created a deep-rooted aversion in our young men against entering upon whole-time Christian work.

"This unfortunate situation has not been without its redeeming features. It is true it has roused a passion for lay service amongst us, deepening our responsibility for self-support and self-extension, the outstanding illustration of the latter being the founding of the National Missionary Society of India, and has given an impetus to our desire for an Indian Church. But the tragedy of Indian Church life consists in this that the more seriously we have grappled with the problem of evangelizing our country, the more thoroughly we have realized how utterly impossible it is for the Indian Church alone to accomplish it, even as it is for the Missions to achieve it single-handed, and that the only hope lies in a coalescing of the forces of the Church and the Mission and a consequent fusion of their organizations.

"But right here we are to part by the ring-fence of 'policy' which, in the name of the interest of the Church, shuts the Indian out from the councils of Missions and control of its funds. To accept Mission work, with these bars against us, 'for the sake of Christ,' as we are enjoined by our Missionary friends, to do, would not only be sinning against our national self respect, but giving a distorted interpretation of Christ to India, and doing a disservice to our Lord and Country. It will be treason alike to both, and we dare not be a party to it.

"We do not think we are using exaggerated language when we say that the anomalies and indignities of the present situation are too great for any self-respecting people to bear, let alone higher considerations of the Christian ethic. To enumerate all the disabilities would be a long and woeful tale to unfold, but we shall run over some of the salient points in brief:

"(1) We have, under this system, the Mission and not the Church legislating about mass-movement methods. . . .

"(2) This system is also responsible for a certain Secretary coming out from America to decide on important Mission matters, *conferring only with Missionaries,* and ending up by straying into the province of the Church, and making recommendations vitally affecting it.

"Another illustration of the same type is furnished by the June, 1920 Conference in New York, which also supinely ignores Indian representation, though decisions vitally affecting the Indian Church and Missions in India are expected to be arrived at in it.

"(3) This system also has presented us with the spectacle of our College men[8] being vehemently urged to enter *Mission service* when there is in reality no place for them in the Mission. Appeals, under such conditions, 'became a solemn farce'."

This letter is a good sample of many similar protests levelled at the policy adopted by Mission Boards in America, and by the Presbyterian Church in particular.

Some of the missionaries have sympathized with their Indian brethren and from time to time striven to secure the appointment of representative Indian ministers as members of their

[8] Indian Christian Professor.—E. M. W.

Mission, occupying a place of entire equality with the American missionaries. Such action might have forestalled the agitation voiced in this letter. The nearest approach to the recognition of the Indian Presbyterian church was the appointment of two Indian evangelists as consultative members of the Punjab Mission but without a vote. A still further step has been the election of the head masters in our Mission schools as members of the education committee for boys' schools, with a voting power equal to that of the missionary members. In like manner Indians are elected members of the Board of Trustees of the Forman Christian College. It is to be hoped that the democratic spirit of our American church will enable it to solve the problem of mission and church to the entire satisfaction of all parties concerned. The sight of Indians and Europeans working side by side in perfect unity would give joy and efficiency to the Christian world and at the same time mightily impress non-Christians everywhere.

CHAPTER XXVIII.

Reopening of the Mission College Lahore

FIFTEEN years had gone by since the suspension of the Mission college at Lahore. Many a time the question was asked "When shall we reopen the Mission College?" but no one seemed able to answer this question. And so year after year passed with nothing accomplished.

It was left to the enterprise of a young man but three years in the field, Rev. James M. McComb, Principal of the Christian Boys' Boarding School at Lodiana, to initiate the movement for the reopening of this college. Fifteen students of the Mission High School, having passed the matriculation examination, were ready to enter college. The only college in the province open to them was the Government college at Lahore. To enter there would mean the unlearning of many of the lessons they had learned in the Mission school. After consultation with a number of the older missionaries and learning the general opinion of the Indian Christian community that the Christian college so long suspended should be reopened, Mr. McComb began a college class in June, 1885. At the Annual Meeting in the following January he read a paper on the question of starting anew the Christian College. The whole question was then discussed and definite action taken to reopen the Christian College at Lahore, with Dr. C. W. Forman as Principal and Rev. H. C. Velte as a joint Professor. Accordingly the fifteen students were transferred from Lodiana to the Rang Mahal at Lahore. The College Charter not having lapsed, the Lieutenant Governor of the Punjab approved the action of the Mission.

It now became necessary to find separate quarters for the College and to erect new buildings outside the city walls. A vacant lot of some five acres belonging to the Government lying just outside the Anarkali gate was chosen for the college campus and the site for the new buildings. This site was acquired with the aid of the Lieutenant Governor. A building grant was also given by the educational department. In the interim, a building was rented and made suitable for class rooms.

A Board of Directors was elected by the Mission consisting of nine members.

To serve three years,	C. W. Forman
	K. C. Chatterji
	John Newton
To serve two years,	H. C. Velte
	George Lewis
	J. M. McComb
To serve one year,	J. H. Orbison
	Mr. Maya Das
	Robert Morrison

Rev. Kali Charan Chatterji, D.D. was elected Chairman of this Board, a position which he held for twenty-five years, until the day of his death.

The next year by request of the Principal Rev. C. W. Forman, D.D., Rev. J. C. R. Ewing, D.D. was chosen to be Principal of the Mission College at Lahore.

Dr. Ewing had some years' experience in educational work as principal of the Mission High School in Allahabad; and also as a professor in the theological seminary in Saharanpur. By education and training he was eminently qualified to be principal of the Mission College. When he received the formal call to become Principal of the Mission College, he accepted it as a call to duty. In the year 1888 he entered upon his new sphere of service.

The Christian College had during its short career sent forth some of the first B. A. graduates in the Punjab. Two and a half years had now passed since the reopening with a class of eighteen. At the beginning of each year a new class was added so that there were now three classes with a total of 121 students. Almost all of these had been educated in the high schools carried on by the American Presbyterian Mission in the Punjab. A noticeable fact was the large proportion of Muhammadan students. A Christian graduate of St. Stephens' college, Delhi, had been added to the staff of instructors. Indian Christians had shown their sympathy and practical interest from the beginning. Special mention is made of indebtedness to Dr. Caleb, Professor of Pathology in the Government Medical College, and to Mr. F. Goloknath Chatterji, B.A., Assistant Professor in the Arts College, who gave valuable assistance without charge; one in the Department of Science and the other in that of Mathematics.

All the teachers were now Christians except the Pundit and Maulvie. It was the aim of the principal and professors to make the institution thoroughly Christian in its character and influence. "No period in the daily routine was more interesting then the bible period, when the facts, doctrines, and principles of Christianity were insisted on. What other results may follow from these teachings may be doubtful, but it can hardly be doubted that many who were to be leaders in native society acquired favorable opinions of the Christian religion, and that their lives were more or less modified by them."[1] These words voice the spirit of the Mission College, consistently maintained for 33 years by Principal Ewing and his faithful colleagues, American and Indian.

New lecture rooms and a boarding house were formally opened on November 25, 1889 by His Excellency the Viceroy, in the presence of the Lieutenant Governor of the Punjab and a large audience composed of invited guests and college students. Two years later sixteen students were sent up for the B. A. degree, ten of whom were successful. In the intermediate examination, thirty out of forty-seven candidates were successful. The enrollment was now 156. Two years later, 1893, there were 244 names on the roll, of whom 135 were Hindus, 62 Muslims, 25 Sikhs and 22 Christians.

[1] *Lodiana Mission Report*, 1888, p. 7.

At this stage in the history of the Mission College a change occurred in the missionary staff. The Rev. H. C. Velte went to England and America on a well-earned furlough. Of this work the Report[2] says:

"He came to the institution at its reopening in 1886, and to his painstaking and efficient labours very much of the educational success achieved has been due, while by his life and words, he in no small degree impressed his pupils, and led them with interest to engage in the study of God's word."

To supply the place made vacant by Mr. Velte, the Rev. J. M. McComb was transferred from Lodiana. He took charge of the department of Mental and Moral Philosophy. During the year an incident occurred which was both a trial of the faith of the college staff and of the loyalty of the students to the college. One of the students had frequently declared his purpose to be baptized. About this time a young man from Multan came to Lahore and asked for baptism. This man was greatly persecuted by his relatives, who tried to get hold of him by legal process. Their attempt, however, failed. During the progress of this trial the young man took refuge with the principal of the college.

"The other young man, . . . was greatly stirred by the sight of the persecution the youth was courageously enduring; and spent a large portion of the time with him during the critical days, and before the end he too insisted on being baptized. Anticipating serious trouble, he asked to be allowed to leave the Hindu Boarding House and to go to the Mission Compound. From Monday morning until Wednesday evening he lived in the house of Mr. McComb, where his friends were allowed freely to see and to talk with him. After two days of pleading his relatives hit upon the idea of bringing the youth to believe that his father was at the point of death. By sending successive messengers in hot haste to call him, they finally succeeded. Although the missionaries were not convinced, they felt it was right that he should go to his father, whom he imagined to

[2] *Report of the Punjab Mission Conference*, 1893, p. 38.

be dying, if he wished to do so. As soon, therefore, as he expressed such a desire, he was taken by one of the professors to the City. He went promising to return, but never came back.

"The young man from Multan was baptized and has since been a student in our College.

"These cases created great excitement. Telegrams were sent all over the country. Parents and guardians, believing their sons to be in danger, wanted them to leave College. A mass meeting was held in the City. Speeches 'patriotic' and otherwise were made; resolutions adopted, published and circulated throughout the Province calling upon parents to save their families from the Missionaries! Some of the students asked permission to withdraw and were allowed to do so without a word of protest, though the number who actually left was very small, and many who at first, under excitement, wished to go away, came back within a few days and begged to be allowed to remain. New classes were being formed at the time and a definite effort was made by the members of the Arya Samaj to dissuade young men, coming from the High Schools of the Province, from entering our College. These efforts were in many cases successful, and as the result some of the classes were appreciably smaller than last year."[3]

During this year, the College lost its founder and life-long friend Dr. C. W. Forman. While the College was domiciled in the Rang Mahal in connection with the high school he held the place of Principal, but when it became necessary to separate the College from the old home in Rang Mahal, he resigned the Principalship of the College and remained in Rang Mahal high school as the superintendent. Here he had spent nearly half a century. Thousands of young men had received an education under his direction. No one had such a wide influence upon the educational life of the Province. His students were to be found everywhere in the various departments of the Government service. The College he had founded was ever dear to him and its Principal ever found in him a wise and faithful counsellor.

After a long illness Charles W. Forman passed away at

[3] Punjab Mission Report, 1894, pp. 32-34.

Kasauli on August 27th, 1894. His body was brought down from the mountain for burial at Lahore. The following account of his funeral clearly voices the hold which he had upon the hearts of the people among whom he spent his life:

"The funeral services took place among the people, whom he had long and tenderly loved. A stronger testimony than that which was given of the high regard in which he was held by the non-Christian people, could scarcely be desired. The gates of the City were thrown open, a thing which had never happened before, and instead of objecting to its passage as might have been expected, the inhabitants vied with each other for the honour of having the funeral procession pass along their streets. They followed the procession to the grave and there manifested genuine sorrow, for they knew that they had lost a true friend."

During his illness many were the requests that came from his old friends and pupils, wishing to see him and inquiring after his health. When he was gone a general feeling of sorrow pervaded the city and a proposal was made, by the non-Christian community, in which the leading men joined, to erect a memorial, as a mark of gratitude from the city of Lahore, for his life and services.

"It may be doubted whether any officer of State, no matter how high in the service, ever endeared himself to such an extent in the hearts of the people of the City."[4]

As a memorial the name of the college was changed from Mission College to "Forman Christian College in memory of the late Dr. Forman, the pioneer of education in the Province and the first Principal of the College."

The progress of the college for the remaining years of the nineteenth century was rapid. Three Indian Christian professors were present on the staff. A graduate of the class of 1883, who had been deeply impressed by the bible teaching returned to Lahore three years later and was baptized. He had suffered much persecution for his faith, but remained steadfast

[4] *Punjab Mission Report*, 1894, p. 24.

giving promise of great usefulness in the Christian church. Ten additional rooms for Christian students had to be added to the Kennedy Hall. The total attendance had now risen to 322, of whom 175 were Hindus; 84 Muhammadans; 31 Christians; 29 Sikhs; and 3 Zoroastrians.

Principal Ewing closed his report for the year 1899 with these words:

"The purpose of the College is two-fold. It aims to bring the knowledge of Christ to the non-Christian youth of the Province, who resort to us in great numbers; and to educate the young men of the Christian Church, that they may be fitted to take their places as leaders in the great task of evangelizing this country. Young men come to us from all quarters of Northern India, and our daily opportunity for influencing them is a most enviable one. A fair number of non-Christian students are seriously studying their Bibles, and from amongst these some will, we trust, be led by the spirit to a fuller faith, and ultimately to a public profession of their personal allegiance to Jesus Christ."

CHAPTER XXIX.

Higher Education for Village Christians

THE rapid growth of educational institutions for boys and young men naturally led on to the establishment of schools and colleges for girls and young women.

The customs prevalent among Hindus and Muhammadans made it necessary, at least at first, to limit such institutions to the Christian community.

Mention has been made of the excellent work done at the Dehra Christian school for girls. This institution had become a high school, sending forth annually classes prepared to pass the matriculation examination for entrance to the Allahabad university. There was connected with it a normal training school in which young ladies were given the education and training necessary to become teachers in the grade schools. This school was opened in 1913.

"Its staff includes Miss Chatterji, B. A., for many years Principal of the Crosthwaite Girls' School, Allahabad, and Miss Maya Das, who is a specialist in Kindergarten, having graduated from Columbia University, New York City."

The graduates of this school are found in many places of honor in various callings throughout Northern India.

Another school for girls is the Lady Kinnaird school at Lahore. This institution was fostered by the missionaries at Lahore, but was carried on by the Zanana Bible and Medical Mission, an English society, which works as an auxiliary to Protestant Missions. In 1895 this school became a College carried on by a board of directors representing the Zanana Bible and Medical Mission and the Punjab Mission of the Presbyterian church in the United States of America. This College is open to both Christians and non-Christians.

Experience in the conduct of educational work during a half century made it quite clear that certain classes of people were unable to receive the education planned for in the high schools and colleges. Pupils thus defective were found to be injured by the effort to educate them beyond their limitation. Not only so but their presence in a class became a drag upon the other members of the class. Many scholars would make satisfactory progress up to the close of the primary department and stop there. Others would get along fairly well until near the end of the middle or grammar school course and fail in the final examination. Ambitious parents would send them to school for a second year or even a third year in hope they might pass the middle school final examination, but usually it was all for naught. For boys this was most disastrous because they were disqualified for the paying places in government or railway service, and yet were ashamed to dig. In the case of girls the outcome was different. They could be useful as teachers or Bible readers both before and after marriage.

To provide for these classes, schools were opened in which the teaching was in the vernacular language only. The course included training of the girls in sewing, knitting and cooking. The school was a large family in which the scholars took turns in the performance of household duties. The education was that of a primary school. The chief objective being that of character building along with education sufficient to make them intelligent wives and mothers. A few of the brightest girls would be given special lessons in the art of teaching in a primary school. Such schools for girls were established as boarding schools at Jagraon, Hoshyarpur and Ambala—the latter being a middle school with a normal training class. Similar schools for boys were established at Lodiana, Khanna and Saharanpur. In connection with these schools, manual training was carried on so as to enable boys to learn a trade, carpentry, shoemaking, weaving and gardening.

At Moga, a training school was established for the special purpose of training young men for Christian service as teachers in village schools or for a village pastorate. To this an agricultural department was added with a view to enable these village teachers and preachers to become advisers and helpers to the farmers and so increase the production of food and fodder in village communities. This institution was first started at Firozpur by the Rev. John N. Hyde, but afterwards transferred to Moga. Under the care of Rev. R. H. Carter the institution grew rapidly. Buildings were erected and land was acquired for agricultural purposes. The students willingly contributed labor. They levelled the ground about the compound, moulded bricks and built walls, thus saving large outlays of money, while at the same time showing a practical interest in an institution which should minister so much to the welfare of their village communities. Moga has now become the center of a wide-spread scheme of village education. W. J. McKee, Esq. C. E. for some ten years principal of the Rang Mahal high school in Lahore, has been appointed to the principalship of the Moga Training School and has been made inspector of village schools throughout the Punjab Mission. Students of the Moga school have gone forth as teachers in village schools or as candidates for training in the Saharanpur theological seminary, as village pastors.

The girls' middle school at Ambala city, now known as the Mary E. Pratt Middle School,[1] educates girls in the vernacular languages. It is a distinctly Christian school, giving a thorough education, qualifying its students to teach in other schools offering the vernacular middle course.

It will appear from this general description of Mission

[1] This School and the building in which the girls are housed as well as taught owes its being to the energy and generosity of Miss Mary E. Pratt, who, after years of faithful service in Dehra, devoted the remainder of her life in India to this Christian training school.

schools, that the girls are being placed in line to receive practically the same kind of education as the boys. Primary schools become feeders to the middle schools and these in turn become feeders to the high schools and to the training schools. Looking at the subject from the social standpoint, women are being trained to become wives for educated young men, and thus education serves to lift up all classes to a higher place in the social scale. What has been said of education in the Punjab may also be said of education in the Northwestern Provinces and in the Kolhapur state in Western India.

CHAPTER XXX.

Education in North India

THE Mission school for non-Christians at Allahabad, primarily established by the Government, but afterwards made over to the Mission and placed under the Rev. Joseph Owen, was continued under the management of missionaries. This school afforded the children of Indian Christians an opportunity to secure a good education. The establishment of Muir College by Sir William Muir, Lieutenant Governor of the Province, enabled Christian young men to secure a college education without leaving their homes. There were now many young men from other towns in the Province, who were obliged to live in the city. This made for them an environment in no wise helpful for moral and spiritual development.

To provide for this claimant need two plans were possible: one, to build a hostel specially for Christians to be superintended by one or two missionaries, who would live with the students, in order to guide them in their studies and encourage them in such sports as would help to develop a strong and manly character and at the same time shield them against demoralizing influences.

Another plan was to establish a Christian college in which both Christian and non-Christian students coming from Mission schools located in the larger stations might continue their college studies under Christian influences. This was all the more important because the government schools and colleges while ostensibly neutral were really non-Christian,—no religious instruction being permitted. It often happened that the so-called neutral attitude of the professors was in all respects anti-Christian. A Christian convert, and a protégé of the writer, once told him that a European professor was so enraged at him, because he had made a remark about God his Saviour, that he obliged him to write the word "God" eight hundred times as a punishment for using it in his class. He was then warned never to use that word again in his presence. A Muslim student in another college reported a personal experience, to the effect that a noted German oriental scholar had cursed him for uttering a pious remark *Insha állah* (God willing) telling him never to use God's name in his presence again.

Because of such conditions, American missionaries felt constrained to provide Christian schools, wherein the religion of Jesus Christ might be expected to exercise a benign influence upon the minds of the pupils. For the accomplishment of this purpose, the Mission determined to establish a college. The Mission compound on the banks of the Jumna river was designated as the site for the college campus.

Rev. Arthur Ewing, D. D., was called to become the Principal. The Rev. J. J. Lucas, D. D., was a chief mover in this endeavor. By united effort the new college scheme was brought to the notice of the Government and in spite of considerable opposition, it received recognition and substantial aid. Through the benevolence of an American gentleman, commodious buildings were erected and the Christian College entered upon its career. Suitable buildings were erected on one side of the campus to perpetuate the old Mission School. A preparatory school for Christian boys was also added. Additional land was acquired to provide sites for professors' houses and laboratories. Later on, an agricultural department was added, of which Professor Samuel Higginbottom, M. A., was made Principal. An extensive tract of land was secured on the opposite side of the Jumna river and buildings were erected there to house the professors and students, stables for cattle and farm implements were built.

Eventually it seemed wise to separate this Agricultural Institute from the Arts College. The importance of this institution as a missionary asset will be understood, when the rapidly growing Christian communities in the rural districts are taken into account. To enable the farmers to double and treble the productive power of their lands is the surest way to domicile Christianity among village peoples, and to make village churches self-supporting. The extension of Christianity through the mass movement, which tends to isolate vast numbers of village people, because of the caste boycott, involves the endeavor to find some way by which the people may continue to live independently in spite of persecution.

As in the case of schools and colleges, which provide first for the needs of the Christian people, the benefits of education were bestowed upon non-Christians also, so in the effort to aid the village Christians, the benefits of an agricultural training were passed on to the non-Christians also.

At this writing (1920) the Principal of the Agricultural College at Allahabad is practically the superintendent of agriculture in the native principality of Gwalior. In return for this service the State pays an annual grant of $5,000 to the Mission.

The principal of the Christian college, Allahabad, Rev. Arthur Ewing, D. D. was permitted to see most of his plans carried to completion. His energy and enthusiasm seemed to enable him to forge ahead overcoming difficulties that would have staggered many another man. But the sands of time were running fast and his days were comparatively few. He succumbed to a sudden attack of spinal meningitis at Allahabad September 13, 1912, having spent 22 years in the Mission field. His funeral was second only in extent to that of Rev. Charles W. Forman of Lahore. The students insisted on hauling the hearse through the city and to the cemetery, where in the presence of hundreds of Indian Christians and students, the body was laid to rest. In honor of its noble founder, the college was now called *The Ewing Christian College.*

The Allahabad Christian girls' school had been located upon

a portion of the Mission premises made over to the college. It became necessary to provide a separate compound and new buildings somewhat separate from the college. This was accomplished through the generosity of Mr. John Wanamaker of Philadelphia, who had gone on a visit to India and, by invitation came to Allahabad, where the plans for the college and girls' school were placed before him. He had already given large sums for the Y. M. C. A. work in Madras and Calcutta, but generously gave fifty thousand rupees to build a school building for the girls, located on the cantonment side some four miles distant. This arrangement provided for the girls' school a most beautiful and commodious building, sufficiently large to house both the scholars and their teachers. Its location far from the city secures the inmates from any sudden attack by rioters in the city. The school is now known as the *Mary Wanamaker Memorial School.*

By this arrangement, Mr. Wanamaker added the old school buildings and their compound to the college campus. He also undertook to pay the salaries of two science professors in the college. It is difficult to estimate the importance of such gifts in the interests of the Indian church and the general cause of education in India.

These two institutions stand at the head of the missionary educational work in the United Provinces of Agra and Oudh. The high schools for boys in Fatehgarh, Mainpuri, Jhansi and Allahabad are feeders to the college. In like manner girls' schools at the various mission stations are enabled to promote the higher education of girls by sending them on to the Mary Wanamaker High School.

The result of the entire system of education has been the elevation of the Christian community in the social and intellectual scale. Many of them have secured lucrative employment in places of trust. Some of them are employed as teachers and head masters and mistresses in Mission schools. Christian ladies have proved themselves efficient teachers in public as well as private schools. A few have become doctors and midwives and are appreciated as assistants in both Christian and non-Christian service. Many Christian women are employed in Hindu and Muslim families as private tutors in the home, and also as teachers in their schools.

All this kind of service has justified Mission schools and colleges as definite evangelistic agencies.

CHAPTER XXXI.

Progress in the Western India Mission

THE work at Kolhapur continued to progress slowly and steadily undermining caste prejudice. The education given in the State school for boys, although carefully guarded against Christian influences, yet by broadening the minds of the pupils along the lines of western education, was preparing the ground for other than Hindu culture. The desire for female education was growing. The manifest superiority in the mental and moral accomplishment of the Christian girls could not but impress thoughtful men. The Christian school began to admit a few non-Christian girls, who became accustomed to the society of Christian classmates and their teachers. The Christian teaching could not fail to leaven the heart life of such Indian girls, and also to impress the minds of their relatives.

Under the fostering care of the Missionary teachers and especially of the late Miss Esther Patton, the outcome of this work was the establishment of a new school for girls in the city. This was to be a high school open to all classes, Jains, Marathas and Christians. A hostel was to be erected and placed under the care of the Christian community, "and would be for the occupancy of any indigent Christian students, either of Rajaram College, Irwin Christian High School or other institution."[1] The Maharajah proposed to the Mission that they should undertake the management, and expense at least in part. The Missionaries in reply to this proposal expressed their gratification at the honor done them and accepted the proposal as far as feasible, viz:

"That the station, while having no full time Missionary at once available, would undertake to spare some of its workers

[1] *Western India Notes*, No. 4, p. 3.

for this service, and see that it was properly supervised. In regard to the financial side of this proposal, the Missionaries were regretfully obliged to say they were unable to enter upon such an undertaking at present, and therefore the building and equipment would have to be found apart from the Mission."[2]

This liberal spirit is quite unique among Indian princes, but it is certainly sincere as may be seen in the following proclamation posted on the door of a public building in Kolhapur:

"Be informed that all public buildings, charity rest houses, State houses, public Government inns, etc. and river watering places, public wells &c., no defilement on account of any human being is to be taken account of.

"Just as in Christian buildings, and at public wells, and as the Doctors Wandless and Vail, in the American Mission, treat all with the same love, so also here they are to be treated as not esteeming any unclean.

"If not, the town officers, the Patel and *Talarti* will be held responsible. Therefore make the arrangement."[3]

This notice is of special interest as indicating the Maharajah's emancipation from caste and his desire to emancipate others.[4]

The Maharajah has also enacted advanced divorce laws, and a law providing for the free education of non-caste women. He has also made a law entitling a woman to damages for any sort of ill-treatment by her husband.[5]

These enlightened rules, abolishing caste distinctions aroused opposition. At a village Shirgaon, a Christian teacher of a low caste school marched his children to the main school in the town, whereupon the caste children were withdrawn; seventy-five of them, and twenty little "untouchables" remained! Two Brahmin teachers, being left without pupils, were suspended leaving the Christians in full charge.[6]

Such changes for the better are full of encouragement for

---

[2] *Idem.*
[3] *Western India Notes*, Vol. II., No. 2.
[4] *Idem.*
[5] *Idem.*
[6] *Idem.*

those who have labored long with apparently little to show for their faithful endeavor to lift up their people into a higher plane of Christian life and civilization. Many years of effort remain but success is as sure as the promises of God.

The Ratnagiri station, after occupation by Mr. and Mrs. Barker, was taken over by Mr. Seiler, who labored for four years until he went on furlough. During his absence, Rev. Mr. and Mrs. Graham carried on the work. In 1881, Mr. Seiler returned bringing Mrs. Seiler with him. They remained here until 1884 when they were appointed to Kolhapur.

Miss Esther Patton went to Ratnagiri for a part of the year 1882. Mr. and Mrs. Tedford were transferred to Ratnagiri in 1885 and remained there until 1887, when the station was temporarily closed.

Calling to mind the very strong endeavor of Dr. Wilder to maintain the high school as a necessary agency for the evangelization of the people of India, it becomes a pleasure to notice the success of the schools established by him in Kolhapur and of other schools which have been established in the State since. In Vengurla there is a high school in which are more than one hundred pupils enrolled. In Sangli there is an industrial school for Christian boys, in which the following trades are being taught: Agriculture, carpentry, pipe-fitting, blacksmithing and mechanics. Students attend school classes one half of the day and spend the other half at their chosen trades.[7] In every village center a school is provided that Christian children may be taught to read and write.

The greaetest institution in this Mission is the Medical College and Hospital at Miraj, with Dr. William J. Wandless in charge, whose skill as surgeon draws patients from all parts of India. This institution was begun in 1892 as a dispensary. Two years later the hospital was opened. During the first quarter century of its life, the hospital cared for 32,000 in-patients, with a total attendance of 847,400 out-patients. In this period 49,458 surgi-

[7] *Western India Notes*, Vol. II., No. 4, p. 2.

cal operations were performed. In this service Dr. Wandless was aided by 14 different physicians.

"Of the patients who come to the Hospital from the North, East, South and West, the bearded and red-fezzed Muhammadan, the short keen-eyed Marvadi with his much bejewelled wife, the clean-looking Maratha, the rambling Goanese, and the big Pathan from North India . . . all mingle in the common cause of healing."

No statement could more graphically portray the wide reaching influence of a medical mission in a non-Christian land.

CHAPTER XXXII.

Development of Village Evangelization: Reform Movements

THE pioneer Missions had all been begun in large cities or towns. This was certainly true of all Protestant Missions. The first cities occupied in India were those situated on the coast: Calcutta, Madras, Bombay, Rangoon. Other and smaller towns were situated on the great rivers, where were built factories and other accessories to commerce. Here were located the cantonments, with Courts of Justice, barracks to house the soldiery, and the offices of Government. Here were begun the schools and colleges of learning. Here were assembled many of the most intelligent people of the country drawn together by the emoluments of office, civil and military, or by the opportunities of trade and manufacture. The missionaries, like the apostles and evangelists of the early ages of the Christian church, began their work in these centers of physical and intellectual activity. Here they established schools and organized congregations of believers. Here they opened dispensaries and hospitals and asylums for the poor and for orphan boys and girls. Here they set up printing presses and opened book stores and reading rooms. When the way opened, they extended the work into the surrounding towns and villages. By and by when native preachers and colporteurs had been trained they began to organize new stations under native management, modelled after the pattern of the parent stations.

For a whole generation, effort was specially directed towards the building up of an indigenous Christian community, which should become a powerful spiritual influence, spreading out by contact with the surrounding villages and towns. Because of the boycott of the caste system, separate individuals and even families in villages were obliged to take refuge in the town, and even in the houses on the Mission premises. This situation made it comparatively easy to shepherd the scattered members of the flock. Classes were formed for Bible study or even for teaching the converts the art of reading and writing. Family prayers were held at stated periods and so the foundation was laid for a Christian community. The children were gathered into schools where they were taught how to read and how to sing. Congregational worship was undertaken on the Sabbath days and the midweek prayer-meetings. The brighter women and their husbands were given such training as would fit them to be helpers in teaching primary classes in the home or in the school. We have seen in previous chapters of this narrative how much was done to teach and to train bands of Christian workers.

The time had now come when effort should be made to domicile the Christian church. Converts were urged to remain, where possible, in their own village homes. When possible, two or more families were baptized together and an Indian teacher or evangelist was located in the village to teach the catechumens and to lead in family and public worship. Some such arrangement became possible when the convert could secure work as a hand on the farm of a village landlord, or when he could farm a piece of land on the shares, or possibly could cultivate his own fields. Artisans, pedlers and domestic servants could become quite independent by adding to the family outfit a loom for the weaving of cotton cloth, or the plant for the raising of fowls for the sake of the eggs for their own use and for sale. Many Christians were enabled to live in their own villages. When their fellow caste people found them prospering in business, saw their children growing up in intelligence, clean and happy in their games, they began to seriously consider the religion which seemed to be the cause of this change in their condition.

For awhile such Christian communities seemed like oases in the surrounding region, but by and by other families in other villages began to adopt the Christian role. Then separate believers from outlying villages began to join in worship at the central meeting places. It was along in the seventies and eighties that the way opened in the Northwest Provinces, and in the Punjab for the baptism of converts in their own villages, with the expectation they would live among their own people. In the Lodiana Mission, small communities of Christians were organized as churches or congregations at Khanna, Morinda, Rupar, Jagraon, and Moga. The Indian leaders at these centers, who shepherded these scattered flocks were Rev. Jaimal Singh. Rev. Ashraf Ali, Rev. Mattias, Rev. Ahmad Shah and others. In the Jalandhar district, central towns were chosen and evangelists were put in charge of the Mission work established there. Some of these were licentiates: Maulvi Jamal ud-Din at Kapurthala, Sirdar Buta Singh at Kartarpur, Rev. Henry Goloknath at Phillour, Rev. Ralla Ram pastor at Jalandhar city.

The Hoshyarpur district, with Rev. Kali Charan Chatterji, D. D. in charge, was divided into nine sub-stations, in which Indian ministers or licentiates were placed, including the following,—Dasuah, with Rev. Nizam-ud-Din in charge; Hariana, Gardiwala, Tanda, Ghorawaha, Mahalpur, Podhiana Mukerian and Garshankar with Rev. Amir Khan, Rev. Agya Masih, Rev. Wazir Shah and others in charge.

In the Lahore district, similar sub-stations were occupied, all outside Lahore city. They were Kuimira, Bhama, Ganjih, Muzang, Niaz Beg, Shahpur, Sharakhpur, Khudpur, Nawanpur and Chak Warburton. These stations were the centers of evangelistic endeavor where worshipping assemblies met. Some of the leading evangelists were Rev. G. L. Thakurdas, Rev. Talib-ud-Din superintendent of home Missions and Rev. Ghulam Masih. These, with catechists and scripture readers, held stated services for the native congregations and schools for the children.

A special evangelistic work was begun at Kasur, an old Muhammadan city, once famous, but now fallen into decay and ruin. The first Indian evangelist was Rev. P. C. Uppal. The work in the District became so extensive that a European missionary was also appointed at this center. The Rev. Charles W. Forman, Jr., M. D., opened up the work and after him Rev. Robert Morrison, who erected a Mission house on a compound outside the city and organized a church. In the district many Christians were organized into congregations and for these village schools were opened. On Dr. Forman's going on furlough, the work of village education was carried on by Rev. A. B. Gould, who established schools at various village centers, each school ministering to Christian people in the circle about the school. As many as ten or twelve schools brought primary education within the reach of most of the Christians in the Kasur district. Later on the work of evangelization was carried on with enthusiasm by Rev. F. B. McCuskey, Mrs. McCuskey and Miss Sarah M. Wherry. Travelling from center to center with a large tabernacle, which accommodated several hundred people, they held special meetings for several days at each center. Inquirers were brought in from surrounding villages and examined with a view to receiving baptism for themselves and their children. During a single campaign, as many as five or six hundred names would be added to the roll of membership in the church. From time to time communion services were held. These holy services were held in the church tent. The bread used was the unleavened cake (native bread) and raisin juice made by soaking raisins over night and straining through a muslin cloth in the morning. Such remembrance of the Crucified Lord was just as solemn and impressive as if held in a palatial cathedral. The Christians in that district number over 13,000 souls. During the great war several hundred men volunteered as soldiers to serve in Mesopotamia and Persia. They have supplied a large quota in the Christian regiment (71st Punjabis).

The Firozpur station was another center of evangelistic work.

It was at first occupied as an out station from Lahore. The Rev. Jogandra Chandra Bose was placed in charge, but later on it was occupied by Rev. F. J. Newton. Mr. Newton having studied medicine opened a dispensary. Later on a hospital for women and children was built and became a strong evangelistic influence in both the city and the surrounding district. A church was organized for the Indian Christians in the city and cantonment. Extensive tours into the district led to the establishment of village communities at Muktasar, Zera and Fazilka. The Indian evangelists in this district were Rev. Isa Charan, Rev. J. C. Bose, Rev. R. C. Dass, Rev. Amar Dass with assistants, catechists, teachers and readers. Rev. N. Prem Dass has been pastor for many years in the City church. Medical work has been carried on in the district by Dr. Newton and his wife and daughter, Dr. Helen Newton (now Mrs. A. B. Gould). This great district comprises some 1,500 villages with 956,657 inhabitants, a field large enough to employ the strength of the whole Lodiana Mission. Educational work was limited to a few primary schools for the Christian community.

Another great field in the Lodiana Mission was that of Ambala. The district comprises 1,908 villages, including seven towns of 10,000 or more inhabitants. The village work is carried on in seven circles, with centers in Mubarakpur, Lalru, Ambala City, Naraingarh, Sadhoura and Raipur. The plan was to place a preacher or a teacher in each one of these centers who should carry on a work of visitation in his own circuit.

The Indian workers were Rev. William Basten, Rev. Sundar Lal, Catechist Geo. H. Stuart, Mr. Moti Lall and Mr. T. B. Singh.

The work in the Saharanpur, Dehra and Rurki districts was conducted along lines already described. High schools were carried on successfully. Branch schools in the cities were maintained as primary auxiliaries to the high school. Comparatively few boys were allowed to remain long enough to enable them to enter the middle grade or the high school. The great purpose of the schools was to some extent attained and the boys received a considerable knowledge of the Bible and other Christian literature.

At Saharanpur, the Boys' Industrial School continued to care for a large family of children rescued from the horrors of famine. Some of these were trained to be teachers and preachers.

At Dehra, the Girls' School continued its efficient work for Christian girls, most of whom took up the burden of Christian homes. Many were able to undertake the work of teaching in other schools. A few were able to teach in Hindu and Muhammadan homes.

At Dehra, the missionaries were able to care for many lepers in an asylum built by local and Government aid.

The missionaries and Indian preachers carried on evangelistic services in the towns and villages. During the cold season extensive tours were made to the sacred places, especially the annual melas at Hardwar. A sub-station was established at Muzuffarnagar in the Saharanpur district, managed for awhile by Indian evangelists. In 1884 this was made a central station with Rev. W. Calderwood in charge.

The station at Rurki was in charge of Rev. Joseph Caldwell, a man of unusual learning and especially well acquainted with the vernacular languages in this district, Urdu and Hindi. He was sent out by the old Covenanter church. He gave himself to the work of teaching and preaching to the people in the bazars and melas. Occasionally he wrote tracts for distribution among the people. Of his children one son went to America for his education, where he united with the United Presbyterian church. After graduation he was sent to India as a missionary and joined the staff of village preachers in the Punjab. His wife and a daughter are still with him in Pathankot after 42 years' service.

After the death of Rev. J. Caldwell at Rurki in 1878, the station was abandoned. About this time the Presbyterian Board in America discontinued its connection with the Reformed Presbyterian church and concluded to abandon Rurki, but having learned of the purpose of the Reformed body to undertake a missionary work in India, on their own account, they agreed to make over to them the entire property at Rurki. It will be remembered, as already explained in an early chapter, that a number of the early missionaries sent out by the Presbyterian Board in New York, were stationed in Saharanpur, Dehra Dun and Rurki. The understanding, as to their relation to the Board, was that the Covenanter churches would support their missionaries, while the Presbyterian Board should provide the houses and lands upon which the houses were built. By and by, the Reformed churches in America were unable to provide even the salaries of their missionaries. During the Civil War in America, there was a schism in that church, which led their missionaries in India to secede. The entire Saharanpur Presbytery withdrew from the parent church in America, but retained their Presbytery as an independent church. Some of the old churches in America began to set up claims for the property in India, but investigation, and a friendly conference, ended in an agreement, that the Presbyterian Board should give over to the Reformed Presbyterian Church the Rurki property, on condition that all further claims to property by the Reformed Presbyterian Church in America should be abandoned. The native Indian Presbytery has since carried on an independent missionary work with a number of churches in Rurki, Dehra, Muzuffarnagar, Pattiala and Rajpur. They have received some financial support from the Reformed Presbyterian Church in America. Two American missionaries were sent from America early in the present century. Of these one man and his wife are in charge at Rurki. These, although quite separate from the Presbyterian church in India, are working in fellowship with their neighbors. Their one strong church in Dehra is quite self-supporting, having an endowment in support of its pastor.

The village evangelistic work in North India had been conducted along the lines adopted by the pioneers who survived the Sepoy Mutiny in 1857. For some years the Mission was employed in a work of reconstruction. The sufferings of the Christians, which obliged them to seek refuge in the villages, revealed the fact that they had friends in the villages who were ready to protect them and to minister to their wants. This may in some measure, have been due to the influence of the village schools supported by the Christian Maharajah Dulup Singh. It was also due to the visits of the missionaries and their Indian workers on the tours made to the towns and villages during the two decades preceding. A number of villages soon became centers from which Indian catechists could accomplish something like a regular course of visitation and so visit converts and enquirers in their own homes.

The example of the American Methodist missionaries, who authorized their evangelists to baptize any of the people, who were ready to openly declare their faith in Jesus Christ as their Saviour, led the Presbyterians to adopt the methods at least in part. The influence of the evangelists, who were given to the first Methodist missionaries, men like Joel Janvier, who soon became a noted leader, could not but inspire a similar holy zeal and enthusiasm among the Presbyterian workers. The fire of missionary zeal began to glow. The writer well remembers an address made by request of a Presbyterian, asking the Rev. Mr. Thoburn to give some account of the village work then claiming the attention of missionaries everywhere. We were urged to adopt the methods of wise fishermen, who ever sought the places where the fish would bite. The question of where to fish was not that of a comfortable place under a spreading tree where one might sit quietly in the shade and wait for fish to come and take our bait. The question should be whether there are any fish there, and if there, whether they will bite. The man content to waste his time and bait looking for fish which are not, or which will not take the bait, has mistaken his calling.

The effect of that address was to arouse us to call in question some of our ideals of fitness for service. The practical lesson was to turn away from the jabbering crowds in the market places of the city and go into the quiet villages and seek a hearing from the sons of the soil and the children of toil.

Several stations were given to the practical work of evangelism, where direct effort to acquaint the people with the facts of the Bible was made by preaching. These stations were Etawah, Mainpuri, Fattehgarh and Fattehpur. From these centers extensive tours were made among the towns and villages. One of the most zealous of these itinerant missionaries was a young man, Rev. E. H. Sayre, in charge of the work at Etawah. His career was not long, covering only six years. He spent the cold season in traveling from village to village visiting as many as 500 villages each year. His work was that of soul saving. He was followed by the great hymn writer, Rev. J. F. Ullmann, who influenced his Indian helpers to carry on the work. Rev. Nabi Bakhsh, a convert from Islam, became pastor of the church at Etawah, but undertook a good deal of work in the district also.

For some years Etawah has been in charge of Rev. Mr. Fitch, an Indian pastor. At Mainpuri, in addition to the high school for non-Christians, there has been established a training school for Christian boys and young men. These schools have been conducted by Rev. Dr. W. T. Mitchell and Mrs. Mitchell. The schools for non-Christian girls and zenana schools for women have been continued. Preaching in the villages and the circulation of books and scripture portions in the Hindi, have been carried on by Indian workers. Small groups of believers have been organized and placed in charge of Indian catechists and teachers.

The work in the villages in the districts of Fattehpur and Fattehgarh were carried on with great energy by Rev. Dr. and Mrs. Bandy and many people were added to the church.

Here too the first two generations of missionary life and work were preparatory. They were spent in the laying of the foundations. A Christian atmosphere had to be created. This was accomplished by raising up, through Christian sympathy and education, a new cult superior to that of philosophic Hinduism and Muslim scholasticism. The impact of western life and teaching had dealt a fatal blow to the caste system. The rise of democracy among the men of the younger generation, the leaven of Christianity, based upon the teaching of the Christian scriptures, could not but arouse a new spirit of social and national aspiration—could not but disintegrate the whole structure of caste, which had for millenniums enslaved the masses of the common people under Brahmin domination, both in body and soul. The translation of the scriptures into so many languages and dialects and a wide distribution of these scriptures and the exposition of their fundamental teaching in the schools and by preaching and the printed page, had inaugurated a movement among the people. Some had heard the call and broken away from the prison doors.

A larger body of men were striving to reform the old religions. A Christian church had been established in the land. As yet it was an exotic. Its organization more or less allied to the foreign powers of control and dependent upon foreign support, but daily growing in numbers and influence. The congregations and churches were united under ecclesiastical government, wherein the Indians were made to realize their intellectual freedom and the power of Christian unity and fellowship. Through the efforts of ministers and missionaries they were able to unite churches and Presbyteries into Synods and Assemblies and they were thus taught to realize their liberty.

The advance in literacy, through the general growth of the Government and Mission schools in India, ministered to the spread of Christian ideals. Western education, although despised by the proud Brahmins and Muslim priests, was the chief way to Government employment. The introduction of the railways, telegraph and postal systems, led to a nation-wide use of the English language. Newspapers and magazines sprung into being in all the principal cities and towns. The extension of trade and manufacture found ways of entry into all parts of India. The Indians who for centuries had been denied the privilege of a journey across the *Black water*[1] were now keen to avail themselves of the opportunity. The effect of intercourse with Western nations was the birth of a new national spirit and a growing desire for social and national independence. The handicap of illiteracy and the antagonism of caste could not but be recognized. But there were many Hindus and Muslims, who objected to Mission schools because of their Christian influence. Muslims also objected to Government schools because of their godlessness. The solution of these difficulties was for each to establish schools of their own. The Hindus were the first to act. They sent their boys to both Mission and Government schools and then set up their own schools. A paternal Government encouraged these schools, giving them the same grants as were given to Mission schools. Muslims were more conservative, but when they saw that they were losing opportunity to enter the more lucrative professions, because of the ignorance of their boys, they began to establish Muslim schools on modern lines. The general spread of education, however, in spite of special denominational schools, obliged a still further advance. The educated young man could not be held within the narrow limits of orthodox Hindu and Muhammadan belief. Some were lost by their acceptance of the Christian faith, but many more lost faith in the religion of their fathers and so became agnostics or atheists. "The new wine had burst the old wine skins." To save their religion and to save the young from alien influence, effort was made to reform the old religions.

The first reform was that of Brahmoism inaugurated by Rajah Ram Mohun Roy. Later on the Brahmo movement was divided into two sections. One under the leadership of Babu

[1] The ocean.

Keshub Chandar Sen and Babu P. C. Mozumdar, rightly called the progressive section, because of its near approach to Christianity. The other section called the Sanathan Dharma is known as the conservative samaj or society. This section is really a reformed Hinduism free from the gross idolatry of the old faith.

This movement served to sidetrack the young men in Mission schools and yet enable them to take advantage of Western science as taught in Government schools.

A still later reform movement of Hinduism was that of Pundit Dayanand, known as the Arya Samaj. This reform was one of interpretation and adaptation of the vedas. It was claimed that all modern culture, science and invention are nothing more than a rediscovery of the ancient Hindu science and art found fully described in vedic lore. This is a definitely anti-Christian movement. It is an active Hindu propaganda, which undertakes to educate young India away from Christianity, and strives to win back any who have been drawn away by Christian teaching. They condone caste, but are not bound by Brahmin bonds. Naturally they are anti-foreign as well as anti-Christian.

This movement has for a while succeeded in sidetracking many who might have become Christians. These reform movements have become political propaganda.

The Muslim community has established its Anjumans or societies, which, while standing for orthodoxy, nevertheless strive to legislate for such changes in their social life as will serve to hold the Muslims to a loyal support of their religion. They have established their own schools and endeavor to educate their children so as to fit them for Government offices. The stress of political life has availed to make these Anjumans the centers of Muslim propaganda.

Among the village population, there is as yet but little education. Only a few Mission schools have been opened. There are some Government schools, but for the mass of working people of low caste these schools are practically closed. The door is open to the *"untouchables,"* but few of them have the courage to enter in. If they do enter, the caste boys make the place too hot for them. For the fifty millions of out-caste people, the missionaries and the Indian Christians are their best friends. Many realize that the only way of escape from caste rule is to become Christians. Like the poor people who heard the lowly Nazarene gladly, so the poor out-caste people hear the gospel gladly.

In all Presbyterian Missions, the majority of converts have come from the depressed classes. The few converts gathered from among the higher classes have become teachers and preachers. Many of them like the foreign missionaries have waited long to see the seed spring up and bring forth a harvest. But the time was now at hand when the converts should come out in great numbers under what is known as the "mass movement."

CHAPTER XXXIII.

Mass Movements

THE history of religious movements in India seems to prove that they are socialistic rather than individualistic. For long perods, while individuals may be deeply influenced, yet few have the courage to stand alone. Many hold off waiting the action of others. When many have been convinced by the teaching and an able leader appears, the stream so long pent up suddenly breaks forth. Thus the long and faithful services of the "Lone Star" Mission of the American Baptists in South India, seemed to have been so fruitless that the Board seriously considered the question of abandonment. The one remaining missionary, Dr. Clough, tired and discouraged still held on. His school and training class pressed upon him as a heavy yoke. His comfort was in the energy of his Indian preachers, who arose to the occasion and undertook to carry on the village work if he would keep the school agoing. Presently the Indian preachers reported many people who were ready to be baptized. Dr. Clough was unable to make the long tours necessary to visit the candidates for baptism in their own villages, but suggested a grand rally and asked his fellow-workers to prepare the candidates for baptism and then bring them together at the central station. Then followed a wonderful movement, when a multitude poured into his compound from among which upwards of three thousand persons were baptized in a single day. The stream continued to flow until some sixty thousand were added to the church.

The movement thus began was not confined to the limits of this one Mission field; nor of the church. The same phenomenon characterized the Arya Samaj. Pundit Dayanand travelled throughout India lecturing upon his new interpretation of the vedas and holding discussions with Christian missionaries.

Many students were influenced, but orthodox Hinduism was not pleased with his teaching. Their antagonism served to stay the movement for awhile, until a vast number of disciples made the great teacher popular. Then the new Samaj was proclaimed and thousands accepted the new teaching as the utterance of a prophet. The Mahatma became a Swami.[1] Apostates from Hinduism began to return to the fold. A bath in the incense of the purifying sacrifice of melted butter and sweet smelling spices (hom), removed the defilement of alien touch and the candidate was received anew into the sacred fold of Aryaism. Multitudes avowed themselves to be Aryas. Great conventions and noisy processions paraded in the streets.

It was in line with this same principle, that in various places in India, when many of the people became convnced that Jesus Christ was the Great Guru (teacher) and the Incarnation of God, that the restraints of caste were no longer able to hold them. Wherefore, in many parts of India, certain classes were able to throw off the bonds of the old cults and to declare their faith in Jesus Christ as their Lord and Saviour, and by Christian baptism to announce their abandonment of idols and false religion. This was especially true of the Churahs or Pariahs, and other allied classes, who are regarded as untouchable by Hindus and who are without the pale of even the lowest of the castes of Hinduism.

These classes number about fifty million. They are "hewers of wood and drawers of water," a class of laborers annexed to every town or village. They, like the serfs of Russia in the olden time, were treated as slaves and even now under British government are generally dependent upon the landlords and the products of menial service for a living. They have risen in economic value because of the vast schemes of railroad, canal and agricultural improvement. They in general have made vast strides and many have become Christians. They have been degraded by centuries of oppression. Few of them know how

[1] *The Religious Leader* became a *Saint* or *Divinity*.

to read or write. Generally speaking they are anamists, but many have adopted in part the teaching of Hindu and Muslim reformers. For long this class was blind to the gospel of Christ through their ignorance. They have naturally been the chief to suffer on account of famine and disease. For this reason too they became the recipients of the charity which sought to heal the sick and to save the poor. To them was proclaimed that grace of God which has provided a way of salvation for the poor and needy. To them especially did the appeal of the gospel bring hope and salvation both for this life and that which is to come; and when the evangelists brought to them the invitation of God's love, many responded. Often whole villages would agree to come over *en masse,* asking that some one should be sent to teach and guide them in the way.

In the Punjab, the Rev. Dr. Charles Newton and his brother, E. P. Newton, were for some years leading evangelists among these people; first in the Lodiana district and later in the Jalandhar district. They were assisted by a number of Indian ministers and evangelists; in the Lodiana and Firozpur districts Rev. John N. Hyde, Rev. F. J. Newton, Rev. A. B. Gould, with their Indian preachers; Rev. N. Prem Dass, Rev. P. C. Uppal, Rev. Ahmad Shah and others gathered large numbers of converts into the churches.

This mass movement has characterized the work of village evangelization almost everywhere. The movement in many villages has been traced to the endeavor of Christians to convert their non-Christian relatives. In some instances it has been due to the personal effort of a man converted away from home, who, when he had returned to his own village, very naturally strove to bring his own people to believe on his Saviour. It frequently transpired that the greater part of the people in a village would become believers before the missionary or evangelist knew of the movement.

In the Presbyterian Missions in North India and Western India, wonderful movements occurred in the districts of Fattehgarh, Etawah, Mainpuri, Etah, Fattehpur, Jhansi and Khasganj in the Northwest provinces; and at Kodoli, Sangli and Ratnigiri in the Kolhapur state.

The result was that a large part of the labor expended in the villages was that of shepherding the scattered communities of Christians, and in carrying on educational work to lift up an illiterate community into an intelligent literacy, so as to make the light of a Christian community shine in the darkness of the numerous non-Christian homes round about.

Among those who were leaders in this wonderful work of village evangelization, mention should be made of one who, after a comparatively short life of intense service, has gone to his heavenly reward. The Rev. John Newton Forman was a grandson of one of the pioneer missionaries at Lodiana and Lahore. He was a co-worker with Robert Wilder in the founding of the Student Volunteer Movement which has accomplished so much in America and Britain to bring in recruits for Mission service in foreign lands. The distinguishing characteristic of his ministry was his emphasis by word and example upon the prayer life in evangelistic work. Everywhere he carried with him a personality wholly consecrated to the service of the Lord Jesus Christ. This devotedness manifested itself in prayer. His life was an inspiration to all of his co-workers.

The spirit of prayer and intercession marked every act of his life. He not only brought blessing wherever he worked in his own Mission, but was called to numerous conventions throughout the land where he brought special blessing upon his hearers. He was asked to address the young people in schools and colleges and theological seminaries. Multitudes in India, in Britain and America remember his kindly face and his earnest words as he led them into the presence of his Lord in supplication and praise. The Holy Spirit used him to greatly increase the spiritual life of the church.

CHAPTER XXXIV.

The Missions' Council

THE gradual development of the three Missions of the Presbyterian Church, U. S. A. had culminated in three separate organizations, all of which were connected with the Presbyterian church in India. For three-quarters of a century each Mission had its own officers and held separate annual meetings and reported their work to the Board in New York. Located as they were within three distinct Provinces, the Punjab, the United Provinces of Agra and Oudh, and the Bombay Presidency, they were separated by several lines of division. There were the long distances between them, marked by climate, race, religion and language. Then there were the ideals of the pioneers, which placed special emphasis upon special forms of service, education, preaching, medicine and the press. Various institutions had been founded in each of these Missions due to the lack of means of travel or transportation. Very naturally something akin to rivalry began to appear. In applications for grants to be supplied from the home base, it was always possible to press the claims of one Mission to the detriment of another. Then the whole work of the three Missions was more than could be well handled through correspondence by one secretary at the home office. The work of a second secretary might seem to conflict with the judgment of the first. It soon became clear that some organization on the field was needed to consider the various claims of the whole field and to co-ordinate the claims of all and make up a budget agreeable to all and thus seek the highest ends of the missionary work. After careful consideration both by the Missions and the Board, it was decided to constitute a

Council of the three Missions, consisting of six missionaries, two from each Mission, and a Field Secretary elected by the Missions and approved by the Board. The first Secretary was Dr. H. D. Griswold, with a Council consisting of Rev. H. C. Velte and Dr. J. C. R. Ewing from the Punjab Mission; Rev. W. T. Mitchell and Dr. C. A. R. Janvier of the North India Mission; and N. J. Wandless, M. D. and Rev. W. H. Hammun of the Western India Mission.

This council arranges the dates for the annual meetings, so that the Secretary may be present at each one in succession. The minutes of the meetings are scrutinized, and, if necessary, are amended so as to co-ordinate their action. The budgets are examined, and, when necessary, are made to agree with the rules of the Board. When ready, the Secretary sends the whole to New York. The importance of the work done by this Council is apparent to all who desire a scientific conduct of business, a wise expenditure of money, and a masterful array of the forces employed. Another important result of this Council's work is the practical method by which the whole Mission staff, European and Indian, is divided up into Committees, or groups, to manage the various departments of the Mission service; e. g. the Boys' Schools' Committee; the Girls' Schools' Committee; the District Work Committee; the Medical Work Committee; etc. Every branch of the work is thus carefully examined and legislated for.

The review of the three India Missions of the Presbyterian Church for four years, (1913-1917), compiled by the Secretary of the India council (Dr. H. D. Griswold) presents facts which may be relied upon as a conservative statement:

"In round numbers there is a population of 15,000,000, occupying a territory of 50,000 square miles, for which our Missions are responsible. The average density is 300 per square mile. The Christian community in this area, in 1913, numbered 46,533. But in 1917, the number had increased by 20,305, making a total of 66,838. The total number of Foreign preachers in 1917 was

210 and of Indians 230. The total attendance in Sunday Schools was 14,952. In addition to the members of the Church, there were 26,726 catechumens, or candidates for baptism."[1]

This summary will suffice to show the progress made and afford a basis for the estimate of work to be carried on during the new era now begun.

In the year 1918, Dr. Griswold went on furlough and Dr. J. C. R. Ewing was appointed Secretary to the India Council in his place, with headquarters at Lahore. From this center annual tours are made, when the Secretary visits the stations and principal village centers, holding conferences with the missionaries, Indian evangelists and pastors.[2] Such work in no way encroaches upon the prerogatives of Presbyteries or Synods.

During the hot season the Secretary resides in a mountain retreat, where he is able to make up his reports and prepare for the next year's conferences. The establishment of this Council, with a Field Secretary, marks the completion of the organization of the three Missions in India. The stations are united by the Missions. The Missions are united through their representatives in the India Council. The routine business of the stations is transacted at the station meetings and the executive committee of the Mission. The whole business of the stations, comes under review at the annual meetings of the Missions. The Field Secretary and his Council review the minutes of the three Missions and bring the findings of the Missions into accord with the rules of the Board, after which the whole is sent to the Mission office in New York.

The complete minutes of the annual meetings of the Missions are printed, including the estimates in detail. By this arrangement, every Missionary may have a copy for his own use.

---

[1] *Minutes of Fifth Annual Meeting of Council*, December 1918, p. 29.

[2] In 1922 Dr. Ewing retired from active service in the field, and was succeeded by Dr. Griswold.

In like manner, the Council prints a full report of its proceedings annually, and copies are supplied for the use of the members of Council and of the stations in all the Missions.

The effect of this complete organization is seen in the greatly increased efficiency and enthusiasm in the work, and has secured a more careful and economic administration of Mission forces and money. It has also gendered a deeper devotion in the great work of evangelizing and training the people in the life and work of the church.

CHAPTER XXXV.

Our Missions and the Great War

THE outbreak of the great war brought to Missions in India conditions fraught with intense anxiety and danger. The danger for the missionary first revealed itself when Germany attacked the merchant and passenger ships on the high seas. This danger was specially felt, when the German cruiser, the Emden, hovered near the ports of Madras, Calcutta and Rangoon. The danger from submarines on the Atlantic threatened to block travel for a time. Then the necessities of the war made it difficult to secure passage, some people having to wait for a year to get a berth. Many travelled to and from America by the Pacific route. When possible, all missionaries decided to remain in India until hostilities should cease.

But life in India was not undisturbed. Effort was not wanting to create a rebellion in India against British rule. Rumor now had it that the Moslems would declare a Holy War. More than once, warnings were given out in certain places that the Indians were about to rise in order to throw off English rule. Here and there British officers were assassinated. Once an effort was made to seize the fort at Firozpur in the Punjab, which failed. An assault was made upon the Mission at Rawul Pindi and some fleeing women were pelted with stones; but the prompt arrival of a park of artillery from the cantonment quelled the rising, but not until considerable damage had been done to Mission property.

The mose serious rising was at Amritsar; where several banks were attacked and European officers were killed. Churches were looted and burned, and Europeans, and even native Christians only saved their lives by taking refuge in the fort. At Kasur, trains were halted and army officers dragged out of the cars and slain. The railway station was set on fire. The rising was only quelled, when armed men came up from Firozpur. At Wazirabad a similar rising occurred simultaneously with those elsewhere, when the English church was burned and a missionary's house destroyed. The coming of an aeroplane saved the day at Gujranwala. A few days later, a more determined rising was made at Amritsar, which was quelled by General Dyer, when several hundred men were slain. Threatened risings at Lodiana were nipped in the bud, by the stern attitude of the Lieutenant Governor of the Province.

There were similar outbreaks in other parts of India, especially in South and Western India. The outbreak in Delhi and the Moplah rising in the South were the most serious. The loyalty of the great mass of the people, and the watchful, as well as tactful management of the defense forces preserved the general peace and quiet of the empire.

The facts of the great war and the reality of the tragic conflict were kept before the people by the constant dispatch of recruits. The daily papers in many languages brought the latest news from the front. Crowds of people awaited the incoming trains to learn the latest news from the battlefield. India had sent scores of thousands of soldiers. Even the small Christian community had sent its battalions to the front in Mesopotamia and Persia. Many sons of missionaries had volunteered; and some had given their lives on the field of carnage. The wives and daughters in the home and the school were busy knitting gloves and stockings for the boys in gray. Plainly, it was impossible not to realize the distracting influences of the war. The gospel was preached and scriptures and books were circulated, and churches and chapels were filled at the stated services, and souls were converted and wounded hearts were comforted, and thus it went on, until the glad, day, when the armistice was proclaimed.

The question arises: What have been the results of this world cataclysm upon the Missionary work in India?

The India Council of Missions undertook to answer this question of the actual and potential results of the war and how they will affect Missions in the near future. The report says:

The war has in most cases, doubtless, only accelerated processes which in the long run would have probably, even without the war, led to the same results. The by-products, then, whether wholly or partially due to the war, are as follows:

(A) *India Inter-nationalized.*

This is meant only in the sense that the war has broken down the natural isolation of India, as nothing else has ever done. The rapidly increasing literacy in English has contributed to this, while at the same time a considerable number of Indian students have studied in Britain and America. But as a result of the war, not merely the select few, but also the rank and file of India's population from multitudes of villages all over the land have come into touch with the outside world. Indian soldiers in large numbers have served in Mesopotamia, Palestine and France; among them a fair number of Indian Christian soldiers. What is the significance of this fact? For one thing, it means that, for good or evil, India is and will be more and more closely bound up with the other nations of the earth. Mutual influences will be exerted. It is, humanely speaking, probable that there will be a new and larger preparedness on the part of the Indian people to consider all sorts of messages, including the Gospel messages. Probably communities now closed to the Gospel will become open.

(B) *A New Standard of Giving.*

The war has shown what sacrifice people are capable of when they thoroughly believe in a cause. Billions upon billions of dollars have been subscribed in America for war purposes: and the choicest young men of the land have been offered freely to fight the battle of human liberty. Hence a new standard of the sacrificial dedication of sons and daughters, and the sacrificial giving of money has been set. Doubtless multitudes of Christians are now saying to themselves: "We have never yet given, as we ought, but we are now going to give." May we not confidently expect, then, that our new and enlarged program of work for India will be matched by a new and enlarged standard of giving on the part of our Church at home?

(C) *A New Consciousness of the Need of Church Unity.* The war has emphasized the fact that Christianity is able, at such a crisis, to present no united front to the world, no united message and appeal. The best Christian ministry for the soldiers during the great war has been the ministry of an interdenominational organization, the Young Men's Christian Association, through which the churches have worked. The final unity of military command under General Foch demonstrated its wisdom by victory. The lesson to the Christian Church is obvious. We must aim at a closer union of the forces of the Gospel. It is a matter of thanksgiving that both the Presbyterian Church in the United States of America and the Presbyterian Church in India have, at their last General Assembly meetings, expressed themselves as ready for a larger union. The organic union of the Presbyterian, Congregational and Methodist Churches in Canada is a good omen. The system of the National Council of Missions in India, with the various Provincial Councils has strengthened the spirit of unity by promoting acquaintance and appreciation. We shall do well to further in all reasonable ways this tendency and movement towards unity. In view of these things, the *World Conference* for the consideration of questions touching Faith and Order is most timely."[1]

The minds of missionary leaders were naturally full of anticipation of progress in regard to all forms of Christian endeavor. The hope of a larger liberty for the people, of co-operation between the Denominations and especially between the Missions and the Indian Churches, was to some extent realized. The larger undertakings of the Independent churches and a clear recognition of the responsibility of Indian Christians for the propagation of the gospel among their countrymen were most encouraging signs of progress and a sure prophecy of final victory.

[1] *Report of the India Council*, 1918, pp. 39-44.

CHAPTER XXXVI.

The Indian Church and Foreign Missions

THE close of the great world war ushered in a new era in the world's affairs. Mighty empires had been overthrown. Others were shaken to the verge of destruction. All nations were visibly affected. The great work of the world was that of reconstruction. The spirit of democracy seemed to have conquered the world. The nations which escaped the onslaught of revolution were those which had recognized the rights of the people and had given them a share in the government. In the new era, popular government generally took the place of autocratic rule.

These changes have not occurred without long periods of preparation. Nor have they achieved the hope of stability except as they have accepted the basic principles, which have been inculcated by the gospel of Jesus Christ. The strength of the British Empire has survived the cataclysm only because it has, as a limited monarchy, conserved the principles of democratic government. In India, the spirit of democracy has been seen in the spread of education by the establshment of a system of schools, wherein not only the vernacular languages are taught and even the classics; the Sanscrit, Persian and Arabic are taught; but for all classes, the English language has been made the language of letters and culture for the entire nation. Colleges and Universities have been established throughout the land. In this great work, as we have already described, the Foreign Board of Missions has from the beginning taken an important part. What has this policy meant but that through this agency a large class of Indians, without reference to any special class or cult or religion, should be trained to take part in the conduct of Government offices and institutions for the welfare of the Indian people.

Under this system of Government, the work of Missions has been carried on. The churches have been organized by the missionaries and multitudes of men and women with their children have been gathered together to worship God and to propagate the teachings and life of Jesus Christ. Indian Christians have been trained in schools and colleges for the work of leadership; and many have been ordained as ministers and elders. As rapidly as possible, Indians were ordained as pastors of the organized companies of believers. In due course, Presbyteries and Synods and General Assembly were constituted. In these ecclesiastical bodies, Indian and foreign ministers and elders are present on an equal footing. The democratic government in the Presbyterian church is seen in the fact that every pastor is chosen by the members of his church. Every member of Presbytery clerical or lay is a representative of the people's church, and so too, in the higher courts, the members of Synod or General Assembly are remotely representative of the people. Under such a system, it is easy to understand how there may be friction in the working out of a missionary program. So long as Indians are strangers to their privileges and responsibilities, they will be ready to live on in the church much as they did before as Hindus or Muslims, doing what they are told to do by their leaders and be satisfied with a perfunctory round of duty. But when they awake to a sense of responsibility, they naturally rise up to the privilege of self-help and self-direction. Up to this date, foreigners had conducted nearly all of the duties of pastor, presbyter and the business of Synod or General Assembly. Young missionaries came out from America and soon appeared as leaders in the church, while Indians sat in deferential silence. The business was for the most part transacted through the medium of the English language. Indian elders were often mere figure heads. The only sign of equality in evidence was the ignorance of the vernacular on the part of new missionaries and ignorance of English on the part of the Indian. But as the years went by, the second generation of Indian Christians grew up and was educated in English as well as in the vernacular. This generation was prepared to assume the rôle of membership in session and Presbytery on the basis of equality.

This assertion of rights, although indisputable, was sometimes regarded as impertinence. This was the judgment of the older Indian elders or pastors, who preferred the humbler subservience to the manor-born. Education and the democratic principles of Christianity were bound to prevail even in India, the caste-ridden land of the Vedas. Efforts were made to reconcile the East and West by several expedients. One was to withdraw the foreign missionary from the Indian Presbytery: this was to jeopardize the existence of the Indian Presbytery. Another plan was to make some of the stronger Indian ministers full members of the Mission: this was considered to be inexpedient, because it would create a special caste of Indians and so create jealousy among the Indian Presbyters. For awhile, a few Indians were asked to attend the Mission meetings as observers or advisers, but without a vote. The real difficulty in all these plans was the inequality of personality. The Indian does not want patronage. He wants liberty and love. This can only be attained by mutual confidence and co-operation.

With a view to make a plan for co-operation between the Presbyterian church U. S. A. and the Presbyterian church in India, a representative conference was called to meet in Saharanpur U. P. India, from March 30 to April 2, 1921. Rev. J. C. R. Ewing, D. D. Secretary of the India Council, presided. Quoting from the record, we read:

After the most careful consideration, by duly constituted Committees, of the Report of the Post-War Conference held in Princeton, N. J. in June, 1920, an Article on the Church in Japan by Rev. A. J. Brown, D. D. and a letter from Dr. R. E.

Speer addressed to certain members of the Allahabad Presbytery, the following basic principles were unanimously adopted:

PRINCIPLES ADOPTED BY THE CONFERENCE

1. That while we have commonly used the phraseology 'Mission and Church' yet the real question at issue is the relation between the Presbyterian Church in India and the Presbyterian Church in the United States of America.

2. We affirm the principle of independence of the National Church, "An Indian Church not identified with an American Church but independent, national, free, related to the Churches of other lands on an equal footing working with them to save and unite mankind." The independence of the Church need not exclude connection of the missionary with the Church courts in India. When the Church on the field desires it, the ordained members of the Mission should become members of the Presbytery in full and regular standing, and the lay members of the Mission, men and women, are advised to become members of the local churches.

3. The Church has a right to a voice in all work carried on within the bounds of its organization or closely related with it.

4. The Church, as a Church, should be self-sustained and governed; and the Missions as Missions have a vital work to do in co-operation with the Church. The supreme and controlling aim of foreign missions is to make the Lord Jesus Christ known to all men as their Divine Saviour and to persuade them to become His disciples; to gather these disciples into Christian churches which shall be self-propagating, self-supporting and self-governing; to co-operate so long as necessary with these churches in the evangelizing of their countrymen and in bringing to bear on all human life the spirit and principles of Christ.

5. We believe that the aim and development of the Indian Church will best be realized, when the Church and Mission are united in the closest co-operation and when such co-operation is the dominating principle in all forms of their work.

While advocating mutual co-operation between the Church and the Mission, we yet believe that the best results of Mission work in India will be attained when right lines of distinction are observed between the functions of the Indian Church and those of the Foreign Mission; the Mission contributing to the establishment of Indian churches and looking forward to passing on into unoccupied regions when its work is done.

While there has been a measure of co-operation in the past, we recognize that it is a living movement in which we are engaged, and our present effort is to formulate the terms of co-operation under which such living and sympathetic adjustments can be made as will meet the present needs and be capable of such further modification as the changed conditions of the future will be sure to necessitate.

6. Holding this view, it would seem to us that the solution of the present problem is to be found, not in disparaging the Indian Church, nor in dividing its strength, nor in diminishing its responsibilities, but in just the opposite course; by increasing its authority, by expecting more of it, by making it the great agency of evangelization. Instead of transferring a few strong Indian leaders from the Indian Church to become members of a Foreign Mission, in order that they might share in the administration of money from America, we would transfer the administration of the money to the Indian Church for work which the Church is prepared to take over, or to some such joint co-operative body as proposed by the Church in Japan. Along with the taking over of joint authority over the resources of the American Church, there rests upon the Indian Church a peculiar responsibility to take a great forward step in her benevolence. In recognition of this principle, there should be some ratio between the gifts of the Church for missionary work, and the share she takes in the administration of funds from America.

Wherever such funds are made over by the Board, it should be on the basis of an adequate organization, for budgeting, administering and accounting for this money, and definite provision by the body to which the funds are committed for a continuous and steady growth in self-support by the Church.

Personal and voluntary evangelism and service in the interest of the Church and the systematic giving of money or time, as the equivalent of money, should be from the beginning encouraged in believers, and any financial or other aid given through the Mission should be carefully set forth as provisional and gradually rendered unnecessary by the ever-increasing contributions by the Church. We commend to the Church the study of indigenous methods of giving.

7. The transfer of functions and activities from the Mission to the Church should provide in some way for the full participa-

tion of women in the administration of work to which they contribute equally with men.

A Plan to secure more effective Co-operation between the Church in America, working through the Missions, and the Church in India.

Subject to the approval of the Presbyteries, Missions and Board of Foreign Missions, it was decided—

I. *The Presbyterial Committees*

1. That the Board of Foreign Missions through the India Council be requested to ask each Presbytery to constitute a Committee to which shall be entrusted the evangelistic work now carried on by the Mission, educational work carried on in and for the villages, and Zenana work.

That this Committee shall be elected by the Presbytery and shall be composed of foreign missionaries and Indians, so chosen as to secure representation for each district: one-third of the total to be women, missionary or Indian, elected by the Presbytery on nomination by the Women's Presbyterial Society.

That representation shall be based upon the amounts contributed by the Board of Foreign Missions and the Presbytery respectively. If the Presbytery contributes for pastoral and evangelistic work within the bounds of the Presbytery 1/5th of the total spent by the Presbytery and the Board for such work, this plan may be adopted, and the Presbytery shall have the right to elect Indians as members of the Committee up to one half the total membership of the Committee. As the contributions of the Presbytery increase a different ratio of representation is to be worked out.

That the Presbytery shall agree to elect Indians for membership in this Committee, who are members of the Church within the bounds of the Presbytery; possess the educational qualifications of a Matriculate, except by 2/3rd vote of the Presbytery, or the certificate of a recognized Bible or Divinity School, and who have had at least five years' experience in Mission or Church work.

That the Board of Foreign Missions shall agree that only missionaries shall be eligible to membership in this Committee, who have a working knowledge of the language and who have had at least five years' experience in India.

2. Work and Funds to be transferred;—

a. That the Board of Foreign Missions agree to transfer through the India Council or the Missions to the Committee of Presbytery all men's evangelistic work, Class IV, and educational work carried on in and for the villages and institutions having a distinct connection with evangelistic work; all Indian workers ordinarily required to maintain and conduct that work; and all funds now appropriated to that work.

b. That the Presbytery shall agree to conduct Every-Member-Campaigns in order to educate the Church to give more freely to the support of evangelistic work.

3. The Organization and Powers of the Committee;—

a. That the Committee shall be authorized to organize itself with the understanding that the Treasurer of the Mission shall be the Secretary-Treasurer of the Committee.

b. That the Committee be empowered to prepare estimates for the work entrusted to it, administer the funds (not including the fixation of salaries) assigned by the Board and the Presbytery; appoint, transfer, dismiss agents and employees (reserving for the latter the right of appeal to the Presbytery), determine the policy of the work, to recommend through the Intermediary Board to the Property Committee of the Mission extensive alterations or remodelling in existing buildings and prepare an order of preference for new property. The rules and regulations concerning the appointment, transfer, dismissal, pay, increments of agents, working under the Presbyterial Committee shall be the same as those of the Mission within whose bounds the work is carried on. At the end of two years if changes are desired they shall be made in consultation with the Mission. Salaries of all agents except of those, who are members of the Intermediary Board, which shall be fixed by the India Council, shall be determined by the Intermediary Board.

c. That this Committee shall budget the travelling expenses of its members at Intermediate Railway Fare rates.

4. Audit, Review and Report—

a. That all, who administer funds, under the Presbyterial Committee, shall submit their accounts together with the vouchers to an Auditing Committee of three to be elected by the Presbytery, one member of which shall be the Treasurer of the Committee. This Committee shall have the authority to employ a certificated accountant, if deemed desirable.

b. That the Presbyterial Committee shall require that all

workers submit—at regular intervals—reports of development and progress of the work.

c. That the Presbyterial Committee shall encourage the transmission of quarterly letters to the Secretary of Specific Work, New York.

d. That the Presbytery shall present to the Intermediary Committee a copy of the Proceedings of its Committee and an Annual Report of the expenditure of the funds given it by the Board of Foreign Missions together with a report of its Auditing Committee on the same, and detailed estimates for the next fiscal year.

e. That the Presbyterial Committee shall transmit through the Intermediary Board to the Board of Foreign Missions an Annual Narrative.

5. Women's Work—

That Women's Presbyterial Societies shall be formed; membership to be open to all women missionaries, Bible women and representatives from each organized church.

II. *Joint Committees, Education and Medical*

1. a. That the Educational work be committed to a Joint Educational Committee for each Mission area. High Schools and Anglo Vernacular Middle Schools shall be entitled to one missionary representative each on the Committee. Colleges shall be entitled to two missionary representatives each. The total number of missionary representatives shall be at least 8, the Presbyteries to elect an equal number of men or women, who are representatives of the above-mentioned institutions, their election being based on nominations made by the institutions.

b. That the Medical work be committed to a Joint Medical Committee for each Mission area. Each institution shall be entitled to one missionary representative on the Committee. The total number of missionary representatives shall not exceed five, the Presbytery to elect an equal number, men or women, who are connected with Medical institutions, their election being based on nominations made by the Institutions concerned.

c. That any member of the Mission, or any Mission agent, or any member of the Presbyterian Church in India, willing to undertake to be present at the meetings of the Committees, shall be eligible for election to membership in these Joint Committees.

Members of these Committees shall be elected for a term of three years.

2. Powers of these Committees—

a. That these Joint Committees shall, subject to the regulations hereinafter defined, be authorized to prepare estimates for the work entrusted to them, administer the funds, assigned by the Intermediary Board, appoint, transfer, dismiss agents and employees; reserving for them the right of appeal to the Intermediary Board, and determine the policy of the work. These Committees shall be competent to recommend through the Intermediary Board to the Property Committee of the Mission extensive alterations or the remodelling of existing buildings, and prepare an order of preference for new property. These Committees shall budget the travelling expenses of their members at Intermediate Railway Fare rates.

b. That proposals regarding the location of missionaries shall ordinarily originate in the Joint Committees and in the Presbyterial Committee and be presented through the Intermediary Board to the Mission.

3. Funds at the Disposal of these Committees—

That appropriations for Class V, except so much as shall be made over to the Presbyterial Committee, shall be at the disposal of the Joint Educational Committee. Class VI appropriations shall be at the disposal of the Joint Medical Committee.

III. *Intermediary Board*

1. That there shall be an Intermediary Board composed of 9 members, one of whom shall be the Treasurer of the Mission who shall be ex-officio Secretary-Treasurer of the Committee, 5 members to be elected by the Mission, 2 from Presbytery, to be elected from Presbytery's representatives on the Joint Committees from each Presbytery in areas where there are two Presbyteries, and 2 by each Joint Committee from among its members.

That the members of the Committee shall be elected for two years (with due consideration for rotation) with the right of re-election for one term.

2. Powers of the Intermediary Board—

That the Board shall act as a Finance Committee to receive, modify, and transmit estimates through the India Council to the Board, to allocate sums to the Joint Committees, to arrange for the audit of accounts, and other financial work; to hear cases of appeal from the Joint Committees, to review the proceedings of the Joint Committee, with a view to co-ordinating all branches of the work. If the Intermediary Board disapproves of any action of a Joint Committee, it shall re-commit that action to that Committee with explanation, after which it must receive a two-thirds vote of the Committee to be adopted.

The Board shall receive from Presbytery (see 1-4, d. e. above) the reports of and estimates for work carried on by the Presbyterial Committee. It is understood that this Board shall exercise the greatest care to safeguard the ecclesiastical rights of Presbytery.[1]

This plan was accepted and practically adopted by the Punjab Mission and the Presbyteries of Ludhiana and Lahore. The North India Mission was agreed as to the general principles outlined by the conference held at Saharanpur, but differed somewhat as to the constitution of the representative or joint committees. The Presbyteries had not (at this writing) taken action on the subject. The action of the North India Mission is given in Appendix V. Similar action was taken by the West India Mission and the Presbytery of Kolhapur.

There is every reason to hope for a speedy consummation of the co-operation of the Missions and the Indian Presbyterian church on the basis of the Saharanpur plan.

Henceforth the Indian church will receive recognition as the center from which the great work of Indian evangelization will be carried on.

---

[1] See ***Report on India and Persia*,** **Appendix 10, p. 680.**

CHAPTER XXXVII.

Our Contribution to the Church of Christ in India

THE achievements of our missions in India cannot be catalogued in statistical tables. The ministry of service which has resulted in the moral and spiritual uplift of the people of India cannot be accredited to any single agency, or any one group of agencies at work in obedience to the great commission "Go ye, therefore, and teach all nations." The 165 Protestant organizations at present working within the bounds of the Indian empire have done a wonderful work. But even they have not accomplished all that has been done. The Roman Catholic Church, and the Syrian Church in Mysore have been witnesses for Christ to millions of people even before the advent of Protestant Missions. Many great missionaries have lived and labored and died in the service and others have entered in and reaped where they have not sown.

We too have entered upon the fields, where Kiernander, Ziegenbalg, Schwartz, Carey, Ward and Marshman and other apostles of Missions in India, toiled and prayed and died. We have carried on the good work and shall pass on to the rest that remaineth. Others will follow and help create the history of the Church of Christ in India. One soweth and another reapeth, but the day will come when they and we shall rejoice together in the great harvest of the Kingdom of God.

The records which tell of the Christian community within the bounds of the Missions of the Presbyterian church U. S. A. fix the number of church members at 85,225. The church organizations include 801 groups of believers, scattered among some 4,000 villages and towns.

The entire evangelistic force is scattered about 33 centers:

14 in the Punjab, 12 in the United Provinces and seven in Western India. There are 151 sub-stations in village communities, occuped by 246 missionaries, men and women; and 1,288 Indian evangelists, teachers and workers.

Such a statement fails to indicate in any adequate measure the accomplishment arrived at. We must include the widespread influence of our educational system affecting many thousands of the youth and children, young men and women, of the best classes of society. Such schools and colleges advance the general knowledge of large communities and train men and women for better citizenship and better service in the church, a higher civilization and a purer morality and a deeper spirituality in life.

The hospitals and dispensaries, too, exert a wonderful influence for good. Much suffering is alleviated and lives are saved. Especially is this true of women and children. The practical help which the Mission brings in time of famine and plague, or of epidemics of disease of any kind, adds incalculable joy and comfort to both the Christian and non-Christian people. Ability for self-help is bestowed upon multitudes who rarely understand whence the blessing comes. The introduction of people into the use of Western remedies for various ailments, the gospel of soap and hot water, the cleanliness of the home and sanitary surroundings and many similar matters which add so much to the health of the people have been brought by the missionaries. Then again the promotion of many industries and much of handicraft and the teaching of the value of improved machinery for farming, better methods of weaving, sewing and cooking have added materially to the income of both men and women. During the terrible famines which periodically visit India, when a paternal Government or the benevolence of Christians in England and America make provision for relief, it is generally the Missions which are chosen to administer the relief. Thousands of lives have thus been saved. Helpless orphans have been rescued, and, when possible, returned to their relatives, or failing to find them, refuge has been given in orphanages, where they have been tenderly cared for and where many have received education and training for life's work.

Perhaps nothing has done more for the physical well being and manhood in India than the training given in Mission schools and collges in the various sports,—cricket, foot ball and hockey, which have become the delight of every Indian school boy. A similar service has been rendered by the ladies, who have introduced through the schools for girls the games of badminton and tennis, besides the physical training which does so much for the development of the body as well as of the mind. To all of this must be added the establishment of Christian home life with its reverence for God, purity of thought, kindly treatment of children by Christian parents and loving service of parents by their children, religion in the home and stated attendance on the public worship in the churches, the regular observance of the Lord's Day in the midst of crowds who never observe the Holy Day, in short all that distinguishes the Christian from the non-Christian.

The goal of the church is a Christian civilization with glory to God and well being to men as the purpose of life.

These homes and churches are now as lights shedding light and life upon the multitudes who yet dwell in darkness. The living God in a living church is the hope of the world.

Appendix I.

Pioneers in Christian Literature

1. Rev. James Wilson is mentioned as one of the pioneer missionaries at Lodiana and Subathu, but was transferred to Allahabad to take up the work of that new mission in succession to Rev. James McEwen. His special work in the production of a vernacular literature was accomplished there and at Agra during a period of sixteen years. His work was done through the medium of the Urdu and Hindi languages. As pastor he realized the need of better translations of the sacred scriptures. He took part in the earlier translations of the New Testament and the books of Isaiah and Daniel in the Old Testament. This was revised by Rev. J. A. Schurman of Benares.

A translation of the *Westminster Shorter Catechism* was made and published by James Wilson, Joseph Owen and J. Warren. Mr. Wilson also translated from the English a *Catechism for Young Children*. He wrote a tract on Nicodemus in Hindi. Early in his life as a missionary he made a study of Muhammadanism. He published in Urdu and in the Roman character a translation of the Quran with annotations, also in the Roman Urdu. This was done for the benefit of Christian preachers. He also wrote a book in English, entitled, *The Rise, Progress and Decline of Muhammadanism*. Two treatises on the *The Trinity* and *The Lord's Supper* complete the list of books written by this devoted missionary.

2. Rev. John C. Rankin who was sent with James Wilson to open the new station at Agra in the year 1844, was also one of the champions for Christianity against Islam. He wrote a notable reply to a memorable assault upon Christianity by a Moslem Maulvie in a book entitled *"Reply to Saulet-uz-Zaigkam."*

3. REV. JOSEPH WARREN founder of the Mission Press at Allahabad, was the author of a number of books written in the Urdu language. He collaborated with several Indians, who became noted authors. His own books were *The New Birth; The Crucifixion of Christ; History of Ruth; The Way of Life* (Translated); *The Fountain of Life* (Translated); *On Prayer; On Wisdom.*

4. JOHN HARI, a disciple of Mr. Warren, translated Bunyan's *Pilgrim's Progress* into Urdu and wrote a tract entitled *The Comforter.*

5. LEVI JANVIER translated in collaboration with Mr. Warren, *The Confession of Faith.* He translated into Punjabi *Genesis and Exodus 20 Chapters, The book of Psalms.*

6. JOSEPH PORTER wrote a discourse on *The Ten Commandments,* and tracts on *Justification,* on *Repentance, The Worth of the Soul.*

7. REV. W. S. RODGERS translated into Urdu a tract on *Holiness; The Happy Water Man; Poor Joseph; The African Servant; The Roll Call; The Young Cottager; The Barren Fig Tree; What is Your Religion; Divinity of Christ; The Two Old Men; Don't Put It Off; The Dairyman's Daughter; On Happiness; A Refutation of Muhammadanism; The Brazen Serpent.*

8. JOHN NEWTON, SR. wrote in *Urdu the Day of Judgment; Integrity of the Scriptures; Salvation Not By Works; An Urdu Primer; A Book of Psalmody* (compiled from various authors); *The Sermon on the Mount* translated into Kashmiri under his superintendence; into the Punjabi he translated the *Four Gospels* and *Acts of the Apostles; The Pilgrim's Progress* (abridgement) translated under supervision by native pundit also the following: *Selections from Bible History; The Life of Christ; The Fall and Recovery of Man; Religious Catechism; The Ten Commandments; The Brazen Serpent; Bathing in the Ganges* (By Newton and Goloknath) tracts translated under Mr. Newton's supervision; *Address to Pilgrims; Address to Hindus;*

Poor Joseph; Bob the Cabin Boy; Two Old Men; On Holiness; What is your Religion?

9. Rev. Goloknath wrote a *Treatise on Pantheism* and several tracts in Urdu.

10. Other writers were Mrs. Scott, who wrote *Jesus, the Child's Best Teacher;* Rev. J. R. Campbell, who wrote in Urdu, *Good News; The Two Ways and Two Ends; Parable and Exposition;* Rev. Joseph Caldwell, who translated into Hindi, *Bob, the Cabin Boy;* a tract *On Idolatry.*

Note. These publications were written during the 23 years preceding the Sepoy Mutiny. They indicate the kind of preaching and teaching undertaken at that time. One notes the absence of books for women and children who were almost entirely illiterate. A book for children was probably intended for the few Christian mothers and teachers to enable them to instruct their children in the homes and in the Girls' orphanages. As yet Bible teaching was done orally in the home and the church.

Almost all of this literature was burned up in the destruction of the Mission Presses at Lodiana and Allahabad.

Appendix II.

An Invitation to Prayer addressed to the Church of Christ throughout the World, being an extract from the Minutes of the 23rd Annual meeting of the Lodiana Mission. This paper was presented by Rev. J. H. Morrison, D. D.:

"*Whereas* our spirits have been greatly refreshed by what we have heard of the Lord's dealings with his people in America, therefore:—

"*Resolved First,* That we hereby publicly acknowledge the debt of gratitude we owe to Him, and our obligation to Him more than ever, not unto ourselves, but unto Him who died for us.

And in view of our spiritual necessities, and of the wants of the perishing millions about us, and in the hope of obtaining similar blessings for this land,

"*Resolved Second,* That we will do our best to get Union Meetings, for prayer for the out-pouring of the Spirit, established at our respective stations, wherever we may find two or three willing to meet together in the name of Christ.

And further, being convinced from the signs of the times, that God has still large blessings in store for His people, and for our ruined race, and that He now seems to be ready and waiting to bestow them as soon as asked, therefore:—

"*Resolved Third,* That we appoint the second week in January, 1860, beginning with Monday, the 8th, as a time of special prayer that God would now pour out His Spirit upon all flesh, so that all the ends of the earth might see His salvation; that on the first day, that is Monday, the 8th, be a holy convocation for solemn fasting, humiliation, and prayer, and that on the last day, that is Sabbath, the 14th, be a holy convocation for thanksgiving and praise: that the intervening time be spent in private and social exercise of prayer and praise, as the circumstances of each community may dictate; that all God's people of every name and nation, of every continent and island be cordially and earnestly invited to unite with us in a similar observance of that time; and that from the receipt of this invitation, onward, all be requested, in their secret, family and public devotions, habitually to entreat the Lord to pour out upon all His people so much of the Spirit of grace and supplication, as to prepare them for such an observance of the time designated, as may meet with His approval and secure His blessing."

Lodiana, 29th November, 1858.

Appendix III.

REV. ISADOR LOEWENTHAL.

This missionary martyr was one of the most brilliant men ever sent as a missionary to the Moslem world and deserves a place, along with Henry Martyn, as a Christian hero who sacrificed his life in the path of duty. The church should know more of him and his work. The following brief statement is given on the authority of his pastor, Rev. S. M. Gayley.

The Rev. Isador Loewenthal was born (1827) in the city of Posen in Prussian Poland, of Jewish parents. He was the eldest of a family of eight children. His father had at heart little regard for Judaism, but observed from custom its principal rites and ceremonies. His mother was a strict adherent to the traditions of the Rabbis and instructed her children carefully in the tenets of the Jewish faith, and in the principles of morality. His parents bestowed upon him a liberal education. At a very early age he was placed in a Jewish school, where he acquired the rudiments of science, learned to read the Hebrew text, and to repeat prayers he did not understand. At this period, though but a child, he evinced that love of books and thirst for knowledge, which characterized his maturer years.

From the first he made rapid progress in his studies, and gave evidence of more than ordinary talents. After a few years he entered the gymnasium in his native city, where he studied the higher branches of a liberal education—the ancient classics, natural science, metaphysics, mathematics and to some extent, music, Hebrew, and several of the languages of modern Europe. He had passed successfully through the course of study usually taught in such institutions at the age of seventeen. After leaving the gymnasium he entered a mercantile house in Posen as a clerk. But merchandising was ill suited to his taste which was for books. His leisure hours from business were devoted to his favorite pursuits. He had a strong desire to enter one of the German universities, and had made arrangements to do so, but was prevented by the event that led to his emigration to the United States. He formed association with educated young men of his own age of liberal political sentiments, and became implicated in political difficulties by being so rash as to publish in one of the public journals a piece of poetry of his own composition, containing sentiments adverse to the Government. This brought him under the notice of the police, and, being informed that he was in danger of arrest, he hastily fled from his home. After many difficulties he reached Hamburg, where, after much embarrassment, he procured a passport and took passage on board an English ship for New York, where he arrived in the autumn of 1846. Here he was a stranger in a strange land. He was possessed of little means, and was ignorant of the English language. He tried to find employment in New York City, but was unsuccessful. He then visited Philadelphia, where he met with the same want of success. Leaving Philadelphia, he went to the country and sought employment from the farmers, offering his services for what they chose to give him; but he was again doomed to disappointment. Being of diminutive stature, and having no acquaintance with farm work, the farmers deemed him dear at any price. His funds being now nearly exhausted and every door of employment seemingly closed against him, he became very despondent. But, feeling the pressure of necessity to do something for a living, as the last resort, he invested the little money he had left, in a small basket and a few notions, and, with this on his arm, he started out to the counry as a peddler.

In this capacity, on a cold day in November, 1846, he came to the house of the late Rev. S. M. Gayley, near Wilmington, Delaware, drenched with rain and suffering from the cold.

Having disposed of some of his wares, and being about to depart, Mr. Gayley, noticing that he was thinly clad, and the evening being intensely cold, gave him a cordial invitation to spend the night with him, which he gladly accepted. By conversation with him during the evening, Mr. Gayley discovered that his guest was a young man of no ordinary talents, and one who had received an excellent education; that he had an extensive and accurate knowledge of the ancient classics, Hebrew and several of the modern languages. His sympathies were at once drawn out towards him. He thought it a pity that a young man of such talents and acquirements should be engaged as a peddler, when he might be more usefully employed. Mr. Gayley invited him to remain at his house, while he would interest himself to secure for him a situation as a teacher, which invitation he accepted.

By his efforts he secured for Mr. Loewenthal, through his nephew, now Rev. S. A. Gayley of West Nottingham, Maryland, then a member of the senior class in the college, the position of teacher of French and German in Lafayette College, at Easton, Pennsylvania. Mr. Loewenthal entered upon his duties in the college in the beginning of January, 1847.

At this time he had but an imperfect knowledge of the English language. With untiring industry he addressed himself to its study, and, at the close of that session, he could both speak and write it with classic purity; and, in a very short time, he displayed an intimate acquaintance with English literature. He was a most indefatigable student, not only in his hours of leisure from college duties, but habitually, long into the nights, and frequently whole nights were devoted to study. His usual time allotted for sleep was four hours. Possessed of an iron will, whatever he resolved to do was done if labor could accomplish it. Gifted with a retentive memory he rarely forgot anything he read.

During his stay at the house of Mr. Gayley, he never disclosed his lineage, nor did Mr. Gayley ever suspect him of being a son of Abraham, until Mr. Loewenthal, in a letter to him some time afterwards, informed him that he was a Jew. It was during his residence there that "the veil was rent away" from his heart and that he received the first religious impressions, and became convinced of the truth of Christianity. In a letter to Mr. Gayley in July, 1847, he informs him of his conversion to Christianity, and he gives a history of the means employed by the Holy Spirit in bringing about this change. He states:

"It was by Providence I was sent to your door. When I came to your house it was for worldly gain. Little did I then think I was to receive there what was infinitely better. It was at your house, by your earnest prayers (at family worship) to which I first went half from curiosity, half from politeness, by your humble supplications that I was first awakened to apprehend my danger, to consider I had an immoral soul. I began to open the Bible. I was astonished. I waited with eagerness, morning and evening for the summons to family worship, to hear you pray. I was more and more convinced I was on the wrong path."

During the time he was at Easton, Mr. Gayley corresponded regularly with him, and, although ignorant of what was passing in his mind, gave him religious counsel. These kind words, Mr. Loewenthal states in the above letter, were most seasonable and were specially adapted to his case. In the following autumn, during the vacation of the college, he made a public profession of his faith in Christ as the true Messiah and was baptized by Mr. Gayley, his father in the gospel, and was received into membership of the Rockland Presbyterian Church, to which Mr. Gayley then ministered.

Mr. Loewenthal entered the senior class of La Fayette College in the fall of 1847, and graduated with honor. After his graduation, he acted as tutor in the college for some time. In the winter of 1848, being tendered the situation of teacher of languages in the Mount Holly Collegiate School, under the charge of Rev. S. Miller, he accepted it. Whilst there he devoted his leisure hours to philological studies, in which he made rapid progress; he collected a large library of very rare and valuable works bearing upon his favorite studies.

Being brought to the notice of the Rev. Dr. Phillips, pastor of the First Presbyterian Church of New York City, he tendered to Mr. Loewenthal a scholarship at his disposal in the Princeton Theological Seminary, which offer, after much prayer and consultation with judicious friends, he regarded as providential, and falling in with long cherished desires, he concluded to accept. In the fall of 1852, he resigned his situation at Mount Holly and went to Princeton and was matriculated a student of theology. Theological studies were much to his taste. There he took a high stand. His public exercises were far above mediocrity and augured his future eminence. Whilst there, he still pursued his philological studies, during his leisure hours, and was a contributor to the Biblical Repertory. His able articles published in that quarterly established his reputation as a writer. The Society of Inquiry of the Seminary, selected him as their essayist to read the essay at their annual meeting at the Commencement at which his class graduated. His subject was "India as a field of Missions." It was a masterly production evincing great ability and learning.

At this time his thoughts were turned to India as the field of his future labors. For some time after his graduation at Seminary, he acted as tutor in Nassau Hall, which position he filled with marked ability.

Having decided to devote himself to the service of his Redeemer in the foreign field, he offered himself to the Board of Foreign Missions of the Presbyterian church, selecting India as his field. He was accepted and received an appointment to the new Mission to the Afghans. His eminent linguistic talents and acquirements remarkably fitted him for that post. He was licensed in 1856 by the Presbytery of New York; and, in August of that year, he sailed for India.

When Mr. Loewenthal arrived in India late in the autumn, he went at once toward the station selected for the opening of the Mission to the Afghans. He went by invitation to the city of Peshawur (as has been explained in the text) and entered with ardour upon his duties.

(Here the biographer tells the story of his missionary career, closing with a eulogy.)

Although his missionary life was only seven years, yet he had translated and published the whole of the New Testament in Pashtu, had nearly completed a dictionary of that language, and could preach with facility in Pashtu, Persian, Hindustani, and Arabic. It is certain that few foreigners in India had such thorough knowledge of Asiatic literature as he and none had a more thorough acquaintance with the manners and customs of the people and their political life in the Orient. He had a thorough knowledge of the religious systems of the people; and as a disputant with Muhammadans and other religionists he was a master. He enjoyed the friendship of the first men in both civil and military service in India and was on most intimate and friendly terms with Sir John Lawrence, the Governor-General of India.

It is truly astonishing the amount of intellectual labor he accomplished. Besides his linguistic labor he was actively engaged in preaching in the bazar. He undertook frequent journeys into neighboring districts. Besides conducting a large correspondence, he was a contributor to British and American quarterlies. He possessed a genius in the truest sense. His mind was characterized by great versatility. He had seemingly an equal aptitude for all branches of study. He excelled in whatever he undertook. He was an accomplished musicians, mathematician, metaphysician and preeminently a linguist. He stood in the first rank as a philologist. In the social circle he was a charming companion. He combined a mind thoroughly cultivated and richly stored with knowledge with a genial humour and fine conversational powers. As a Christian he was sincere, humble, devout, and zealous. He was in a word a man of God. Sad was his death, and irreparable his loss to the cause of Missions. The memory of his many virtues is embalmed in the heart of the church of which he was an ornament.

Appendix IV.

"The Rev. Levi Janvier, D. D. whose tragic death at the hands of a fanatic, Akali Sikh, has been described in the text, was born at Pitts Grove, in the State of New Jersey, on the 25th day of April, 1816. His early youth was spent in study under the care of his father, who was pastor of the Presbyterian church in that place. His early studies were directed to the Latin and Greek languages, and these studies soon developed a native aptitude for acquiring language in general. At Easton, where La Fayette College was as yet in its infancy, he studied Mathematics under the instruction of Rev. Dr. Jenkin, and in that branch his proficiency was no less remarkable. From Easton he went to Lawrenceville, where he spent a few months in the school of Rev. Isaac V. Brown. He then went to Princeton where he entered the Junior Class. During his residence there, he studied the French language in addition to the regular course of his class. At the Commencement he gave the Salutatory address and shared with two others the first honor of his Class. While he was in College he joined the Church and felt called of God to the Gospel Ministry. During his course of study in the Theological Seminary, he decided to offer himself as a missionary to the Board of Foreign Missions and chose India as the field of his labor. With the consent of the Board he with his wife sailed for India and arrived in Calcutta in September, 1841."

After his decease, Mrs. Janvier carried on the work at Subathu for some years until conditions of health and the education of her only son made it necessary for her to retire from the work. She took a house in Princeton and made a home for her son C. A. R. Janvier until he completed his education at the college and theological seminary. After a successful pastorate in Philadelphia Mr. Janvier was called to the office of Principal of Ewing Christian College, Allahabad, which became vacant by the sudden death of Rev. Arthur Ewing, D. D. Thus the work begun by the devoted father is being perpetuated by the son.

Rev. Dr. C. A. R. Janvier, D. D., an eloquent preacher in the Urdu language as well as the English; a man who as an evangelist is equally at home as preacher in the Scottish Kirk in Allahabad or the Kellogg Memorial Church in Landour or the Union Church at Simla. He is wanted at the many conferences and conventions held for the quickening of the spiritual life among Europeans and Indians.

The college is now one of the great Christian institutions in India. The prayers and hopes of the martyr and his bereaved widow have been heard and God is glorified.

Appendix V.

A Plan for Co-operation Between the Mission and the Presbyteries.

Adopted by the North India Mission At Its Annual Meeting, Allahabad, October, 1921.

After consideration of the proceedings of the Saharanpur Conference on the *Relation of Church and Mission,* the North India Mission expresses its full sympathy in general with the Statement of Principles outlined by the conference and trusts that the following plan as a modification of the Saharanpur plan and in accord with the principles laid down will be acceptable to all parties concerned and adopts it tentatively subject to the assent and co-operation of the Presbyteries:

The work of the mission shall be conducted by a *System of Joint Committees* responsible to the mission and the Presbyteries.

I. *Composition of the Joint Committees*

1. The joint Evangelistic Committee. This Committee shall be composed of all voting members of the Mission engaged in evangelistic work, and others in charge of evangelistic work directly responsible to the Joint Committee. On nomination by this committee other voting members of the Mission may be appointed as additional members for a term of two years. Each Presbytery is asked to elect three members to this committee whose educational qualifications shall be graduate of a recognized theological school or University Matriculate, the Presbytery being competent to make exceptions by a two-thirds vote. The term of office shall be for three years, one to be elected each year, and eligible to re-election. Presbytery (on nomination of the Woman's Presbyterial Society) is asked to elect one woman as a member of this committee for a term of two years. Elected members must be members of the Presbyterian Church in India and except by two-thirds vote of the Presbytery (except in the

case of women) must be ministers or elders in the Church. Elected members must undertake to attend the meetings of the committee.

2. The Joint Educational Committee. All voting members of the mission engaged in educational work except that under the control of the Evangelistic Joint Committee, are members of this committee. On nomination of this committee the Mission may appoint voting members of the mission as additional members of this committee for a term of two years. Headmasters and headmistresses of the B. A. or higher grade shall be members of this committee and by a two-third vote the committee may co-opt headmasters and headmistresses of lower grade for a two year term. Each Presbytery is asked to elect two members (one each year for a term of two years) of at least F. A. qualifications. Such elected members must be members of the Presbyterian Church in India, and by a two-thirds vote must (except in the case of women) be ministers or elders of the church. Elected members must undertake to attend the meetings.

3. The Joint Medical Committee. All missionary doctors and trained nurses who are voting members of the Mission and engaged in Medical work are members of this committee. The Mission shall elect three additional voting missionary members for a term of two years. Each presbytery is asked to elect two (one each year for a two years term) of recognized medical or nurses training to this committee, or by a two-third vote may elect one of the two from among those not medically trained.

4. As Presbyteries increase in their financial support of Church and evangelistic work and as their membership has an increasingly large proportion of those not employed out of foreign funds, the Presbyterial membership of these committees may be increased.

II. *The Powers of the Joint Committees*

1. The Joint Committees shall have power to organize themselves with the understanding that the Secretary-Treasurer of the Mission is the Secretary-Treasurer of the Joint Committee (but without a vote on any committee except the one of which he may be a member), the record and accounts of the committee being an integral part of the records and accounts of the Mission.

2. The Joint Committees are expected to survey the whole need of the field of work allotted to them, to consider how much of this work should be done without financial payment, to pre-

pare estimates for the work for which financial provision should be made, to determine how much of the money needed should be provided in India and how much it is right to ask from America, to administer the funds which may be available and to direct the work for which they are supplied (not including the fixing of salaries and grades). They shall appoint, transfer and dismiss agents, make recommendations on policy and methods of work to the Presbytery and the Mission, recommend to the Mission alterations in existing buildings and an order of preference for new property and advance work, including new missionaries. The Committees in administering funds must do so by a two-thirds vote, as is required of the Mission by the Board.

3. These committees shall require all workers and institutions under their control to submit annual reports of the development and progress of the work and in their turn shall submit to the mission and the Presbytery a report of their proceedings, the work done and the use of the funds, either body being competent to express its opinion as to how the work may be improved and mistakes corrected. All the reports prepared by the committees shall be sent up to the India Council with the Mission's and the Presbytery's judgment on them. Council having veto power by a two-thirds vote over the use of funds.

4. To the Joint Committees on Evangelistic work shall be committed the funds designated by the Mission for Class IV and such school work as is carried on in and for the villages and institution having close connection with evangelistic work and such parts of Class VII as have to do with district work. Where any question shall arise regarding such allocation the Mission shall decide.

To the Educational Joint Committee shall be committed the funds which the Mission shall allot to Class V (except such as are designated for the Evangelistic Committee) and such Class VII items as belong to schools.

To the Medical Joint Committee shall be committed the funds that the Mission shall assign to Class VI and such part of Class VII as is connected with medical work.

Any powers, funds, or work not specifically handed over to these committees shall remain with the Mission as heretofore.

Two Indian members representing each Joint Committee will be invited to be present in the Mission meeting when the reports of the Joint Committees are being considered and while the allocation of funds to the various Joint Committees is being made.

Each committee may appoint its own auditing or finance committee to whom all who administer funds must present their accounts with vouchers for audit and sanction. The Secretary-Treasurer shall be a member of each of these committees. These auditing committees shall have power to disallow expenditures not in accord with the appropations and rules, but subject to appeal to the Joint Committees. Where no such auditing committee is appointed the Finance Committee of the Mission shall arrange for the audit.

Index

Index

Index

*Rev. J. E. Freeman and Mrs. Elizabeth Freeman, Rev. D. E. Campbell and Mrs. Campbell, Rev. A. O. Johnson and Mrs. Johnson, Rev. R. McMullen and Mrs. McMullen, two children of the Campbells.

Index

Index

---

*"He began the Christian Boys' Boarding School at Lahore which was removed to Lodiana. He was superintendent of High Schools at Rawulpindi, Jalandhar, and Lodiana for most of his lifetime."

**He was the author of many books and tracts in the Punjabi language. He was also editor and reviser of the Psalms and other portions of Scripture in Punjabi. He carried on a school for Christian boys and the Khanna Industrial School.

Index

Index

*Of the principals of Woodstock School and College, very special mention should be made of Rev. H. Marston Andrews and Mrs. Andrews, under whom the High School became a College.